Sport, Civil Liberties and Human Rights

What is the relationship between sport and human rights? Can sport protect and enhance the human rights of competitors and sport workers? Can it also undermine those rights?

These topical issues are among the many that are explored in this groundbreaking volume which analyzes how sports both contribute to, and undermine the human rights of participants, spectators and workers. The papers are written by esteemed academics whose work is at the cutting-edge of this burgeoning area of study. Experts from around the world have contributed to this important work, examaning controversial issues such as:

* sexual harassment
* racism
* freedom of movement
* sport as popular protest.

This book was previously published as a special issue of *Sport in Society*.

Dr David McArdle, is with the department of Law at the Aberdeen Business School, Scotland.

Dr Richard Giulianotti, Senior Lecturer in Sociology, University of Aberdeen

Sport in the Global Society

General Editors: J.A. Mangan and Boria Majumdar

Special issue: Sport, Civil Liberties and Human Rights

Sport in the global society
General Editors: J.A. Mangan and Boria Majumdar

The interest in sports studies around the world is growing and will continue to do so. This unique series combines aspects of the expanding study of *sport in the global society*, providing comprehensiveness and comparison under one editorial umbrella. It is particularly timely, with studies in the aesthetic elements of sport proliferating in institutions of higher education.

Eric Hobsbawm once called sport one of the most significant practices of the late nineteenth century. Its significance was even more marked in the late twentieth century and will continue to grow in importance into the new millennium as the world develops into a 'global village' sharing the English language, technology and sport.

Other Titles in the Series

Disreputable Pleasures
Less Virtuous Victorians at Play
Edited by Mike Huggins and
J.A. Mangan

Italian Fascism and the Female Body
Sport, Submissive Women and
Strong Mothers
Gigliola Gori

Rugby's Great Split
Class, Culture and the Origins of Rugby
League Football
Tony Collins

Terrace Heroes
The Life and Times of the 1930s
Professional Footballer
Graham Kelly

Soccer and Disaster
International Perspectives
Paul Darby, Martin Johnes and
Gavin Mellor

Barbarians, Gentlemen and Players
A Sociological Study of the Development
of Rugby Football
Second Edition
Eric Dunning and Kenneth Sheard

Capoeira
The History of an Afro-Brazilian
Martial Art
Matthias Röhrig Assunção

British Football and Social Exclusion
Edited by Stephen Wagg

The First Black Footballer
Arthur Wharton 1865–1930: An Absence
of Memory
Phil Vasili

Sport, Civil Liberties and Human Rights

Edited by

Richard Giulianotti and David McArdle

Routledge
Taylor & Francis Group

LONDON AND NEW YORK

First published 2006 by Routledge, an imprint of Taylor & Francis
2 Park Square, Milton Park, Abingdon, Oxon, OX14 4RN

Simultaneously published in the USA and Canada
by Routledge
270 Madison Ave, New York NY 10016

Routledge is an imprint of the Taylor & Francis Group

Transferred to Digital Printing 2008

Typeset in Times 10/12pt by the Alden Group Oxford

British Library Cataloguing in Publication Data
A catalogue record for this book is available from the British
Library

Library of Congress Cataloging in Publication Data
A catalog record for this book has been requested

ISBN10: 0-714-65344-6 (hbk)
ISBN10: 0-415-46419-6 (pbk)

ISBN13: 978-0-714-65344-0 (hbk)
ISBN13: 978-0-415-46419-2 (pbk)

CONTENTS

vii

Introduction

The Olympic Games display the very best of our common humanity.
Coming together across virtually every line of race, ethnicity, language,
religion, gender and national identity, the athletes – on their own or as
members of a team – will scale new heights, set new records and give
the world a lesson in international understanding. The Games are a true
celebration of humanity. Olympic ideals are also United Nations ideals:
tolerance, equality, fair play and, most of all, peace. Together, the
Olympics and the United Nations can be a winning team. But the contest
will not be won easily. War, intolerance and deprivation continue to
stalk the earth. We must fight back. Just as athletes strive for world
records, so must we strive for world peace.

> Kofi Annan, UN Secretary-General, message to the Sydney
> Olympic Games,
> August 2000

These words from the UN Secretary-General make some strong claims and
assumptions about the role of the Olympic Games, and of sport much more
generally, in assisting peaceful co-existence across the world. Yet, as the
various chapters in this book demonstrate, sport has a far more ambiguous,
indeed contradictory relationship to human and civil rights, and to international
development, within the age of intensified globalization.

At first glance, the work of organizations like the IOC suggests that human
rights, international development and peace are pivotal to sport. Indeed, for
the first Olympic Games in ancient Greece in 776 BC, an Olympic Truce was
agreed, ensuring that warring city-states would cease fighting seven days prior
to the Games up until seven days afterwards, thereby enabling participants and
spectators to travel to and from Olympia in peace.[1] In 1993, almost a century
after the modern Olympics were founded, the Truce, known as *Ekecheiria*,
was revived more formally through the United Nations and observed for the
first time at the Winter Games in Lillehammer a year later, largely with
reference to the war-torn Balkans. UN resolutions have subsequently followed
in support of the Truce. The modern version seeks to suspend all fighting for
the sixteen days of Olympic competition with the ambition that, if respected, it
'can help create the environment and infrastructure for continued dialogue and
renewed hope for reconciliation during the Olympic Games and beyond'.

Yet, almost instinctively, we can suggest other, more violent historical
dimensions of the Olympic Games: the desire of their founder, Pierre de
Coubertin, to improve the military fitness of French youth in the build-up
to war; the 1936 Berlin Olympics hosted by Nazi Germany in a bid to

demonstrate Aryan racial superiority; the violent struggles between athletes from Russia and other Eastern bloc nations, notably Hungary in 1956; the massacre of hundreds of protestors just before the 1968 event in Mexico; the assault on Israeli athletes by PLO gunmen in 1972; the Cold War posturing that led the USA and its allies, then the USSR and its supporters, to boycott consecutive games; the selection of Beijing to host the 2008 games, despite its human rights record; and the long-standing connections of Olympism's leaders to neo-fascist movements and regimes. While official discourses regarding sport emphasize cosmopolitanism and universalism, there are numerous others that spotlight histories of xenophobic nationalism and international strife. If the practice of sport is to possess universalist and humanist dimensions then, as the ancient Olympians would have recognized, such a goal can only be attained within circumstances conducive to the preservation of human rights.

Human rights and civil rights can be distinguished for analytical purposes although the two categories are strongly inter-related. Human rights refer to those inalienable rights that all individuals possess according to natural law, and which must not be removed through any kind of social exchange. The 1948 Universal Declaration of Human Rights, the inspiration for the work of the United Nations, contains thirty articles that begin from the premise that is article 1: 'All human beings are born free and equal in dignity and rights. They are endowed with reason and conscience and should act towards one another in a spirit of brotherhood.' Other conventions, such as the 1950 European Convention on Human Rights and the 1990 Convention on the Rights of the Child, establish additional frameworks for articulating and safeguarding inalienable rights.

Civil rights refer more particularly to the legal rights and entitlements that people gain through their membership, as citizens, of a specific society. These might include formal rights conferred by the state through legislation or the provisions of a written constitution, the laws promulgated by supra-national entities such as the European Union and, in the United Kingdom and elsewhere, common-law rights developed by the judiciary. Thus, while civil rights are cross-culturally variable and may not apply to all people within a nation's borders, human rights are taken to apply universally and without compromise. There are civil rights that are reinforced by the natural law of human rights. For example, in most market societies, citizens have civil rights to their own property, to the right of assembly, to the right to privacy; these are also covered by the Universal Declaration in articles 12, 17 and 20.

However, as the leading human rights commentator Richard Falk observes, 'It is now more critical than ever to embark upon a fundamental rethinking of the Western human rights paradigm.'[2] In regard to making these and other articles in the Universal Declaration function effectively, it could be argued that we need to do more than guarantee the legal and formal political freedoms of individuals. We must consider how these rights might acquire substance in political economic terms. In peering into the growing chasm between the northern and southern hemispheres, we confront the dark truth that without adequate development there may be little point in enshrining 'rights' that are assumed to be inalienable within the developed world but a relative luxury to much of the developed world. According to the United Nations Development Programme, extreme poverty afflicts a quarter of the world's population. How important is it to guarantee a human right like the right to privacy when one is threatened with starvation on a day-to-day basis? How meaningful is article 24 of the Declaration, confirming the right to 'rest and leisure, including reasonable limitation of working hours and periodic holidays with pay', when a civil war has erupted across the local village? Thus the formal enforcement of human and civil rights cannot work unless the material and developmental inequalities of the world are systematically reduced.

Sport provides one important site for the exploration of new horizons in human and civil rights. Sport is the popular cultural forum *par excellence* in which the normative bases of human relationships are dramatized and debated. Sports institutions provide for popular senses of membership, belonging and participation that are analogous to those of citizenship. More practically, sport can contribute to the consciousness-raising required by international organizations in seeking to promote the development that is required to assist in the everyday realization of human and civil rights. For example, as one of its eight 'millennium development goals', the United Nations' members are committed to halving global poverty by 2015. At the forefront of the UNDP's publicity programme has been the 'Teams to End Poverty' campaign, introduced through full-page advertisements in over two hundred newspapers across the world. The campaign has been endorsed by many global sports celebrities, notably the leading football players Ronaldo and Zinedine Zidane. This is one of the many examples of partnership between sports celebrities, institutions and humanitarian NGOs.

Yet sport continues to highlight how our practical freedom to enjoy particular rights, including those to leisure, are relatively differentiated according to material resources. Little wonder that a nation like Finland, with high human development scores and low social inequalities, was the first to legislate on sport as a human right.[3] There is a direct correlation between levels of development and opportunities to participate in sport, particularly at school. The least developed nations, by definition, have the lowest per capita figures for physical education teachers, sports clubs, and elite-level athletes.[4] Even in many developed societies, particularly those that privilege the market, the 'freedom' to practice particular rights is closely connected to one's possession of particular material resources. More seriously, there are systematic practices within sport that countermand our human and civil rights: athletes' bodies are subjected to abusive forms of domination and control by coaches, agents and physicians; sports spectators have their personal liberties curtailed by police and security officials; sports authorities undermine the civil liberties of athletes and spectators in relation to dope-testing and dissemination of information; and international sports organizations work cosily with oppressive and expansionist states.

This collection of essays seeks to disentangle and analyze these complex substantive and theoretic issues by forwarding the first detailed, critical examination of sport, civil liberties and human rights.

We begin with these articles that explore children's labour and abuse within sport. Peter Donnelly and LeAnne Petherick provide a forceful and wide-ranging critique of the various ways in which child labour is brought to bear within sport. The most extreme manifestations involve the exploitation suffered by poor child workers in the developing world who are employed to manufacture sports goods such as footballs for sale by transnational corporations. There are the athletes from the developing world whom Western agents and sports clubs recruit on oppressive contracts or who are abandoned in strange locations after failing to make the grade professionally. Even in more developed societies, abuses of children's rights are apparent in the rigorous training programmes endured by young athletes. Donnelly and Petherick note that little in sport has been done to challenge these abuses, although international campaigns against the employment practices of transnational corporations in the developing world have had some impact. We are some way from having international sport bodies and governments agree to a raft of special rights or codes of best practice regarding children in sport.

The essay by Celia Brackenridge examines the protection of children and women from abuse within sport. Of particular concern is the position of male coaches in developing relations of trust and responsibility with young athletes, providing the potential context for sexual abuse. Only belatedly has the sexual abuse of athletes emerged as a serious issue within major sports organizations. Brackenridge argues that this public attention to child abuse in sport has ironically served to set back concerns with gender equity more generally. She notes that, from the late 1980s onwards, sport witnessed a progressive shift towards a rights-based approach towards the status of children, yet women have still found themselves subordinated and likely to be penalized if they challenge patriarchal conventions within sporting organizations.

The critical analysis of the abuse and exploitation of children within sport is given substantive elaboration in Fan Hong's study of the Chinese sport system. Since the late 1980s, China's political leadership has been dedicated to establishing the nation as a sporting superpower, as measured through the international competitive successes of its elite athletes. The result, as Fan Hong argues, has been systematic abuse of childrens' human rights, as young athletes labour intensively within highly oppressive coaching regimes that are intended to churn out champions. Boys and girls endure physical and mental abuse at the hands of coaches, and the violation of young bodies through doping remains a massive problem. Yet potent cultural values regarding national patriotism, the fear of being shamed, and the veneration of single-mindedness serve to silence many potential critics and to pacify the athletes themselves. Unless the Chinese sport system is revolutionized, most likely through external pressures, one can only expect this regime to become harsher as the nation gears up for the Beijing Olympics in 2008.

The inter-relations of human rights, globalization and normative education within sport are considered by Richard Giulianotti. Although recognizing that many sports-focused development projects are operated by international NGOs and sports organizations worldwide, Giulianotti identifies some inherent problems in regard to sport and human rights. The 1948 Declaration makes no explicit mention of any human right to sport, while too many sporting governing bodies would appear to tolerate, if not encourage, the breach of specific articles within the Declaration. Moreover, the historical diffusion of sport across the globe is implicated in severe abuses of human rights. To explore some form of solution, Giulianotti seeks to combine the insights of Roland Robertson on globalization and Richard Rorty on moral education. The 'thematization' of the global human condition takes the partial form, in the West, of a 'human rights' culture. For Rorty in particular, this culture is to be nurtured, to produce future generations whose tolerance and understanding of others are inspired through sentimental education. Giulianotti argues that sport provides a potentially felicitous arena for sentimental education, as we encourage our fellow and future citizens to view other peoples as our fellow players, team-mates and supporters.

The problematic relationship of sports governing bodies to civil liberties comes under critical inspection in the chapter by Helen Lenskyj. Lenskyj focuses specifically upon how, in cities either hosting or bidding to host the Olympics, the local authorities, business interests and media institutions form a pragmatic hegemonic bloc to challenge and suppress critics or organized opponents of what she terms 'the Olympic industry'. Civil and human rights relating to freedom of assembly and freedom of the press, Lenskyj argues, are restricted when the Olympic industry enters town. In Toronto, for example, the local press fell in behind the city's Olympic bid and so failed to inform its readers, the local citizens, of the true financial costs and political issues surrounding the projected Olympic jamboree. In Sydney, new legislation, intended ostensibly to augment security at the Olympics, has been used more widely and overzealously by local police with serious consequences for the civil right to assemble freely in public places.

The article by David Rowe considers the question of cultural citizenship within the developed world. Specifically, Rowe addresses the extent to which our cultural citizenship may be undermined by the increasing commodification of sport. He argues that sport promotes senses of citizenship, yet such forms of popular participation and cultural inclusion are jeopardized by the attempt to turn sports fans into 'consumers'. Citizens in many nations take for granted, as an aspect of their cultural citizenship, their right to watch on television their favoured team in the world's most important sports events. However, as sports governing bodies and teams seek to maximize their profitability, so the sale of sports broadcasting rights to subscription television stations emerges as a serious challenge to this participatory ethic. Rowe appreciates that, while free-to-air broadcasting is unable to match the sports dedication of pay-television stations, there is scope for nation-states and international governmental organizations to safeguard the cultural rights of the citizens that they represent.

Richard Parrish and David McArdle's article on the relationship between sport and the law of the European Union takes as its starting-point the infamous 'Bosman ruling' of 1995. This essay reveals that, far from breaking new legal ground, the *Bosman* ruling merely represented a perfectly straightforward application of existing European Union principles, and there was nothing in that decision that could have occasioned the surprise and consternation that European football authorities expressed. Since *Bosman*, sports authorities and the European Union have attempted to strike a balance between upholding the fundamental rights conferred upon European citizens by EU law – the right to move freely between member states to take up employment opportunities being but one of them – and acknowledging the concerns of sports organisations that an untrammelled application of EU law to sport would be contrary to those organisations' interests. While there is still a long way to go before those competing agendas are reconciled, the contribution stresses that there are several routes by which that goal could be achieved – although many sports bodies still refuse to accept that principles such as persons' freedom of movement are sacrosanct and that sports organizations, rather than the EU, will have to cede the most ground if the relationship between the two is to be anything other than antagonistic.

We turn to two essays on the civil and human rights issues surrounding one of the most controversial issues within sport: doping and drug-testing. The essay by Barrie Houlihan examines critically, from a civil rights perspective, the legal and political frameworks of sport that are geared towards combating doping. Sports governing bodies afford little scope for dialogue or consultation with athletes in shaping and implementing anti-doping strategies. The athletes' rights to fair hearings and to privacy may be seen to have been undermined by contemporary anti-doping strategies. Houlihan's particular focus is on the World Anti-Doping Code and the Court of Arbitration for Sport which, though offering much that protects athletes and the credibility of sports, fail to provide sufficiently for political input from competitors themselves. The Code, notes Houlihan, contains serious lacunae in regard to protecting the rights of children within sport. Houlihan further considers the role of genetic modification in regard to doping, since the former could be seen as another form of corporeal manipulation outside the accepted bounds of sports preparation.

Angela Schneider provides a provocative philosophical analysis of the human rights issues surrounding dope-testing in sport. Specifically, Schneider considers whether sporting governing bodies can defend themselves from the accusations that they infringe the rights of athletes to privacy and confidentiality in the attempt to keep sports 'clean' of drugs. Particular inconsistencies are apparent in sporting bodies' penalization of athletes who have taken marijuana or over-the-counter cold remedies, neither of which would appear to offer any remarkable advantage to competitors. Further problems arise regarding the 'informed consent' to doping controls in sports events involving minors. Arguments regarding the function of anti-doping programmes in preventing harm to athletes are also treated sceptically, particularly given the fact that other, far more serious risks are allowed to remain in sports. For Schneider, one way of retaining doping controls within sport while safeguarding athlete rights is by handing over policy-making on doping to the competitors themselves.

Patrick K. Gasser and Anders Levinsen provide a practical analysis of the role of local sport-based initiatives in challenging the roots of conflict and in promoting reconciliation in war-torn areas. There is a strong professional impetus behind their study: Gasser (formerly of the ICRC) manages UEFA's development programmes while Levinsen (a former professional player) founded the Open Fun Football Schools (OFFS) programme in the Bosnia-Herzegovina region of the former Yugoslavia. It is the OFFS programme which provides the focus of their essay. By 2003, around 20,000 young players from the different Serb, Croat and Muslim communities in the region had participated in the OFFS. Gasser and Levinsen demonstrate that the success of the project has been founded upon a keen awareness of the historical and social complexities of local areas, and also a commitment to the full participation of local people in decision-making and programme implementation. At the very least, as the authors indicate, the programmes have 'broken the ice', enabling inter-ethnic contact and co-operation to take place, as football trainers from different communities help to organize players into multi-ethnic teams.

The cross-cultural ethics of this project, with the remarkable consequences of having former enemies cheering for their children who play on the same team, do provide a telling illustration of sport's capacity to foster universalism through play.

In similar vein, Gary Armstrong's contribution critiques the role of sport in war-torn Liberia, paying particular attention to child labour, human rights abuses and warped notions of masculinity and the role of education. Armstrong discusses the role played by over 100 neighbourhood football teams established in and around Monrovia to provide a diversion for the child victims of Liberia's civil war and operating in conjunction with child Homes and Youth centres. By 2002, over 4,500 children were involved in the football programme, and more than 120 people were employed as outreach workers and in other administrative capacities. While certainly not underestimating the impact that these initiatives have had upon Liberian children's lives, Armstrong concludes with the telling point that "rehabilitation and re-integration projects are doomed to fail if there is no better life offered to the disaffected demilitarized". His sad tale makes that point all too clearly.

RICHARD GIULIANOTTI and
DAVID McARDLE

NOTES

1. In the modern era, the earliest sign of a similar accord came with the famous 1914 'Christmas Truce' during the First World War, when enemy soldiers met in no man's land to exchange gifts, sing songs and play football. See M. Brown and S. Seaton, *Christmas Truce* (New York: Hippocrene Books, 1984).
2. R. Falk, *Human Rights Horizons: The Pursuit of Justice in a Globalizing World* (London: Routledge, 2000), p.93
3. P. Donnelly and B. Kidd, 'Human Rights in Sport', *International Review for the Sociology of Sport*, 35, 2, 2000, pp.131–148.
4. See, for example, W. Andreff, 'The Correlation between Economic Underdevelopment and Sport', *European Sport Management Quarterly*, 1, 4, 2001, pp.88–105.

Workers' Playtime? Child Labour at the Extremes of the Sporting Spectrum

PETER DONNELLY and LEANNE PETHERICK

Workers' Playtime was a BBC Radio lunchtime variety programme, broadcast live from factory canteens around Britain in the 1940s and 1950s. Its title recognized lunchtime as a break from work, a time when workers might play. When applied to children, when children are workers, this title takes on a more sinister connotation. Play is supposed to be characteristic of childhood, and play is considered to be intrinsic to healthy child development – physical, mental, and social. When applied to children who work at sport, and in the industries that supply sporting goods, 'workers' playtime' has a cruel irony. This article is about those children.

The vast majority of the world's nations have ratified the United Nations (UN) Convention on the Rights of the Child (CRC)[1]. By their signature, nations have committed themselves to the best interests of children (defined as all humans under 18 years of age). Forty of the 54 Articles in the CRC deal directly with children's rights, and four refer directly or indirectly to children's participation in sport and physical activity. For example, Article 24 affirms 'the right of the child to the enjoyment of the highest attainable standard of health ...', Article 28 'recognize[s] the right of the child to education ...', physical education being implicit in this right since it was previously affirmed in the 1978 UN Educational, Scientific and Cultural Organization (UNESCO) International Charter of Physical Education and Sport,[2] and Article 29 states that education involves 'the development of the child's personality, talents and mental and physical abilities to their fullest'. However, it is Article 31 that directly recognizes:

1. the right of the child to rest and leisure, to engage in play and recreational activities appropriate to the age of the child ...
2. the right of the child to participate fully in cultural and artistic life and [States Parties] shall encourage the provision of appropriate and equal opportunities for cultural, artistic, recreational and leisure activity.

Given this international recognition of children's rights to participate in sport and physical activity, it may be surprising to note that almost half of the 40 Articles dealing directly with children's rights are occasionally or routinely violated in most countries when we consider children's involvement – direct and indirect – with sports. Human rights are interconnected in various ways, and although this article deals most directly with Article 32 of the CRC (Child Labour), the process of child labour involves violation of many of the other rights acclaimed in the CRC. The essay begins with a short overview of child labour; moves on to consider three specific forms of child labour in sport: children's involvement in the manufacture of sporting goods, child trafficking for the purposes of sport, and children's involvement in high-performance sport; and concludes with recommendations for resolving the issue of child labour in sports.

Child Labour

Article 32 of the CRC recognizes:

> ... the right of the child to be protected from economic exploitation and from performing any work that is likely to be hazardous or to interfere with the child's education, or to be harmful to the child's health or physical, mental, spiritual, moral or social development.

States' Parties are expected to establish a minimum age for employment, regulate the hours and conditions of employment, and set appropriate penalties in order to enforce these standards.

The International Labour Organization (ILO) recognizes that work is normal for children:

> After the age of six or seven, children may have small tasks around the home, run errands, or spend some time helping parents to run the family farm. This can make a healthy contribution to their development ... [with] children learn[ing] to take responsibility and pride in their own activities .... Even in the wealthiest countries, children may be encouraged to work a few hours a week.[3]

Child *labour* is different. In child labour, children 'are being exploited, or overworked, or deprived of their rights to health and education'.[4] Blanchard notes that child labour may be defined as: 'children prematurely leading adult lives, working long hours for low wages under conditions damaging to their health and to their physical and mental development, sometimes separated from their families, frequently deprived of meaningful education and training opportunities that could open up for them a better future'.[5]

The ILO is even more specific about the characteristics of child labour:

- working too young (children in developing countries often start factory work at age 6 or 7) working long hours (in some cases 12 to 16 hours a day)

- working under strain (physical, social or psychological)
- working on the streets (in unhealthy and dangerous conditions)
- working for very little pay (as little as US$3 for a 60-hour week)
- working with little stimulation (dull, repetitive tasks which stunt the child's social and psychological development)
- taking too much responsibility (children often have charge of siblings only a year or two younger than themselves)
- subject to intimidation (which inhibits self confidence and self esteem, as with slave labour and sexual exploitation).[6]

Nobody knows how many child labourers there are in the world. The ILO estimates that 16 per cent of the world's children (some 246 million) are child labourers; that 12 per cent of the world's children are in the worst forms of child labour (approx. 184 million), and that some 186 million are less than 15 years of age.[7] ILO Convention 182 (2001) is specifically intended to end the worst forms of child labour (e.g. sex workers, working in dirty and dangerous conditions, etc.), and the International Programme on the Elimination of Child Labour (IPEC) has been established to monitor progress.

Child Labour in Sport

As noted in the introduction, there is an essential contradiction between labour and sport, especially for children. Children labour in the cause of sport in various ways. Some are workers in the sports equipment and sportswear factories of developing nations, labouring to produce the equipment and uniforms that will be used by others (including other children) to participate in sport. Others are physically talented children in wealthy nations whose talents have been recognized, and who have been encouraged to specialize early on the high-performance sport development track. Between these two are children from poor countries who are bought and sold to be athletes in wealthier countries. The sociology of sport is only beginning to recognize children's involvement in the production of sporting goods, and child trafficking in sport.[8] However, there is a growing body of literature in the sociology of sport on the problems of children in high-performance sport, and that is reflected in the third section below.

Child Labour in the Sporting Goods Industry

The processes of economic globalization that resulted in the downloading of manufacturing jobs to developing nations led to the emergence of two related protest campaigns in the 1990s. The first concerned the conditions of labour, and particular attention was paid to the manufacture of sports shoes and clothing; the second concerned the issue of child labour. While sociologists of sport have paid some attention to the anti-Nike and other campaigns concerning sweatshop work,[9] they have not responded to evidence from NGOs such as Christian Aid and Global March about the widespread involvement of children in the manufacture of sports equipment ranging from soccer and rugby balls to badminton birdies and boxing equipment.

The first reports of child labour in the sporting goods industry appeared in 1995, and the issue started to come to public attention in 1997, with the signing of the Atlanta Agreement and the publication of Christian Aid's research report, 'A Sporting Chance: Tackling Child Labour in India's Sporting Goods Industry'.[10] The Atlanta Agreement was conducted under the auspices of the US Department of Labor, which had reported the employment of children in the sporting goods industry in their document 'By the Sweat and Toil of Children'. The Agreement was signed by the Sialkot (Pakistan) Chamber of Commerce and Industry – Sialkot being the largest producing city in the world for soccer balls – the ILO and the United Nations Children's Emergency Fund (UNICEF). The objectives of the Agreement were to:

1. Prevent and progressively eliminate the child labor in the manufacture or assembly of soccer balls in Sialkot and its environs;
2. Identify and remove children under the age of 14 from work and provide them with education and other opportunities; and
3. Facilitate changes in community and family attitudes towards child labor.

The Atlanta Agreement was joined by Save the Children – UK, which took on the responsibility of funding two NGOs in Sialkot, each working to improve education and the rehabilitation of children and families impacted by child labour.[11] The Christian Aid report, the research for which was carried out in conjunction with the South Asian Coalition on Child Servitude (SACCS), identified child labour in settings such as a tannery preparing leather used in the manufacture of cricket balls, stitching Everlast boxing equipment, and stitching the panels in soccer balls in Sialkot's counterpart in India, Jalandhar. They pointed out that Sialkot produces 35 million balls a year – some 54,945 a day, or 2,289 an hour.[12] Christian Aid urged the British government to hold large corporations accountable for unethical corporate conduct.

Soccer balls became the focus of media attention in the lead up to the 1998 World Cup in France, with a number of newspaper articles around the world reporting that the balls to be used in the World Cup had been hand-stitched by child labourers in India and Pakistan. Two sport sociologists, John Sugden and Alan Tomlinson of the University of Brighton in England, attended a press conference in Paris just before the start of the World Cup (they were involved in a major research project on or FIFA Fédération Internationale de Football), when the first question that was asked concerned the child labour issue. A spokesperson for Adidas pointed out that children's small hands were necessary to carry out the task of stitching together the panels of soccer balls, and that the children were not mistreated. A rather docile audience of sports reporters appeared to accept this absurd explanation. As Sugden and Tomlinson[13] pointed out, it was not credible to think that humans, whose technological know-how had permitted them to land on the moon, could not devise a machine to stitch soccer balls; and the economic realities were that child labour was cheaper than the development of machinery. Christian Aid reported that children received as little as 14p for stitching a ball that sold in the UK for £14.99.[14]

Although children are involved in the manufacture of sports equipment other than soccer balls, and in other parts of the world (e.g. China, softball stitching in Latin America, etc.), the focus has remained largely on the manufacture of soccer balls in South Asia. The issue re-appeared with renewed energy when the organization, Global March against Child Labour, started a major campaign ('Kick Child Labour out of Soccer') leading up to the 2002 World Cup in Japan and Korea.[15] They were able to obtain assurances from Adidas-Salomon that none of the balls used in the World Cup would be products of child labour, and that the company would no longer use child labour in the manufacture of soccer balls. The assurances were part of an agreement between FIFA, the World Federation of Sports Goods Industry (including Adidas-Salomon, Nike, Puma, Decathlon and Reebok), and the Sports Goods Foundation of India (SGFI). The agreement, outlined on the Global March website, involved the following assurances:

1. Limit number of suppliers' stitching centres that are used; all production facilities are audited against child labour and health and safety standards for general compliance; stitching centres must register with the ILO IPEC monitoring programme. The age documentation of workers in stitching centres is checked regularly by the suppliers, local staff, and independent monitors from the ILO.
2. There are four approved manufacturing partners in Pakistan, all located in Sialkot. These manufactured ball components are shipped to registered stitching centres, where footballs are assembled. The finished footballs are returned to the factory for quality testing, packaging and shipping. To prevent footballs from being made in unregistered sites Adidas-Salomon have implemented a product tracking system, which matches ball components with output, delivery records and payslips of workers from each stitching center. Adidas-Salomon staff checks these records regularly.

Various reports suggest that these agreements are routinely violated. For example the India Committee of the Netherlands (ICN),[16] which has been particularly active on this issue, noted that the newly established stitching centres were exempt from the Factory Act in India, which entitled employees to several rights (e.g. a labour contract, an annual bonus, double pay for overtime, etc.). The ICN report, *The Dark Side of Football*, noted:

- There is strong evidence that a few members of the SGFI are hiding a part of their production from the monitoring system, in particular the largest exporter Mayor & Co. This company is supplying balls to Adidas, Mitre and Mundo, as well as to other FIFA/ISL-licensed companies. Mayor & Co. also supplies footballs with a Euro 2000 design for the European market, imported under FIFA/ISL-license by Mookie Toys.
- The contractual agreements between the ISL (the licensing organization of FIFA) and all licensed football importing companies who buy their balls in India are violated on the issues of (hiding) child labour, wages below the official minimum, misuse of advances paid to workers, obstacles to the right to organize, exemption from existing labour legislation and lacking health standards and sanitary facilities.[17]

Global March also focused on violations in its 2002 World Cup campaign, 'Kick Child Labour out of Soccer'.[18] There are photographs on the website, one showing a child stitching the Adidas World Cup panel into a soccer ball; and another of a child stitching the 'child labour-free' panel into a soccer ball. According to Phillippe Roy, Global March's representative in Pakistan, middlemen in Sialkot evade the monitoring system by sending the ball pieces, manufactured for major corporations such as Coca-Cola (promotional balls) and Adidas, to small villages for stitching.[19]

Anti-child labour campaigns began to crystallize around the 2002 World Cup, but also looked to the future. For example, the European Parliament passed a resolution endorsing the Global March campaign, and called on the football industry to eradicate all forms of child labour. The European Parliament also called on FIFA and the national Football Associations to make the next World Cup (Germany 2006) the first international event free of child labour.[20] UNICEF says 'YES for Children Campaign' involved FIFA in their 'Say YES for Children Campaign' the 2002 World Cup. And the ILO' the 2002 World Cup. And the ILO's 'Red Card Campaign' (Red Card to Child Labour) took a much broader focus, and proposed that: 'The ultimate event in the campaign hopefully will be to celebrate the universal ratification of the convention against the worst forms of child labour at the World Cup football tournament in 2006.'[21]

Organizations, such as the ILO[22], the UN[23], Global March[24], the Clean Clothes Campaign[25] to introduce fair labour practices into the international garment industry, and the various organizations of the anti-Nike movement, are beginning to take seriously the problem of child labour in the sporting goods industry, and to work to improve the conditions of work, and to ensure fair wages and release time for education. However, there are clearly more steps to be taken before the 2006 World Cup can be declared Child Labour Free.

Child Trafficking in Sport

The process of trafficking children for the purposes of sport has received even less publicity than child labour in the sporting goods industry. However, during the 1990s, two specific forms of trafficking children in sport began to receive some publicity.

Camel Jockeys. The first was the kidnap and/or purchase of small boys, particularly in Bangladesh and Pakistan, for transport to the United Arab Emirates (UAE) to be trained as camel jockeys. Camel racing is a popular sport, involving a significant amount of gambling, in several countries of the Arabian peninsula. Small children are preferred as jockeys because of their light weight. There is a risk of injury, sometimes death, in falls during training and races, and there is some evidence that the boys may be badly treated and poorly fed to keep their weight low. The Anti-Slavery Organization reports that evidence provided to the United Nations Economic and Social Council (ECOSOC sub-commission on the prevention of discrimination and protection of minorities) suggests that boys are 'underfed and subjected to crash diets to be as light as possible, they are strapped to camels' backs but in a fashion that still permits slipping. Some are dragged and others thrown off; the children suffering injury or death. Children have little control over the camels in races.' Reports indicate that children as young as age two have either been kidnapped, or purchased from parents with promises (usually not honoured) that they will earn money to be sent to the parents, that they will receive an education, and that they will be returned when they reach the age of 11 or 12 and are too heavy to be of further value as jockeys.

Because this is clandestine activity, the actual numbers are quite difficult to determine. Newspaper reports compiled by Lawyers for Human Rights and Legal Aid (LHRLA) suggest that some 19,000 children had been taken from rural and coastal areas in Bangladesh to become camel jockeys, but they were also being used for organ transplants and drug trafficking.[26] The Ansar Burney Welfare Trust International (ABWTI) estimates that 30 boys a month are kidnapped in Pakistan alone to be taken to the UAE[27]. And the *Trafficking in Migrants Quarterly Bulletin* reported that 3,397 children were trafficked from Bangladesh to Gulf states to act as camel jockeys.[28]

LHRLA was the first organization to begin investigating the issue, and it was pressure from this international lawyers' association that led the Camel Jockey Association to change its rules in 1993; the new rules disallowed the use of children under 14 years of age, or under 45 kilos.[29] However, recent journalistic reports suggest that the practice continues, with six-year-olds who are under 20 kilos still participating. Anti-Slavery has also been very active, putting pressure on the UAE to ban the 'import' of camel jockeys, and to end the use of jockeys under the age of 14.[30] Their recommendations include:

1. Carry out regular unannounced inspections to identify, release, and rehabilitate any child who is currently being used as a camel jockey
2. The government must ensure that those responsible for trafficking or employing under-age jockeys are prosecuted under existing laws.
3. Introduce legislation that prohibits the employment of children under age.

The US Department of State, in its 2001 country report on the UAE, made it very clear that none of the new 1993 regulations were being implemented. The report noted that the powerful families who own camel stables are above the law, and the demand for child camel jockeys continues even though some children are repatriated.[31] Anti-Slavery recently found that even though the UAE government states that they are trying to end this abuse, a virtual postcard is, at the time of writing, still on the UAE's official website with a photograph of a young boy riding a camel at a race track.[32]

Most recently, the International Office of Migration (IOM) was asked by the Bangladesh government to assist in the return of children who had been working as camel jockeys in the UAE. The IOM suggested that a medical committee, if established, could check the age and weight of jockeys before races, and airport checks would help stop the trafficking of children into the UAE. They pointed out that integrating children back into society would not be easy; often the children did not know their parents, following long absences since a young age, and they were no longer able to speak their native language.[33] ABWTI has been involved in rescue work, and was able to rescue 49 children from camel stables in the UAE during January to May 2001.

Soccer Players. The second form of child trafficking, which may occur on an even larger scale, is the traffic in child soccer players (from Africa, South America and, to some extent, Eastern Europe) to professional soccer clubs in Western Europe. In the early 1990s, self-styled agents and scouts began to recruit in the newly open countries of Eastern Europe and the former Soviet Union for talented young soccer players for the wealthy soccer clubs of Western Europe. Exclusive contracts were signed with poverty stricken parents in the devastated economies of these countries, and it is believed that many of the children and their families were exploited. Perhaps worse, because of the more extreme poverty and the greater distances (cultural and geographical) involved, is an ongoing traffic in talented young soccer players from Africa and South America. Again, agents contracting with professional soccer clubs in Western Europe sign agreements with parents and bring the children to Europe to try out for and play on the clubs' youth teams. Those who do not make it in the soccer system are often not returned to their homes.[34]

Belgium is often singled out as one of the worst offenders in this regard, with its recruitment of players from Africa. In a paper given to an IOM conference in Brussels, Belgian Senator Paul Wille noted:

> We discovered that Belgium is one of the leading countries to 'import'football players from Africa to sell them on the European market. The problem was that young African boys who didn't receive a contract in a football team ended up illegal on the streets and [often] prostitution was the only way of surviving.[35]

It is believed that many of the homeless children living on the streets of Brussels are abandoned soccer players from Africa. Because of the involvement in prostitution, abandoned soccer players in Belgium were mentioned in the country report of another IOM report on 'Trafficking in Unaccompanied Minors for Sexual Exploitation in the European Union'. The report notes:

> There are known cases of [sexual] exploitation of young football players from Africa and South America in [the professional sportsmen] sector. Untrustworthy agents go to African and South American countries in search of young talent. These young men are lured to the West with the promise of playing for European football clubs.[36] If successful, a contract is signed with a club for a minimal wage for the football player. Often, the length of the contract is not respected so that the football club can own these persons as a commodity ... The issue at stake here is the future prospects of these minors. In case they do not succeed in the football world, what becomes of them?[37]

The situation in Belgium prompted various actions. For example, Paul Carlier started an organization called Sport and Freedom, and lined up an impressive group of human rights and trade union organizations to lobby the Belgium government for legal action. Despite resistance from Belgian professional soccer clubs, new legislation in 1999 prevented the granting of a football license to players under age of 18 who do not have a residence or work permit; increased the rates of pay for non-EU players; and made 'both clubs and agents responsible for the living, medical and travel expenses of non-European recruits for at least 3 years after their arrival'.[38]

Critics in both France and Belgium have referred to trafficking young soccer players as 'the new slave trade'. A BBC news report [39] quoted a leading agent in France who stated that there must be stricter licensing laws for soccer agents, and France was proposing legislation to end transfer fees for players under the age of 18, to limit the activities of agents, and to restrict clubs from placing teenagers under contract. A newspaper report in The Straits Times Interactive,[40] after outlining examples of the traffic and trade of young soccer players between the ages of 10 and 17 (which included the dealings of Arsene Wenger, the manager of English club, Arsenal), notes, 'Amazingly, the selling of minors is not an offence.' A more recent report in the *International Herald Tribune*[41] by Hughes states that, 'Procuring players of school age is rampant and unchecked.' Hughes goes on to note that soccer clubs in less wealthy countries such as Argentina depend on the development and trade of talented young players:

> It is the lifeblood of soccer. It is also a business, a legal speculative trade through which some kids escape poverty. Consequently, some are forced quicker than is good for their physical development and broken in the process. Some find fame, most do not, and countless are left with a hole where adolescent fun and education should have been.

When former Argentine President Carlos Menem declared that he was going to end the trade in young soccer players, he was quickly reined in by the national soccer association, and the traffic in young players continues.

Other Sports. It may be argued that any conditions in professional or pre-professional sports that involve individual athletes under 18 years of age being treated as a commodity, that involve young athletes moving from their homes, and that are unregulated, might be considered as trafficking of children. Kidd and Macfarlane give an example of this kind of practice, which they termed 'child buying', in Canadian ice hockey some 50 years ago.[42]

Community ice hockey programmes, rather than school and university programmes, function as the major talent development system for professional hockey in Canada and, from the late 1940s to the mid 1960s, community teams were tied directly to National Hockey League (NHL) teams. 'As a result, every [hockey playing] boy in Fredericton grew up knowing he was 'Black Hawk property', every boy in Winnipeg 'belonged' to the Boston Bruins'.[43] Agreements between the NHL and the Canadian Amateur Hockey Association (CAHA) were signed in 1947 and 1958, initially during a period of financial hardship for the CAHA. They ensured the sponsorship of teams, and the effective ownership of all young hockey players. The agreements ended in 1966 with the expansion of the NHL.

If we consider the current situation, the data suggest there is still evidence of the exploitation of children in hockey today. Selection drafts replaced direct sponsorship in 1966. However, a type of 'child buying' continues, especially in the form of the 'midget' draft of the best 14, 15 or 16-year-old players to elite, pre-professional 'Major Junior' hockey teams (which maintain a relationship with NHL teams). Although the teams are not technically professional, US universities classify the players as professionals and they are ineligible for interuniversity competition in the United States. The players receive expenses, and are eligible for a bursary to a Canadian university; their games are played before ticket paying audiences. The system ensures that most of the talented adolescent players will have to leave home in order to continue playing. It is a system that makes young players vulnerable to exploitation. For example, they may be exploited by agents befriending parents, and taking advantage of parents' hopes for their children's future as a professional player by signing the children to contracts.

The system of scouting and agents outlined for soccer players above is also evident in ice hockey, and also seems to be growing in basketball. NHL scouts regularly visit Eastern European countries to import talented young players for Major Junior teams in Canada and the US. And in basketball, the trend to signing National Basketball Association (NBA) players directly from high school has started a youth movement that has blossomed in light of the US$90 million contract that US high school player LeBron James signed with Nike (in addition to his NBA salary). Talent scouts and agents are exploring North America and the world now in search of talented young basketball players. We argue that this represents trafficking when the system is unregulated, and when the system caters to the interests of agents, scouts, and professional teams, but makes no provision for the health, education, income protection and social development of individuals who are considered to be 'children' under the UN definition.

Children in High-performance Sport[44]

It is widely acknowledged that adult professional athletes are treated as commodities to be bought and sold, drafted and traded.[45] In the previous section we outlined how these principles have been applied to children, how talented child athletes (or just small children in the case of camel jockeys) are trafficked as commodities in the international system of professional sports. Treatment as a commodity, however, does not always involve trafficking. Talented child athletes in many sports, who train and compete while still living at home, may also be treated as commodities and be implicated in the system of child labour in sports.

Social scientists of sport in Canada and Germany have argued for over 20 years that children's involvement in high-performance sport may be viewed as a form of child labour. Children participate in highly work-like conditions; adults depend on children's work for their own employment and income; the receipt of income, expenses, and prizes formalizes their working status, but many labour in the expectation of future income.

The involvement of children in high-performance sport is relatively recent. The widespread emphasis on early talent identification and specialization in sport may be traced to the Montreal Olympics in 1976, when a 14-year-old Rumanian gymnast (Nadia Comaneci) was awarded the first scores of

10.0 ever recorded in the sport. She, and the large number of medals that were won by Soviet, Cuban and East German athletes, drew attention in the West to the sport system that had been developed in Eastern Europe and the Soviet Union. The system involved a broad base of children's participation in sports from which those who showed signs of athletic talent could be identified. Young athletes so identified were recruited for intensive and specialized training in a particular sport.

East European and Cuban success in Montreal triggered interest in the new system. Sport scientists began to conduct research into talent prediction, and early specialization in sport, and sport organizations began to recruit younger and younger athletes. The early success of the female gymnasts, and victories for young female athletes in sports such as figure skating and swimming, provided an additional incentive for early involvement and specialization. Such early intensive involvement was new to most other sports, and problems began to emerge.

By the early 1980s, commentators such as Cantelon were beginning to identify the new participants as 'child athletic workers', and their participation as 'child labour', and as a social problem.[46] Grüpe summarized the problems for children in elite sport programmes. They:

- are not permitted to be children
- are denied important social contacts and experiences
- are victims of disrupted family life
- are exposed to excessive psychological and physiological stress
- may experience impaired intellectual development
- may become so involved with ... sport that they become detached from the larger society
- face a type of abandonment on completion of their athletic careers.[47]

Donnelly began to study this issue in 1985, conducting a series of retrospective interviews with retired high-performance athletes in Canada.[48] The interviewees represented a variety of sports, and had had successful careers; all had intensive involvement in the sport during their childhood and adolescence; all were given every opportunity to address both positive and negative aspects of their careers; and each spent approximately ten times more time on the negative than the positive.

They reported a variety of problems that they connected directly to their early intensive involvement and specialization. These included:

- family concerns – problems such as sibling rivalry and parental pressure
- social relationships – missed important occasions and experiences during childhood and adolescence

- coach–athlete relationships – authoritarian and abusive (emotional, physical, sexual) relationships, especially male coach–female athlete
- educational concerns – any achievements were earned in spite of the sport and school systems, not because of them
- physical and psychological problems – injuries, stress, and burnout
- drug and dietary problems – some experiences of drug use, widespread concern about disordered eating
- retirement – widespread adjustment difficulties, especially when retirement was not voluntary.

Donnelly also asked the former athletes if they would repeat their careers (10 per cent said no, and 65 per cent gave a qualified yes) 'knowing what [they] know now'; and if they would permit their own children to become involved in intensive training in their sport (40 per cent said no, and the 60 per cent who said yes suggested that their experiences and knowledge would help them to protect their own children from the problems and provide them with a more positive experience).

As a result of these types of critique, and especially following an intensive period of criticism about the US women's gymnastics team following the 1992 Barcelona Olympics (their youth, tiny bodies, and stress fractures gave rise to numerous concerns about eating disorders and other problems), three sports organizations made rule changes. The Women's Tennis Association raised the age for turning professional to 16 years because of the well-publicized burnout of young players such as Tracy Austin, Jennifer Capriati and Andrea Jaeger; and both women's gymnastics and women's figure skating raised the minimum age for international competition to 16 years. However, the new age limits appear to be only token changes. For gymnastics and figure skating they have done little to resolve the problems, and may even have made them worse. Extending the age of international competition without changing judging criteria, or introducing any regulations about health, nutrition, or bone density, may force adolescent girls to attempt to maintain a pre-pubescent body type until they are even older.

Children from all backgrounds, but most commonly now the middle classes, who have shown talent in ice hockey, swimming, figure skating, tennis, gymnastics, etc. – all of the sports that are invested in an early specialization developmental track – may experience the type of problems outlined above. Solving the problems created by early intensive involvement and specialization raises a question of balance. But that balance is difficult when we consider all of the adults who may have a vested interest in a child's success in sport – parents, coaches, sport administrators, educators, sport scientists, sports medicine staff, agents and even media personnel.[49] Such vested interests may range from the often understandable ambition of parents to enable their children to attain the highest level of achievement possible, to more material economic and career advancement interests.

For some of these individuals, their careers and incomes may depend on a child's success; and there are even cases of parents who have taken out a second mortgage in order to finance their talented child's sport development. Kay has demonstrated the stress that supporting a talented child athlete often puts on families.[50] Parents, coaches, and other interested parties are concerned that an over-emphasis on the child having a 'normal' life may lead to failure to fully develop his/her talent (and miss a chance at the Olympics and/or a career as a highly paid professional athlete); but it is apparent that an over-emphasis on the talent can also lead to a variety of problems from exploitation to burnout. It is precisely this lack of balance that led Donnelly to suggest that Canadian national team athletes were the survivors, rather than the products, of our high-performance development system, and that we had to find a way to stop 'sacrific[ing] children on the altar of international and professional sport success'.[51]

Recommendations and Conclusions

The twentieth century was characterized, in part, in the West by increasing concerns about children's rights and child protection. These included restrictions on child labour and the forms of physical punishment that may be applied to children, the recognition of children as a special category under the law and human rights codes, the recognition that adults and the state have a 'duty of care' to the welfare of children, and increasing years of mandatory public education. These are reflected most recently in an increasing 'culture of concern' regarding the safety and supervision of children. We argue that, because of economic and competitive concerns, and because of certain characteristics of the often conservative culture of sport, high performance and professional sport has been out of step with this aspect of social change.

Our analysis of different forms of child labour in sports has emphasized the negative and, in most cases, it is appropriate to emphasize the problems associated with child labour in its various forms. However, it is also important not to overstate the problems, to outline circumstances where there have been successful outcomes, and to develop policies and recommendations that result in even more successful outcomes. For example, while there can be little justification for child labour, the Clean Clothes critique of the Atlanta Agreement noted the following:

• The primary cause of child labour is the poverty of parents, thus children are forced into labour. This is not really taken into account by the [Atlanta Agreement].

- The project as a whole does not properly address the issue – children who don't work for football exporters tend to work in other sectors where working conditions are worse (i.e. brick kilns, and [the manufacture of] surgical instruments).
- The Atlanta Agreement impacts 6–7 thousand working children; there are at least 3.5 million working children in Pakistan (limited approach).[52]

Responses to child labour need to be clearly planned and implemented. The 1990s consumer boycott of clothes made in Bangladesh, following revelations of children's sweat-shop labour in their manufacture, resulted in a widespread closure of factories and many children attempting to survive on the street, often as sex workers. Although Western consumers may feel that an appropriate response to child labour in the sporting goods industry is to boycott products from offending manufacturers, none of the campaigns noted above call for a boycott. All call for an improvement in working conditions and pay scales, a gradual reduction in the use of child labour, and the provision of education for part-time and former child labourers. NGOs now recognize that sudden changes can harm the children and their families (loss of jobs, loss of income in families that may be surviving at a subsistence level), and that a loss of profits can lead to factories closing, and the problem starting up again somewhere else (which requires campaigns to start all over again). Child labour declined in the developed world 100 years ago, during a time of widespread unemployment, when organized labour and social reformers began to work together – trade unions recognized that the use of inexpensive child labour took jobs away from adults. The organization of adult labour in the developing world is likely to have similar effects.

While it is difficult to think of any justifications for the traffic in children as camel jockeys, there have clearly been successful outcomes from the traffic in children in soccer and other sports. Although some have not been able to sign a contract with a club and may have been abandoned on the streets of a European city, and others have been cheated by their agents and exploited by their clubs, a few have gone on to successful professional careers and have been able to help their families in material ways that would not otherwise have been possible. Similarly, many young people who specialized early in a sport, and participated in a high-performance programme that involved intensive training and competitions, thoroughly enjoyed their experiences and went on to enjoy successful, and sometimes materially rewarding careers.

Although we have treated them as part of a continuum and, although there are clear overlapping concerns, in many ways child labour in the sporting goods industry is quite different from the trafficking of talented young athletes and the labour of children in high-performance sports. For the latter, the problem is: how to nurture the talent of highly talented children without exploiting or abusing them or, in other words, how we might assure their all-round healthy development. It is understandable that parents wish their children to achieve their fullest potential, and that talented children will also want to realize their fullest potential, and perhaps receive an opportunity for material success that would not otherwise have been available. Coakley and Donnelly have outlined four possible approaches to resolving the dilemmas raised by these ambitions, each with advantages and disadvantages.[53] We can treat the problem as: an educational issue; a children's rights issue; a child labour issue; or a child welfare issue.

1. Education: all of the adults involved in the lives of elite child athletes need to be educated about child development, and about maintaining a balance in children's lives. Education is the approach most favoured by sports organizations. It is their response to the widespread criticism of problems in their sports (of which they are well aware), but education is also a response that they are able to control. It slows the pace of any changes, thus allowing the status quo, with which all except the children and their parents are familiar, to continue. Education is a slow process with which to effect social change, and while education is necessary, it does not resolve the problems currently being experienced by many young people at present in the system. Criticism, and the resulting education, has brought about some changes (for example, the Canadian women's gymnastics team now boasts that it is the oldest, tallest, and heaviest team in world competition, and that that is preferable to winning medals with 'anorexic children' and the Athens Olympics suggests that such changes may be spreading to other countries), but more drastic measures may also be necessary. Education is also a key to resolving child labour in the sporting goods industry – educated women tend to have fewer children, and to become more economically independent; educated workers are more likely to organize; and provision of education, even on a part-time basis, to child workers will eventually disrupt a system of child labour that is reproduced because of poverty.

2. Children's rights: a children's rights approach forms a bridge between the educational the legal responses to the problems. Galasso produced one of the first children's rights charters in sport.[54] He proposed that children in sport should have:
   • the right to self-determination
   • the right to knowledge
   • the right to be protected from abuse
   • the right to try out for a team or position

- the right to have properly qualified instruction and leadership
- the right to be involved in an environment where opportunity for the development of self-respect, and to be treated with respect, is imperative.[55]

While these are not exclusive to high performance sport, enjoyment of these rights would mean that there had been a significant change in the structure of sport at that level. Such charters raise important issues with regard to children's sport, but they only have moral rather than legal standing and are therefore related more to education and political will. However, the UN Convention on the Rights of the Child[56] does provide a legally binding constraint on signatory governments. The CRC provides a legal means to address violations, and Convention challenges remain an unexplored approach in pursuing children's rights in sport, or children's rights in the sporting goods industry.

3. Child labour: if children's involvement in high performance sport is treated as a child labour issue, the protections invoked by the laws governing workers and the workplace would be available to young athletes. Bart McGuire, CEO of the Women's Tennis Association Tour, acknowledged the concerns about some young professionals: 'If you have both parents who have given up their jobs and are living off the earnings of a player on the tour, the pressure gets to be a concern.... Implicit in the relationship is the fact that if you don't practice for a few days, we don't eat.'[57] Since a number of adults (e.g. coaches, medical staff) may depend on the labour and income of young athletes for their livelihood, they may have more of a vested interest in the athlete's performance than in his / her healthy development. However, while children may be traded as commodities, earn incomes, and play and practice in highly work-like environments, the legal system has been slow to adapt to the rapid changes that have occurred in sport, and this is still an area in which it is possible for authorities to deny that children are working. Thus, there are few protections in the form of limits on training time or the number of competitions, enforcement of the time that athletes devote to compulsory education, securing and investing their incomes, or access to health and safety regulations that govern workers and employers in the workplace. It also appears that such protections are not soon likely to appear. In the entertainment industry (film, television, advertising, dance, music, theatre, and modelling), where it is quite clear that children are workers, such protections for children are beginning to appear as a result of legislation and/or union agreements. Since professional and Olympic sports are arguably part of the entertainment industry, it may be possible to look forward to the day when similar protections are offered to child athletes.

Certainly, the implementation and enforcement of child labour laws, and workplace health and safety laws in developing nations would go a long way toward resolving the problems in the manufacture of sporting goods.

4. Child welfare: child welfare laws are more discretionary than child labour laws. As Tenebaum noted, 'When we can reasonably foresee that others will be affected by our actions the law says that we owe them a '"duty of care" in terms of how we ought to behave...'.[58] This 'duty of care' is considerably higher for children because of their special need for attention and protection. Child welfare laws are intended to protect children from physical harm, negligence, sexual molestation, emotional harm and abuse; and to ensure that they receive appropriate medical care. All of these protections have been violated in the case of children in high-performance sport. However, the agencies intended to ensure child welfare are usually so overworked with respect to, for example, dysfunctional families, or more overt forms of child abuse, that they are not likely to be eager to investigate complaints involving sport. And, even if child welfare laws exist and are enforced in developing nations, the sporting goods industry would have a relatively low priority when compared to the welfare of children involved in much worse forms of child labour.

Of the four possible approaches to resolving the problems of talented children in sports, only the 'educational' approach is currently in play – backed up to some extent by growing criticism of the problems and the moral force of 'children's rights'. Perhaps the threat of legal action, internationally as a Convention challenge, or nationally and locally in terms of child labour or child welfare violations, would be enough to speed up the changes being brought about by education. However, that seems unlikely while adults continue to profit from child athletes, and more direct legal action may be necessary. We think that it is probably best not to think of these as choices, but as a four approaches which, if used in combination, may help to alleviate the problems. In the meantime, all of the forms of child labour in sport may be brought to public attention and resolved, at least in part, by a campaign that focused on the corporate social responsibility of both corporations and international sport federations. The regulation of child labour in the sporting goods industry is the responsibility of both governments and corporations. The choice of sporting goods for use, and the selection of sporting goods corporations as sponsors, are responsibilities of international and national sport federations. The regulation of conditions under which children practice and compete, and under which they are bought and sold, is also a responsibility of international and national sport federations, and of umbrella organizations such as the International Olympic Committee (IOC) and the Commonwealth Games Federation.

Campaigns such as the current (leading up to Athens 2004) Oxfam coalition's 'Fair Play at the Olympics',[59] aimed at national Olympic Committees, the IOC, and manufacturers of Olympic clothing who employ sweat-shop labour, provide a model for challenges to all forms of child labour in sports. Corporations who claim to be socially responsible respond to negative publicity about their use of sweat-shop and child labour. Sport federations have rarely been challenged to act responsibly in this way, but a two-pronged effort from socially responsible corporate sponsors and from social activists might begin to have an effect. The IOC has responded, in recent years, to campaigns to bring about greater gender equity at the Olympics, and to campaigns to produce more environmentally responsible Olympics. Child labour in sports could easily be the next campaign.

We think that the government- and corporate-sponsored sports organizations who run high-erformance sport development systems need to be able to ensure that children are not treated as commodities, and not exploited; that governments and sport organizations should ensure the education and healthy development of children and adolescents in the sport development systems for the sake of the vast majority who will not become professional players or Olympic athletes; and that NGOs and sport organizations need to focus on the issue of child labour in the sporting goods industry.

NOTES

An earlier version of this article was presented as a keynote address at the 2nd World Congress of Sociology of Sport, Köln: Germany, June 2003.

1. United Nations Convention on the Rights of the Child (CRC), ⟨www.unhchr.ch/html/menu3/b/k2crc.htm⟩.
2. UNESCO, *International Charter of Physical Education and Sport* (1978) ⟨www.unesco.org/youth/charter.htm⟩.
3. *World Labour Report* (Geneva: ILO, 1992) p.14.
4. *World Labour Report* (note 3).
5. Cited in the Report by the India Committee of the Netherlands (p.4), *Labour Standards in Sports Good Industry in India – with Special Reference to Child Labour. A Case of Corporate Responsibility.* (New Delhi, July 2000) ⟨www.indianet.nl/tatarep.html⟩.
6. *World Labour Report* (note 3).
7. International Labour Organization. *Red Card to Child Labor: Red Card Campaign* (2002). ⟨www.ilo.org/public/English/standards/ipec/ratification⟩.
8. P. Donnelly, 'Child Labour, Sport Labour: Applying Child Labour Laws to Sport', *International Review for the Sociology of Sport*, 32/4 (1997) pp.389–406. '"...a tale which holdeth children from play:" Exploring negative consequences at both exremes of the physical activity spectrum.' Keynote address delivered at the Annual Meeting of the North American Society for Pediatric Excercise Medicine, Lansing, MI, 1 August, 2002; P. Donnelly, 'Marching out of step: Sport, social order, and the case of child labour.' Keynote address delivered at the 2nd World Congress of Sociology of Sport, Köln, Germany, 19 June, 2003.

9. G. Sage, 'Justice do it! The Nike Transnational Advocacy Network: Organization, Collective Actions, and Outcomes', *Sociology of Sport Journal* 16/3 (1999) pp.206–35. G. Knight and J. Greenberg, 'Promotionalism and Subpolitics: Nike and its Labor Critics', *Management Communication Quarterly* 15/4 (2002) pp.54170.
10. The Atlanta Agreement is cited in numerous sources, including the ILO-IPEC (International Programme on the Elimination of Child Labour) document, *IPEC in Action: Asia* (1998) ⟨www.ilo.org/public/english/standards/ipec/publ/field/asia/pakist98pr.htm⟩; Christian Aid, *A Sporting Chance: Tacking Child Labour in India's Sports Goods Industry* (1997) ⟨www.christian-aid.org.uk/indepth/9705spor/sportin2.htm⟩.
11. Christian Aid (note 10).
12. Christian Aid (note 10).
13. J. Sugden and A. Tomlinson, personal communication (1999).
14. Christian Aid (note 10).
15. Global March against Child Labour, *Kick Child Labour Out of Soccer* (2002) ⟨www.globalmarch.org⟩.
16. India Committee of the Netherlands, *The Dark Side of Football* (2002) ⟨www.indianet.nl/iv.html⟩. India Committee of the Netherlands, *Labour Standards in Sports Good Industry in India – With Special Reference to Child Labour. A Case of Corporate Responsibility* (New Delhi, July 2000). ⟨www.indianet.nl/tatarep.html⟩.
17. India Committee of the Netherlands (2000) (note 5).
18. Global March Against Child Labour (note 15).
19. CorpWatch, *Football Dreams Stitched with Children's Hands* (Corpwatch Holding Corporations Accountable, 2002) ⟨www.corpwatch.org⟩.
20. Global March Against Child Labour. *European Union to tackle child labour in the sports good industry* (2002). ⟨www.globalmarch.org/clns/clns-15-06-2002.htm⟩.
21. International Labour Organization (note 7).
22. International Labour Organization, ⟨www.ilo.org⟩.
23. United Nations, ⟨www.un.org⟩.
24. Global March, ⟨www.globalmarch.org⟩.
25. Clean Clothes Campaign, Sialkot, Pakistan. *The Football Industry from Child Labour to Workers' Rights* (1999) ⟨www.cleanclothes.org/publications/child_labour.html⟩.
26. Lawyers for Human Rights and Legal Aid, *Trafficking in Women and Children* (2002) ⟨www.lhrla.sdnpk.org/trafficking.html⟩.
27. Anti-Slavery Organization, *The Trafficking of Child Camel Jockeys to the United Arab Emirates (UAE).* United Nations Commission on Human Rights. Sub-Commission on the Promotion and Protection of Human Rights, Working Group on Contemporary Forms of Slavery, 27th Session (2002) ⟨www.antislavery.org/archive/submission/submission2002-UAE.html⟩.
28. *Trafficking in Migrants Quarterly Bulletin* 23 (2001) 2–3.
29. United Nations Wire, *Pakistan: Authorities Arrest Alleged Agents of Child Camel Jockeys* (2002) ⟨www.unfoundation.org/unwire/2002/07/09/⟩.
30. Anti-Slavery Organization, ⟨www.antislavery.org⟩.
31. Reported by the Anti-Slavery Organization (note 30).
32. United Arab Emirates. Official website ⟨www.uae-pages.com⟩.
33. International Office of Migration, Bangladesh child camel jockey repatriation (2002) ⟨www.iom.int/en.news/phn200802.shtml⟩.
34. L. Krushelnycky, 'Belgium's Football "Slave Trade"', *BBC News World Edition. Crossing Continents*, (10 March 1999).
35. P. Wille, 'Future Policies on Prevention and Trafficking of Human Beings in Europe' (p.5), paper presented at IOM-Conference on Prevention of and fighting against trafficking in human beings with particular focus on enhancing co-operation in the process to enlarge the European Union (2002).
36. Serge Nijki Bodo, a 17-year-old player from the Cameroon, was abandoned by a Belgian club just as his three-month visa ran out. He stated, 'When you're a youngster in Africa, you watch TV, and you see the beautiful soccer stadiums, and you want to wear the football strip like

the real professional players.' Bodo, who was never paid, found that the contract he signed had been altered to guarantee his agent 50 per cent of his earnings. L. Krushelnycky (note 34).
37. International Office of Migration (note 33) p.41.
38. See L. Krushelnycky (note 34).
39. J. Sopel, 'Football "Slave Trade"', *BBC News* (14 February 2000) ⟨www.peacelink.it/anb-bia/week_2k/2k02224a⟩.
40. *The Strait Times Interactive*, 'In Soccer Bondage' (24 December 2000) ⟨http://straitstimes.asial.com...g/mnt/html/preiership/news-dec-22.html⟩.
41. R. Hughes, 'Nobody Blinks at the Plundering of Tender Young Talent', *International Herald Tribune* (2000) www.iht.com/IHT/RH/rh090299.html
42. B. Kidd and J. Macfarlane, *The Death of Hockey* (Toronto, ON: New Press, 1972).
43. Ibid. p.56.
44. Parts of this and the following sections are adapted from J. Coakley and P. Donnelly, *Sports in Society: Issues and Controversies*, 1st Canadian edition. (Toronto: McGraw-Hill Ryerson, 2004).
45. Robidoux makes this case most explicitly in his analysis of 'farm systems' for the highest level professional sports teams. M. Robidoux, *Men at Work. A Working Understanding of Professional Hockey* (Montreal and Kingston: McGall-Queen's University Press, 2001).
46. H. Cantelon, 'High Performance Sport and the Child Athlete: Learning to Labour', in A. Ingham and E. Broom (eds.) *Career Patterns and Career Contingencies in Sport* (Vancouver: University of British Columbia, 1981).
47. O. Grupe, 'Top Level Sport for Children From an Educational Viewpoint', *International Journal for Physical Education* 22/1 (1985) pp.10–11.
48. P. Donnelly, Problems Associated with Youth Involvement in High Performance Sport in B. Cahill and A. Pearl (eds.), *Intensive Participation in Children's Sports* (Champaign, IL: Human Kinetics, 1993).
49. P. Donnelly (1997) (note 8).
50. T. Kay, 'Sporting Excellence: A Family Affair?' *European Physical Education Review* 6/2 (2000) pp.151–69.
51. P. Donnelly (note 48) p.120.
52. Clean Clothes Campaign (note 25).
53. J. Coakley and P. Donnelly *Sports in Society* (note 44).
54. P. Galasso, *Philosophy of Sport and Physical Activity* (Toronto:Ontario Scholars Press, 1998).
55. Ibid, pp.334–36.
56. UN Convention on the Rights of the Child (1989) ⟨www.unicef.org/crc/crc.htm⟩
57. S. Brunt, Unlike Other Games, 'Women's Tennis is Child's Play', *Globe and Mail* (18 August 1999) p.S1.
58. K. Tenebaum, Daunted Spirits, Mangled Bodies: Children in High Performance Sport (unpublished paper, McMaster University, 1996) p.25.
59. See Oxfam, *Fair Play at the Olympics* ⟨www.fairolympics.org⟩

Women and Children First? Child Abuse and Child Protection in Sport

CELIA BRACKENRIDGE

Introduction

Child welfare and women's rights both feature prominently in contemporary debates on equal rights. Efforts to combat trafficking and domestic violence, for example, have included adult women *and* children since age per se is not a defence against such forms of exploitation. Whereas gender equity has been a policy objective for the past 30 years in sport organizations, child protection has only recently emerged as a sport ethics issue, following several public scandals in swimming and other sports in the early 1990s.[1] The response of the state to concerns about child abuse in sport was initially slow but gathered momentum as the result of grassroots pressure and, arguably, child protection has now leapfrogged over gender equity as a policy priority. In this article, I will outline how child protection initiatives in England have developed since those early scandals and raise some questions about whether the focus on the children's rights agenda in sport has helped or hindered the development of gender equity and women's rights in sport.

The article opens with a discussion of the role of children in sport in relation to opposing ideologies of social control and personal freedom. It then examines the place of women in English sports policy and practice, revisiting some of the well-known feminist critiques of sport. Once child abuse in sport had been recognized, the institutionalization of child protection occurred relatively fast, with a dedicated Child Protection in Sport Unit being established jointly by the National Society for the Prevention of Cruelty to Children (NSPCC) and Sport England in 2001. This development is described and the benefits and limitations of it are assessed and placed in a global context. The shift in theoretical focus from 'women' to 'gender' has been accompanied by a widening of the general social policy focus away from solely heterosexual interests to include the rights of gay men, lesbians, bisexual and transgender people. It is argued here that this shift has not yet occurred in sport policy or practice because of the inherent conservatism of the institution and its continued political marginalization. Child protection has acted as a kind of Trojan horse, wheeled into the centre of sports politics more successfully than women's rights (and gender equity) ever could be and, at the same time, opening up the ethics agenda more widely then ever before. The paradox of child protection, laid out in this article, is that it has simultaneously drawn public attention to issues of abuse and exploitation in sport *and* deflected attention away from the specific issue of women's rights in sport.

Children in Sport

Sport has always been riven with class, gender, race and other social divisions. It is essentially a competitive activity and the striving for supremacy has masked these divisions in a false contest of assumed equals and so-called level playing fields.[2] As a social institution, sport shares many of its basic values with the Christian church. Indeed, in the nineteenth century 'muscular Christianity', whereby missionaries carried both bibles and footballs, helped to disseminate the virtues of both religion and sport.[3] Sport was also used at that time in public schools and corrective institutions for children as part of the disciplinary practices that were consonant with the Victorian ideal of 'spare the rod and spoil the child'.

Parton argues that children were constructed by the Victorian Poor Laws as a delinquent threat since their destitute status rendered them social outcasts.[4] It was not until the 1980s, when, according to Franklin, children's rights 'came of age', that legislation in Britain ceased to objectify the child and instead created the 'child-as-subject', with the right for children to comment on their own lives.[5] The 1989 United Nations (UN) Children's Charter was an international expression of the rights of the child, albeit it within a monocultural context.[6] While this has been adopted across almost all member nations, barring the United States and Somalia, its impact on practice has been variable.[7] Lyon and Parton, for example, argue that the child is now legally defined in order to allow arms-length social and political control over the family.[8] Since the mid-1980s, children have assumed more visibility in English society as their rights as citizens have come to be acknowledged. The citizenship status of the child, however, is still not fully embedded in all spheres of public life, nor in many private settings, since their capability as decision makers is not universally accepted. In sport, for example, it is still rare to find children consulted or represented in the decision-making process, even in matters of direct concern to them.

The cultural construction of childhood varies between nations and, because there is no universally accepted delineation between 'adulthood' and 'childhood', there are also anomalies and disparities between the rights and responsibilities accruing to these statuses. Variations in the age threshold for criminality, smoking, marriage, sexual relations, voting and gun use are just some illustrations of the age-related confusion of rights. Even within the sport community, age and rights are further confounded because 'junior' and 'senior' age definitions vary between sports. Adult athletes are frequently treated like children, with their freedom to socialize, eat, drink and travel curtailed by training regimes and coaches. At the same time, talented child athletes are frequently defined as adults, in relation to the expectations placed upon them to function and perform at a high level. It is therefore unsurprising that there is confusion about both moral and sexual boundaries in sport.

There has been a long association between sport/body and mind, including the adoption of sport within the nineteenth public school system as a mechanism of social control (*mens sana in corpore sano*). The discipline of sport was thus an ideological means to discipline the mind and heart. Ironically, as the child/athlete has been fragmented into his/her physiological, biomechanical and psychological self through sport science, so his/her moral status and its integrated personhood have often been lost. Sport science has perhaps been working, unwittingly, in opposition to the general children's rights movement, representing the child as raw material for performance enhancement.[9] Whereas early twentieth-century physical education focused on development *through* the physical, the most recent sport science credo – Long Term Athlete Development – effectively excludes any concern for individual moral reasoning or political autonomy in the developing athlete as a performance machine.[10] The suppression of individual autonomy through coaching practice maintains the status of the coach-as-controller.

Indeed, in his analysis of child labour in relation to labour laws, Donnelly uncovered exploitative practices in sport that would never be tolerated in educational or employment settings.[11] Because of the laxity with which children's rights have been applied in sport, various other types of exploitation, such as sexual abuse, have been facilitated.

Women in Sport

The history of women's struggles for recognition in sport has been fully and convincingly recorded by feminist sport historians and sociologists.[12] While such authors have now corrected the record of women's invisibility in sport, they have not yet succeeded in helping to transform the institutions that perpetrate exclusionary sporting practices. In England, there was no policy on women and sport until 1993 and even then the policy was the first ever to be rejected by the Sports Council (the UK sport's ruling body) when it was first presented for approval.[13] Once accepted, and despite its relatively liberal tone, the policy became one of the foundation stones for international advances, leading to the Brighton Declaration in 1994.[14] This Declaration is a ten-point set of principles for women's sport which emanated from the 1994 Brighton international conference on women and sport. It addresses:

- equity and equality in society and sport
- facilities
- school and junior sport
- developing participation
- high-performance sport
- leadership in sport
- education, training and development
- sports information and research
- resources
- domestic and international competition.

The Brighton conference was followed by world congresses of women and sport in Namibia and Montreal at which international progress on the endorsement of the original declaration by government and non-government bodies was reported.[15] Notwithstanding the significance of achieving an international template for women's sports development, critics of the Declaration argue that it, along with a number of parallel organizational and pressure-group initiatives for women's sport, merely reflect, defer to and therefore perpetuate, a patriarchal sporting system.[16] In its attempts to move from exclusion (not being allowed to play), to inclusion (being allowed to play but have no power), to equity (playing with parity), to transformation (humanizing the structures and practices of sport) I would argue that British women's sport has become stuck somewhere between inclusion and equity.[17]

Although England and the other 'home countries' of the UK each developed sport policies for women and girls they left the patriarchal sub-structure of sport intact. A couple of Regional Sports Council and Standing Conferences of Sport were brave enough to mention sexuality in their own policy documents but, in essence, policy formulations for women's sport stalled. This is because they were seen, in and of themselves, as radical within the institution of sport yet were hopelessly behind the times when measured against wider political and feminist developments. In short, women in sport were seen as relevant neither to sport (which was and is male) nor to women (whose conservatives eschewed it as unfeminine and whose radicals eschewed it as anti-feminist).

Birrell and Theberge summarized the main aspects of cultural struggle facing women in sport in fairly familiar ways, as *social justice* issues (adapted below):[18]

- patriarchal privilege (sexism and male violence)
- unrestricted capital accumulation (classism)

- white skin privilege (racism and sectarianism)
- compulsory heterosexuality (homophobia)
- reproduction of privilege (social exclusion)

While women working within the sport community failed to connect with these wider social justice concerns, it is no wonder that their efforts for recognition and status went largely unrewarded. Heterosexuality is still an 'organizing principle' in sport with sex segregation embedded in its constitutive systems and in the ideological and cultural domination enjoyed by heterosexual men.[19] In recognition of this, a number of pro-feminists (male supporters of critical feminist analysis of sport) have attempted to reformulate our understanding of the gender order in sport and to draw attention to the cultural constructions of gender and sexuality that afford privilege to males but that *can* be reconstructed to challenge such privilege.[20] The politicization of the female athlete has also been an ongoing project for radical feminist critics of sport.[21] According to such critiques, only by challenging the depoliticization that appears to be a by-product of the coaching process *and* by emphasizing the individual agency of the female athlete will women's sport ever succeed in defining its own future. Importantly, it was these feminist researcher advocates who prepared the way for pro-feminist men to receive acclaim for their 'gender work' in sport. What might subsequently have been lost in the process of acknowledging 'gender' in sport is the value of the pioneering work on 'women'. It is arguable whether the sudden rise of child abuse and protection up the sport policy agenda has helped or hindered the process of women's recognition and representation in sport. It is to this issue that we now turn.

Child Abuse and Protection in Sport

The sexual exploitation of children has been one of the more successful radicalizing issues in sport. Sexual exploitation and abuse are not, of course, new dangers in Western society but they are relatively new to the sport community which has previously preferred to see sport as something of a moral oasis. Interestingly, the 'moral panic' generated by the issue is closely linked to homophobic fears about the breakdown of normative (that is heterosexual) morality and the nuclear family.[22]

The traditional autonomy of the voluntary sport sector has effectively shielded it from external scrutiny and from the regulatory systems that characterize workplace industrial labour relations. Even major human rights legislation on behalf of children has yet to make an impact on certain exploitative sporting practices.[23] The permissive context of child exploitation – whether sexual, physical or emotional – in sport, arises from the symbolic separation of sport from social and legal regulation. Individual abuses take place within a network of personal and organizational relationships that are historically resistant to outside interference. These networks collectively place athletes, whether children *or* adults, in an exploitative relation to authority figures and thus increase their susceptibility to exploitation.

David describes 1989 as a

> ... crucial benchmark in the field of child protection as it marks the year the United Nations General Assembly adopted the Convention on the Rights of the Child. For the first time ever, a legally binding international treaty recognized, to persons under 18 years of age, a full set of human rights ... [and] moved child protection from the traditional welfare approach to a more modern and dynamic one, the rights-based approach.[24]

Notwithstanding the legislative force of the UN Declaration, David also suggests that 'the promotion and protection of the human rights of young athletes in the context of competitive sport has received almost no recognition and has rarely been discussed ...'.[25] While recognizing the undoubted potential benefits of sport for children, in terms of health, well-being and self-determination, David identifies five main situations that have the potential to threaten the physical and mental integrity of child athletes: involvement in early intensive training; sexual abuse and violence; doping; economic exploitation through the transfer market and trafficking; and limitations on access to education.[26]

Prior to the UN Declaration, throughout the 1980s, there was increasing public awareness of the problem of child abuse in UK society resulting from a number of serious disclosures and legal cases. A national telephone help line, the charity-funded ChildLine, was first established in 1986 and subsequently merged with the NSPCC's own helpline service. In sport, some work on codes of ethics and conduct was done in the mid-1980s.[27] But child protection was not named as an issue in UK sport until the late 1980s.[28] Even by the early 1990s, there had been virtually no child protection work in UK sport organizations, and there was widespread denial of the issue. The arrest in 1993 of a former British Olympic swimming coach first brought child protection to the attention of sportspeople in a dramatic way. Paul Hickson was eventually convicted in 1995 for sexual assaults against teenage swimmers in his care over about a 20-year period. His prison sentence – of 17 years – was the longest ever sentence for rape imposed in an English court at that time (subsequently a sentence of 20 years was passed for sexual assaults by a man in the context of equestrian sport). What became known as 'the Hickson case' was a defining moment in the history of sexual exploitation in sport.

The moral panic around sexual exploitation in sport served to expose the processes of social control in sport. Many of those at the top of sporting organizations ridiculed allegations, claiming that cases of abuse were 'just a one-off' or suggesting that this was a problem of society and not one that sport itself could address.[29] Over a two or three year period during the mid-1990s, however, the fear of paedophile infiltration of sport grew to such an extent in Britain that many local government departments and governing bodies of sport began to develop their own, separate policy initiatives, duplicating both effort and resources.[30] After several years of upward pressure on government sport authorities by those with little power, such as sports development officers, parents and club officials, a National Child Protection in Sport Task Force was convened by Sport England in 1999.[31] (At that time only about half of the governing bodies of sport that received government grants had in place a CP policy.)[32] This represented a major breakthrough in the strategic efforts to deal with sexual and other forms of exploitation in sport. It led to a jointly-funded NSPCC/Sport England Child Protection in Sport Unit (CPSU), which began work in January 2001 on implementing the Task Force Action Plan.[33] The primary functions of the CPSU, which is based at the NSPCC's National Training Centre in Leicester, are to:

- act as one-stop-shop for governing bodies
- develop policy and procedures
- operate a 24-hour helpline
- advise sport organizations on case management
- run a research group
- liaise with Government
- set national child protection standards together with Sport England
- assist funded sports to develop child protection policies and Action Plans
- accredit and quality assure training.

The Unit addressed a number of these strategic priorities within its first year of operation, including: the establishment of policy standards for sport bodies, the establishment of working groups for education and training, research and policy and functional relationships with a wide range of sports clubs, federal bodies and individual national governing bodies of sport.[34]

A crucial stage in the acceptance of child abuse as a legitimate concern for sport was when 'paedophiles' – external to the sport system – were defined as the *cause* of the problem. Illicit (predominantly heterosexual) sexual relationships between under-age athletes and authority figures (mainly male coaches) had gone on for years and had been tacitly condoned but the moment 'the paedophile' became labelled as the folk devil, a perfect scapegoat was offered to members of sport organizations who then rallied together to express their growing concern about the external threat of sexual exploitation to children.[35] For some women who had observed at first hand their past discriminations and sexual excesses against female athletes this hypocrisy was hard to bear.

In addition to the false externalization of abuse threats, sometimes described as the 'othering' of the abuser, another consequence of the moral panic surrounding abuse in sport has been a preoccupation among some sport leaders with the possibility of so-called false accusations or false allegations against them or their colleagues.[36] The rights of the 'professional' thus appear to have been elevated over those of the child, despite very little empirical evidence to substantiate such concerns. One framework for understanding the dynamics of child protection in sport is offered in Figure 1.[37] This framework sets out four dimensions of protection that sport leaders or professionals should attend to in relation to child abuse:

1. **Protecting the athlete from others:** that is, recognizing and referring anyone who has been subjected to abuse or sexual misconduct by someone else, whether *inside* sport (by another staff member or athlete) or *outside* sport (by someone in the family or peer group).
2. **Protecting the athlete from oneself:** that is, observing and encouraging good practice when working with athletes in order to avoid perpetrating abuse.
3. **Protecting oneself from the athlete or others:** that is, taking precautions to avoid false allegations against oneself by athletes or their peers or families.
4. **Protecting one's profession:** that is, safeguarding the good name and integrity of sport, coaching, sport science and management.

FIGURE 1

FOUR DIMENSIONS OF PROTECTION IN SPORT

Where:

Sport leader	= the athlete's coach, teacher, physio or other authority figure
Athlete	= athlete in dependent relationship to sport leader/professional
Family or other	= primary carers, siblings, peer coaches and peer athletes

This depiction of four dimensions of protection has potential benefits. For example, as empirical evidence is gathered to support or refute the weight of concerns along each dimension, the model could be used to re-balance policies and practices for child protection in sport. In addition, it should assist with clarifying the interests of the key stakeholders in a way that helps to: allay fears (of adults concerned about false allegations): focus the attention of leaders in sport on their referral responsibilities (abuses perpetrated outside sport); emphasize good practice (in coaching, teaching, sport science and so on) as a protective measure; and, most importantly, set protection within the broad context of sport ethics. There are examples of interventions in sport relating to all four dimensions, largely promulgated through education and training workshops from Sportscoach UK, the NSPCC and some of the major governing bodies of sport, including The Football Association. Since April 2001, all Exchequer-funded governing bodies of sport in England have been required to have in place a child protection action plan in order to qualify for grant aid.[38] This single change, alone, has had a major positive impact on the uptake of protective interventions. It has forced governing bodies of sport to engage with child protection with an intensity that some have found very challenging indeed. However, it has also helped to take many sport administrators through the 'denial barrier' that previously prevented them from accepting the possibility of child abuse in their sports.

Similar initiatives in sport are not easy to find outside the UK, although in Canada, where social welfare objectives in sport have always been comparatively strongly supported by state agencies, there are local and national initiatives to support zero-tolerance towards harassment in sport and where the national equivalent of the UK's Women's Sports Foundation, the Canadian Association for the Advancement of Women in Sport and Recreation (CAAWS), developed its harassment polices as long ago as 1994.[39] Interestingly, the Canadian Red Cross also published one of the first advice and procedures documents on child protection.[40] In Australia, a series of policy documents on harassment-free sport was published in 1998 and has recently been followed by more recent policy directives on child protection.[41]

European attitudes towards gender equity are much more advanced than those elsewhere, with state involvement in gender equity work since the 1980s and a long-standing European Women and Sport Working Group and representing most of the established and some of the emerging European nations.[42] The same cannot be said of child protection in sport. Here, the Council of Europe began to take an interest in 1997 through a national 'survey' (in reality, a set of self-report items from member states). Desk studies of sexual harassment of women and children in sport were commissioned by the Council of Europe in 1998 and 1999 and followed by the adoption of a directive at a meeting of European Ministers for Sport in

Bratislava.[43] A SPRINT seminar, with 27 member states present, was held in Helsinki in 2001 that attempted to cover issues of welfare and protection for both women and children.[44] The Council of Europe has acted more quickly on this issue than its counterparts in the European Parliament. Some Members of the European Parliament (MEPs) attended a reception in Brussels in May 2002 with staff from the NSPCC and the Child Protection in Sport Task Force, as a result of which child protection was proposed as a theme for the forthcoming 'Year of Education Through Sport' in 2004.[45] The International Olympic Committee, while adopting a set of proposals on harassment at its Paris conference on Women and Sport in March 2000, has not addressed child protection per se, perhaps overlooking the fact that some Olympic performers fall within the legal jurisdiction of 'child' in some countries.[46]

Concern for the welfare of children and young people in sport is gradually surfacing in some non-European countries, for example through, research work in Japan, but there has not yet been a coordinated effort to collate this work globally.[47]

Gender Equity in Sport

Sport has been described as a prime site for the (re)production of heterosexual masculinity by many eminent feminists and pro-feminists.[48] The segregation of sports on grounds of sex is reinforced by powerful ideological and political mechanisms. The heterosexual imperative privileges particular expressions of masculinity above others and above all types of femininity, thus perpetuating the social domination of particular kinds of men and particular expressions of masculinity. However, in recognition of the pointlessness of a hierarchy of equalities (such as white, male, heterosexual over black, female, disabled) theorization has recently shifted away from biologically determined differences to focus on culturally diverse and relational conceptions of gender and sexualities.

Alongside the shift in theoretical focus from 'women' to 'gender', social policy is also shifting to account for much more differentiated conceptions of sexual and gender identity (gay, lesbian, bisexual and transgender) than were recognized under hegemonic heterosexuality. It is argued here, however, that this shift has not yet occurred in sport policy or practice because of the inherent conservatism of the institution towards matters of sex and gender and its continued political marginalization.[49] Mainly driven by employment and legal concerns, active consideration is being given to the establishment in the UK of a single equalities body to replace the different commissions (such as the Equal Opportunities Commission, Commission for Racial Equality and so on). In Ireland and Northern Ireland this has already happened with the setting up of the Equality Authority and the Equality Commission for Northern Ireland respectively. The intention of such new bodies is to allow for multiple discriminations to be more effectively addressed and for more prominence to be given to previously marginalized equality 'strands'. The proposals set out six strands for a new UK body: age, disability, gender, race, religion and sexual orientation.[50] Sport England lists only three strands (or 'target groups' as it describes them) in its equity guidelines – 'ethnic minority communities, people with disabilities, women' but it does acknowledge that '. . . inequality manifests itself in many ways and that these are not the only sectors of the population that are excluded'.[51] Given the non-statutory status of sport and leisure and the private and voluntary settings of most sports clubs, it might seem impossible that sport could be brought within the spirit of these organizational changes. As with their child protection advocacy, however, the Irish have already led the way by stipulating compliance conditions for private sports clubs.[52]

Both sexuality and gender have been differently constructed for women and for men, with sports for men being congruent with masculinity and heterosexuality but sports for women being dissonant with both femininity and heterosexuality.[53] Almost 30 years after Felshin first wrote about the female 'apologetic' in sport, women athletes still adopt overtly feminine clothing, jewellery or other trappings of traditional heterosexuality in order to rebut the threat to their (hetero)sexual identity posed by their participation in sport.[54]

The project of maintaining the privileges of heterosexual masculinity in and through sport has been fiercely pursued by those who perceive equity as a zero-sum game, in other words white, middle-class men who fear losing their power if diversity becomes an imperative for sport. Diversity has many faces but, for these privileged males, is most powerfully repelled if it comes in the form of women gaining prominence in sport, the exposure of homosexuality in sport, or by individual men's own failure to live up to the heterosexual masculine standard. The ideological challenges to men's dominance are thus managed through men's homophobic responses. In this way, as Griffin has demonstrated, all women in sport become labelled (and vilified) as lesbian, regardless of their sexual orientations and 'out' gay males in sport are deemed the most threatening of all since they embody athleticism yet express homosexuality.[55] They therefore present a direct challenge to the heterosexual imperative.

Individual and collective violence (through discrimination, harassment or abuse) constitutes one response to these perceived threats. The heterosexual imperative ensures that, even when men are absent, women in sport are under constant surveillance, with their adherence to social expectations being monitored. Dress, language, gestures and interpersonal behaviour are all targets for subordination and social control. If women choose to resist such control they hazard their access to competitive opportunities, funds or facilities since men control the financial and political infrastructure of sport.

Stereotypical notions of masculine and feminine have been traditionally split along the gender divide. More recently, however, queer theorists have examined the false binaries that characterize sport ideology, the male–female, gay–straight, win–loss relations of sporting practice. In general, however, the material social relations of sport are still far behind queer theorists' analysis and politics. The shift from 'sex' into 'gender' as a focus for theoretical and political debate, while giving a platform for more socially inclusive sports policy across *all* equity strands, has also masked lack of progress (and some would even argue regression) in *women's* rights. It is ironic, therefore, that the impetus for child protection in sport has gained in strength while that for women's rights has declined. For example, in 2001–02 a grant of £130 k, plus a later top-up of £15 k, to the Women's Sports Foundation, the voluntary body that has promoted opportunities for women and girls in sport since 1984 '...appear[ed] to be the total amount of Exchequer funding committed by government [directly or through Sport England] to women's sport', less than the turnover of the CPSU in only its first year of operation.[56] Interestingly, in its annual accounts, Sport England lists a total contribution of £1,720 k to 'Sports equity and social inclusion' but this is not disaggregated.[57] Further, Bennett reports that the English Federation for Disability Sport applied successfully to the TSB Bank Communities Fund but an application from the WSF failed with the organization being told that women were 'too mainstream'.[58]

The relative deceleration of women's rights in sport, compared with the acceleration of child protection, may be due to the widely-publicized backlash against feminism and the women's movement.[59] The backlash argument is that equal rights are now perceived as a 1970s and 1980s issue and that equality is no longer a concern for civil society which is characterized by diversity, plurality, choice and contingency in gender relations. Whether an equivalent backlash will occur in child protection is an interesting question. Finkelhor's contribution to this debate suggests that there will be no decline in public interest in child abuse and protection since its moral force is so powerful and enduring.[60]

Conclusions

If sexual exploitation is only deemed to be problematic when perpetrated against children, then there is a hypocritical distortion of rights at work in sport. The phrase 'child sexual abuse' has been proven to be an effective motivational device with sport practitioner audiences who have, in contrast, shown limited concern about 'sex discrimination' or even 'sexual harassment'. Equally, the use of the word 'child' instead of 'athlete' could be said to have detracted from wider concerns about athlete empowerment for *all* ages.

A rights perspective in sport could have a significant beneficial impact on sporting practices. For example, it could lead to the empowerment of individual athletes, better representation, reductions in their hours of training, increases in financial rewards and insurance protection, and better provision for their long-term education and career planning. But a rights perspective that perpetuates a hierarchy of (in)equalities will do little to advance the cause of women in sport.

Child abuse has risen to consciousness within UK sport over relatively short and inglorious few years. No advocate of children's rights could argue against the advances in policy and practice that have accompanied this development, and the transformative effect that it has had on ethical reflection in sport. But it is important to recognize that a false hierarchy of inequalities favours nobody in the end. The relatively narrow focus of the CPSU on children, defined as under 18 years old, draws attention and resources away from those over that age boundary, including many people with disabilities and, especially, adult women in sport. Child abuse is shocking and degrading and child protection, whether in sport or elsewhere, should be the right of every child. It may be too early to tell, however, whether child protection has hijacked sport as a strategic imperative but it certainly seems to have gained a firm footing in the UK, if not global, sport agenda.

Policies for women and sport, both in the UK and in Europe more generally, have not been as effective as they could have been because of apathy towards gender equity. Child sexual abuse, on the other hand, grabbed the media headlines in the UK and has the potential to open up debate on related rights issues across the equality 'strands'. As the rise and rise of sports ethics continues in response to the many violations apparent in modern sport (doping, fraud, exploitation, violence and others) it will be interesting to observe whether 'gender equity' succeeds where 'women in sport' failed. Child protection may turn out to be the lever for change that has eluded those groups seeking to promote women's rights in sport. At the same time it might deflect both attention and resources away from women's sport.

NOTES

1. C. Brackenridge, *Spoilsports: Understanding and Preventing Sexual Exploitation in Sport* (London: Routledge, 2001).
2. S. Bailey, *Leisure and Class in Victorian England* (London: Routledge & Kegan Paul, 1978). B. Carrington, and I. McDonald (eds.), *Racism and British Sport* (London: Routledge, 2001). S. Scraton and A. Flintoff (eds.) *Gender and Sport: A Reader* (London: Routledge, 2002).
3. J. Clarke, and C. Critcher, *The Devil Makes Work: Leisure in Capitalist Britain* (London: Macmillan, 1985).
4. N. Parton, *The Politics of Child Abuse* (Basingstoke: Macmillan, 1985).
5. B. Franklin (ed.), *The Handbook of Children's Rights: Comparative Policy and Practice* (London: Routledge, 1995).
6. United Nations, *Children's Charter* (New York: UN Office of Public Information, 1989).

7. P. David, 'The Promotion and Protection of the Human Rights of Child Athletes', paper presented to the Council of Europe *Seminar on The Protection of Children, Young People and Women in Sport: How to Guarantee Human Dignity and Equal Rights for These Groups* (Hanaholmen, Finland, 14–16 September 2001).

8. C. Lyon, and N. Parton, Children's Rights and the Children Act 1989 in B. Franklin (ed.) *The Handbook of Children's Rights: Comparative Policy and Practice* (London: Routledge, 1995).

9. M. Weiss, and D. Gould (eds), *The 1984 Olympic Scientific Congress Proceedings*, Vol. 10, (Champaign, IL: Human Kinetics, 1984). R. Magill, M. Ash and F. Smoll (eds.) *Children in Sport*, 3rd Edn (Champaign: Human Kinetics, 1988). V. Grisogono, *Children and Sport: Fitness Injuries and Diet* (London: Murray, 1991).

10. I. Balyi, 'Long-Term Athlete Development, the System and Solutions', *Faster, Higher, Stronger* 14 (2002) 6–9.

11. P. Donnelly, 'Child Labour, Sport Labour: Applying Child Labour Laws to Sport', *International Review for the Sociology of Sport* 32/4 (1997) 389–406. A. Tomlinson, and I. Yorganci, 'Male Coach/Female Athlete Relations: Gender and Power Relations in Competitive Sport', *Journal of Sport and Social Issues*, 21/2 (1997) 134–55.

12. C. Oglesby, *Women and Sport: From Myth to Reality* (Philadelphia, PA: Lea & Febiger, 1978). H. Lenskyj, *Out of Bounds: Women, Sport and Sexuality* (Toronto: The Women's Press, 1986). J. Hargreaves, *Sporting Females: Critical Issues in the History and Sociology of Women's Sports* (London: Routledge, 1994). M. Hall, 'Feminist Activism in Sport: A Comparative Study of Women's Sport Advocacy Organizations' in A. Tomlinson (ed.) *Gender, Sport and Leisure: Continuities and Challenges* (Aachen: Meyer and Meyer Verlag, 1997) 217–50.

13. Sports Council, *Women and Sport: Policy and Framework for Action* (London: Sports Council, 1993).

14. Sports Council, *The Brighton Declaration on Women and Sport* (London: Sports Council, 1994).

15. Sport England, *Windhoek Call for Action* (London: Sport England, 1998). ⟨www.canada2002.org⟩. A. White and D. Scoretz, *From Windhoek to Montreal – Women and Sport Progress Report 1998–2000* (Montreal: Sport Canada, 2002).

16. M. Hall (note 12).

17. C. Brackenridge, 'Think Global, Act Global': The Future of International Women's Sport, *Journal of the International Council for Health, Physical Education, Recreation, Sport and Dance* 11/4 (Summer 1995), 7–11.

18. S. Birrell and N. Theberge, 'Ideological Control of Women in Sport' in D. Costa and S. Guthrie (eds.) *Women and Sport: Interdisciplinary Perspectives* (Champaign, IL: Human Kinetics, 1994), p.362.

19. L. Kolnes, 'Heterosexuality as an Organising Principle in Women's Sports', *International Review for the Sociology of Sport* 30 (1995) 61–80.

20. M. Messner, *Power at Play: Sports and the Problem of Masculinity* (Boston: Beacon Press, 1992). M. Messner and D. Sabo (eds.) *Sport, Men and the Gender Order* (Champaign, IL: Human Kinetics, 1990). M. Messner, and D. Sabo, *Sex, Violence and Power in Sports: Rethinking Masculinity* (Freedom, CA: Crossing Press, 1994).

21. M. Hall, *Sport and Gender: A Feminist Perspective on the Sociology of Sport*, CAPHER Sociology of Sport Monograph Series (Ottawa, Ontario: Canadian Association for Health, Physical Education, and Recreation, 1978). M. A. Hall, How Should We Theorise Sport in a Capitalist Patriarchy?' *International Review for the Sociology of Sport* 1 (1985) 109–13. C. Ogelsby (note 12). J. Hargreaves (note 12). H. Lenksyj (note 12).

22. S. Cohen, *Folk Devils and Moral Panics: The Creation of the Mods and Rockers* (London: MacGibbon and Kee, 1972).

23. P. Donnelly (note 11). P. David (note 7).

24. P. David (note 7) p.1.

25. P. David (note 7) p.3.

26. P. David (note 7).

27. C. Brackenridge, 'Problem? What Problem? Thoughts on a Professional Code of Practice for Coaches', paper presented to the Annual Conference of the British Association of National Coaches, Bristol, England, December 1986. C. H. Brackenridge, 'Ethical Concerns in Women's Sports', *Coaching Focus*, National Coaching Foundation Summer (1987). National Coaching Foundation, *Code of Ethics and Conduct for Sports Coaches* (Leeds: NCF Coachwise, 1995).
28. C. Brackenridge, *Child Protection in British Sport: A Position Statement* (Cheltenham: Cheltenham and Gloucester College of HE, 1998).
29. C. Brackenridge, *Spoilsports: Understanding and Preventing Sexual Exploitation in Sport* (London: Routledge, 2001).
30. Sport England, 'Child Protection – Task Force Formed', Press release, (London: Sport England, 25 October 1999). Sport England, *Child Protection in Sport Task Force, Draft Action Plan*, unpublished paper (London: Sport England, 5 April 2000).
31. C. White, 'Progress Report on Child Protection Policy Development in English National Governing Bodies of Sport', unpublished document presented to a workshop at the NSPCC (14 June 1999).
32. Child Protection in Sport Unit, ⟨www.sportprotects.org.uk⟩ (2002).
33. Child Protection in Sport Unit, *Child Protection in Sport Unit: Business Plan 2001–2004* (Leicester: NSPCC and Sport England, 2002).
34. C. Brackenridge (note 29). S. Cohen (note 22).
35. C. Brackenridge (note 29).
36. C. Brackenridge, 'Ostrich or Eagle? Protection and Professionalism in Coaching and Sport Science', keynote speech to the annual conference of the British Association of Sport and Exercise Sciences (Newport, September 2001).
37. S. Boocock, The Child Protection in Sport Unit in C. Brackenridge and K. Fasting (eds.) *Sexual Harassment and Abuse in Sport – International Research and Policy Perspectives*, Special issue of the *Journal of Sexual Aggression*, 8/2 (2002) 37–48.
38. Canadian Association for the Advancement of Women and Sport, *Harassment in Sport: A Guide to Policies, Procedures and Resources* (Ottawa: CAAWS, 1994). Canadian Association for the Advancement of Women and Sport, *What Sport Organisations Need to Know About Sexual Harassment* (Ottawa: CAAWS, 1994).
39. Canadian Red Cross, *It's More Than a Game. The Prevention of Abuse, Harassment and Neglect in Sport* (Gloucester, Ontario: Canadian Red Cross, 1997).
40. Australian Sports Commission, *Harassment Free Sport: Guidelines for Sport Administrators* (ACT: ASC, 1998). Australian Sports Commission, *Harassment Free Sport: Guidelines for Sport Organisations* (ACT: ASC, 1998). Australian Sports Commission, *Harassment Free Sport: Guidelines for Athletes* (ACT: ASC, 1998). Australian Sports Commission, *Harassment Free Sport: Guidelines for Coaches* (ACT: ASC, 1998). Australian Sports Commission, *Harassment Free Sport: Protecting Children from Abuse in Sport* (ACT: ASC/Active Australia, 2000).
41. Women and Sport European Working Group.
42. C. Brackenridge, and K. Fasting, *An Analysis of Codes of Practice for Preventing Sexual Harassment to Women and Children* (Strasbourg: Council of Europe/Committee for the Development of Sport, 1999). C. Brackenridge and K. Fasting, *The Problems Women and Children Face in Sport with Regard to Sexual Harassment* (Strasbourg: Council of Europe/Committee for the Development of Sport, 1998). Council of Europe, Sexual Harassment and Abuse in Sport, Especially the Case of Women, Children and Youth', resolution of the ninth conference of European Ministers responsible for sport (Bratislava, 31 May 2000).
43. Council of Europe/Committee for the Development of Sport, *Report on the CDDS Seminar on: The Protection of Children, Young People and Women in Sport: How to Guarantee Human Dignity and Equal Rights for these Groups*, held at Hanasaari, Espoo 14–16 September (Strasbourg: Council of Europe/Committee for the Development of Sport, 2001).
44. Resolution of the Ninth European Sports Forum, Lille, October (www.sportsprotects.org.uk 2002).

45. International Olympic Committee, Resolution of the Second IOC World Conference on Women and Sport, Paris (www.Olympic.org/ioc/news/pressrelease/press_255.e.html 8 March 2000).

46. Personal communication, Takako Iida (email: 11 February 2003).

47. H. Lenskyj, 'Sexual Harassment: Female Athletes' Experiences and Coaches' Responsibilities', *Sport Science Periodical on Research and Technology in Sport*, Coaching Association of Canada, 12/6 (1992), Special Topics B-1. M. A. Hall, *Feminism and Sporting Bodies: Essays on Theory and Practice* (Champaign, IL: Human Kinetics, 1996). S. Thompson, 'The Games Begins at Home: Women's Labor in the Service of Sport' in J. Coakley and P. Donnelly (eds.), *Inside Sports* (London: Routledge, 1999), pp.111–20. M. Messner, *Power at Play: Sports and the Problem of Masculinity* (Boston, MA: Beacon Press, 1992). M. Messner, 'Studying up on Sex', *Sociology of Sport Journal*, 13 (1996) 221–37.

48. M. Messner, and D. Sabo (eds.) *Sport, Men and the Gender Order* (Champaign, IL: Human Kinetics, 1990). S. Scraton and A. Flintoff (note 2). N. Theberge, Sport and Women's Empowerment, *Women's Studies International Forum*, 10/4 (1987), 387–393. B. Pronger, *The Arena of Masculinity: Sports, Homosexuality, and the Meaning of Sex* (London: GMP Publishers Ltd, 1990). M. Hall, *Feminism and Sporting Bodies: Essays on Theory and Practice* (Champaign, IL: Human Kinetics, 1996).

49. Department of Trade and Industry, *Equality and Diversity: The Way Ahead* (London: HMSO, 2002).

50. Sport England, *Making English Sport Inclusive: Equity Guidelines for Governing Bodies* ⟨www.sportengland.org/resources/pdfs/people/equity/pdf⟩ (2000) p.3.

51. Child Care Northern Ireland, *Our Duty to Care: Principles of Good Practice for the Protection of Children* (Belfast: DHSS, 1995). Irish Sports Council/Sports Council Northern Ireland *Code of Ethics ands Good Practice for Children's Sport* (Dublin: Irish Sports Council/Sports Council Northern Ireland, 2000). B. Merriman, 'Single Equality – Speaking from Experience' presentation to a conference 'The Future for Equalities: The Implications for Scotland of a Single Equalities Body', Royal Society of Scotland, Edinburgh (25 November 2002).

52. M. Messner, 'Studying up on sex' (note 47) pp.221–37.

53. J. Felshin, The Dialectic of Woman and Sport; E. Gerber, J. Felshin, P. Berlin and W. Wyrick (eds.) *The American Women in Sport* (London: Addison-Wesley, 1974) p.203.

54. P. Griffin, *Strong Women, Deep Closets: Lesbians and Homophobia in Sport* (Champaign, IL: Human Kinetics, 1998). B. Pronger (note 48).

55. R. Acosta and L. Carpenter, *Women in Intercollegiate Sport: A Longitudinal Study – Twenty Five Year Update 1977–2002* (Monograph, Brooklyn College of the City of New York and Project on Women and Social Change of Smith College, 2002).

56. A. Bennett, Personal communication, (email dated 29 November 2002).

57. Sport England, *Annual Report 2000–2001* ⟨www.sportengland.org⟩ (2002).

58. A. Bennet (note 56).

59. S. Faludi, Backlash: *The Undeclared War against Women* (New York: Anchor, 1991).

60. D. Finkelhor, 'The "Backlash" and the Future of Child Protection Advocacy'; J. E. B. Myers (ed.), *The Backlash: Child Protection Under Fire* (London: Sage, 1994) pp.1–16.

Innocence Lost: Child Athletes in China

FAN HONG

> We are the flowers of our motherland,
> We are the children of our socialist country,
> We grow up happily and innocently
> in the New China
>
> – Children's song of the 1960s

It is not a secret that the success of Chinese sport depends on the remarkable system which turns tiny children into sports stars. Lu Li, the Olympic gymnast gold medalist, went to sports school at age of six. When she received her gold medal at the 1992 Barcelona Olympics she was only 13. At the age of 14 she was fighting against injury and pain and wanted to retire. Lu Li is a victim of the sports system. She is not the first, and certainly not the last: there are 80,617 professional athletes in China and two thirds of those are child athletes. In addition, there are 400,000 children trained in 3,000 sports schools throughout China. This article will analyse the system and examine the relationship between child athletes and human rights in the context of culture and politics in contemporary China.

The Elite Sports Training System

One cannot understand child athletes in China without examining China's sports system, which has systematically produced thousands of child stars. In October 1949 the Communists defeated the Nationalists, took over China and established the People's Republic of China (PRC). The Chinese Sports Federation, a non-government sports organization, was established. The function of sport was increasingly recognized by the government. On 15 November 1952 the Sports Ministry was established as a formal government body to promote and control sport.

In 1956 the Sports Ministry issued 'The Competitive Sports System of the PRC'. In consequence, a competitive sports system was formally set up: 43 sports were officially recognized as elite sports; rules and regulations were implemented; professional teams were set up and increased from three in 1951 to more than 50 in 1961. Regional and national championships took place every year and the National Games were held every four years.[1]

From 1957 to 1962 this elite sports system was further developed during and even after the Great Leap Forward (GLF). The GLF officially started in 1957 with the economic goal of overtaking Great Britain within seven years and the USA in 15 years. The Sports Ministry promoted its own Sports Great Leap Forward campaign with the goal of catching the world's best competitive sports countries in ten years. Therefore, the Soviet Union's spare-time sports school model (*Yeyu tixiao*) was copied in order to train and advance talented athletes from a young age. By September 1958, there were 16,000 such schools with 770,000 young athletes.[2]

The failure of the GLF and the Great Famine brought economic disaster and the death of two million people in the early 1960s, but this did not stop the further development of elite sport. In 1961 the Sports Ministry determined to use its limited resources to give focused training in focused sports towards effective international competition. In 1963, the Sports Ministry issued the 'Regulations of Outstanding Athletes and Teams' with a view to improving the system. A search for talented young athletes took place in every province and ten key sports were selected from the previous 43 (athletics, gymnastics, swimming, football, basketball, table tennis, badminton, shooting, weight lifting and skiing).[3]

In the 1970s, during the Cultural Revolution, sport had proved extremely valuable both as a resource and as an arena for diplomacy. As a resource sport enabled the Communists to make approaches to Western enemies through a medium that benefited from its non-political image. The well-known 'Ping-Pong diplomacy' was the best example. Sport was also used to strengthen relations between allies, since it could help effectively to break down national barriers and to establish and promote international contacts between different political systems. 'Friendship First, Competition Second' was the slogan. While other social institutions like education and social services were completely broken down and dysfunctional between 1966 and 1976, athletic training programmes and systems broke down for a far shorter period between 1967 and 1970. They were renewed in 1971 as a consequence of Ping-Pong diplomacy.

In addition, during the Cultural Revolution when many young pupils graduated from their middle schools at 15 or 16 years old they were sent down to the countryside to be 're-educated' by parents. Sport was one of the few ways for them to escape hard labour and return to the city. Athletes were much in demand for entertaining workers in factories and working-units. There were no other cultural events except opera and ballet during the whole Cultural Revolution period for ten years. Sport became a national entertainment, played and watched by millions of people. Therefore, many parents encouraged their children to play sports well when they were young in order to help their future. Despite the unique social, cultural and political circumstances, sport survived and even thrived in China during this period. Sports competitions took place frequently in every city, region and province. Therefore, it was not a surprise when China returned to the Olympic Games in 1984 after the isolation of 32 years, won 14 medals and came fourth in the medals table. The victory stimulated the nation's enthusiasm and motivated people to strive for more Olympic gold.[4]

In the late 1980s the Sports Ministry devised an Olympic strategy and aimed to become a sport superpower by the end of the twentieth century. To achieve that goal, the government continued to channel the best of its limited resources to give special and intensive training to potential gold medallists. For example, the government allocates about a billion Chinese yuan to sports development annually and most of it goes to Olympic events and competitive sports training. In 1990 only 13 million yuan went to sports activities for the general public. Therefore, while a professional athlete's training cost 14,000 yuan a year in 1990, the annual sport funds for an average primary school in Beijing amounted to only 800 yuan, little more than the cost of training a professional athlete for 20 days.[5] National competitions and the National Games, which takes place every four years, are primarily for the purpose of training athletes for international medal-awarding competitions including the Olympics.

Training the Child Stars

The core of the sports system is to produce, systematically and effectively, more elite child athletes. Children from five or six years old are selected to go to specialized sports school where the emphasis is on sports training. They get up at 6:00 a.m. to do exercises such as running and general warm-up for 1–2 hours. They then have their breakfast. After breakfast they have morning session training from 8.00 a.m. to midday. In the afternoon, they study general education courses for four hours. After dinner, they continue their training for another two hours. The training hours generally are 6–8 hours per day. Some senior sports schools would reach 10 hours per day (training during the day and study in the evening after their dinner). From sports schools talented athletes are selected to join professional teams on regional and provincial level. Only the best can make it to the national teams.

The training methods were adapted from the People's Liberation Army in 1963 and are based upon a disciplined, intensive regime of training and practice. Other training methods, emphasizing a more scientific approach to training and the incorporation of rest periods, were criticized as bourgeois. In 1964 a specific Chinese sports training method was introduced which included 'three non-afraids' of hardship, difficulty and injury, and the 'five toughnesses' of spirit, body, skill, training and competition. Since then it has become Chinese sports legend. Vice Prime Minister Chen Yin encouraged athletes: 'Sport is not just playing ball. It reflects our country's image, force, spirit and the superiority of our socialist construction. The achievements in sports are the glory of our country and people. But the glory cannot be achieved without hard training.'[6]

From the 1980s to the present, training methods have evolved to combine the three non-afraids and the five toughnesses with Western scientific training methods. For example, Wang Junxia, the holder of world records from 1,500 m to 10,000 m and recipient of the prestigious Jesse Owens Trophy in 1994, ran 170 km in four days in her training sessions. Almost every child athlete who is working in the national and provincial teams trains for 10–12 hours a day including sports like athletics, gymnastics, swimming, football, basketball, volleyball, badminton and table tennis.

Under this system, child athletes are obliged to devote all their energy and life to their training and performance. They work long hours, train under physical, social and psychological strain and carry much responsibility: winning glory for the nation, the Party, the coaches and their parents.[7] At a provincial sports boarding school, the age range for the boys and girls was from five to ten. Only the fittest could survive and remain in the school or be promoted to professional teams. A British journalist once visited the centre and sighed with emotion: 'I admire these children. I have a daughter of five years old. I can never image that she could endure such a hard life.'[8]

These children are not permitted to be children. They are denied normal family lives and important contacts and experience. They have lost their rights to play like a child. According to the World Labour Report, some characteristics of child labour are: working too young; working long hours; working under strain; working for very little pay; and taking too much responsibility.[9] Child athletes should be regarded as child labour. They are too young to understand that they should have rights to enjoy their innocent ages. They are too young to defend themselves when faced with sexual exploitation.

Sexual Exploitation

Sexual exploitation arguably can include physical abuse, emotional abuse, sexual abuse and neglect. These four types of abuse may connect and overlap. A child may suffer from one, or some, or all of them.[10] Sport frequently involves close personal relationship, both among groups of athletes and between individual athletes and their coaches or leaders. The trust that develops between the athletes and coaches is often regarded as an essential part of training for success. Sometimes, more powerful individuals take advantage of those with less power, using demeaning sexual harassing behaviour – such as sexist jokes or unwanted touching – or in the most extreme cases abusing them sexually, emotionally or physically.[11] Sexual exploitation may be perpetrated by both adult authority figures and coaches. They act as a kind of 'father or mother figure' for the young athletes, especially where the child's natural parents are either absent or show no interest in their sporting progress. The younger the athletes the more vulnerable the victims are because they are easier to control and they have nowhere else to turn.[12] Research conducted in Canada, Norway and Australia points to some athletes experiencing sexual exploitation and abuse in their sporting lives. There are some stories about the 'un-usual' sexual relationships between athletes and coaches and managers in the Chinese sports world. There are rumours about some female athletes running away or taking early retirement to avoid their coaches' sexual abuse. However, due to the tied control of the sports authority and the media, nothing has been proved.

Nevertheless, young Chinese female athletes have always been stereotyped by coaches and academics as willing victims. They have been trained under cruel and inhumane circumstances since the 1960s. The situation has not changed and in some cases it went even further. The famous coach, Ma, and his 'army' can be used as one of the examples. In the 1990s, Chinese women runners emerged as the dominant performers in middle and long-distance races in international competitions. The person credited with this success was their coach, Ma Junren. The team's success has been attributed to his use of traditional Chinese herbal medicine and his rigorous training methods. However, Zhao Yu, a writer, revealed in his book, *The Investigation of the Ma's Army*, the dark side of the story. Ma Junren acted not as a modern athletics coach, but as an ancient gladiator trainer. Girls under his training were 14–16 years old. They had to run 220 km a week – almost a marathon a day. He beat them whenever he wanted to. Wang Junxia, the holder of world records from 1,500 m to 10,000 m and recipient of the prestigious Jesse Owens Trophy in 1994, was beaten by Ma every week, sometimes even in front of TV crews and her parents for her 'inappropriate behaviour'.[13] The same things happened to the other female athletes. Zhao Yu claimed that all girls were subjected to verbal and physical abuse regularly.[14]

Ma also controlled all aspects of their lives. He controlled their wages and did not allow the girls to have money in their pockets. He controlled their reward money and used millions of it to build his training centre. He controlled their medals, rewarded cars and houses and used them to trade for his benefit. He also controlled their personal lives. Girls were forbidden to have boyfriends or to have long hair, face cream, let alone make-up, nice clothes and even bras.[15] On one occasion when Ma noticed Liu Dong, the 5,000 m world champion, wearing a bra he lined the whole team on the training ground, threw her bra on the ground and called her 'a prostitute who wants to attract men'. The humiliation forced Liu Dong to leave the team and retire, while at the peak of her career.

In Ma's training centre there was no music because Ma smashed all records, CDs and tapes by hammer; no books and magazines because Ma burned them all; no educational classes because Ma hated them; no privacy – even private letters were examined by Ma before they reached the receivers. Ma was the feudal warlord. Female athletes had to obey him completely and serve him like slaves. Their duties included washing his feet everyday.[16] Although Ma's cruelty and inhumanity was partially revealed and criticized by the media, Ma was not punished but promoted from a coach to a vice director of Liaoning Provincial Sports Commission and a member of the Chinese People's Political Consultative Conference for his contribution to the Chinese gold medals.

Physical abuse not only happened to young girls but also boys. In a national football boarding-school boys 12–16 years old trained for three years. They suffered verbal and physical abuse every day. Some coaches slapped and kicked boys when they felt like it. They would shout the Chinese proverb while beating the boys that 'Beating means care, abuse means love. If there is no beating and abuse children would not grow up to be useful men.' Bullying and physical abuse were sometimes serious enough to cause young footballers to leave the school. [17]

In both China and Western countries, sport traditionally has shown a high tolerance for violent behaviour on the field of play. This is partially due to the nature of sport, aggression and masculinity (and femininity), and partially due to violence that takes place within the private domain of the locker room and other spaces away from public gaze.[18] However, in the West, tolerance for such behaviour has declined in recent years because of legal challenges.[19] In China, tolerance for violence in sport has increased because of the modern commercialization of sport which brings top sportsmen and women fame and fortune, and because of the firm belief of the traditional culture by their parents, coaches and athletes themselves that 'only those who endure the most hardship can come to the top'.

Therefore, child athletes 'are being exploited, or over-worked, or deprived of their rights to health and education'.[20] When they retired from their sports, at their mid-twenties, the majority face post-sports career crises. In general, athletes have several options. The first is to become officials; the second is to become coaches; the third is to establish sports agencies or companies – but only a handful of world-class athletes with money will be able to follow this route. The fourth is to go to university or college. The government encourages athletes to continue their education after their retirement. World champions can enter universities without passing any examination, while the Sports Law of 1995 claimed that 'national and international champions will be given priority for enrolment in universities'.[21] Some universities and colleges have reduced their entrance scores to attract famous athletes, like Qin Hua University and Beijing Sport University. However, because they received inadequate education in their early years, some athletes who entered universities find it hard to catch up with the rest of the class and have to drop out after their first year.

Furthermore, the above options generally apply only to those who became international athletes. Their fame and fortune provide opportunities denied to the many young athletes who did not reach to the top. They did not have the opportunity to become officials and coaches; they had no money to set up their own business; and they could not take advantage of the lower entry standards to universities and colleges. They became 'waiting to work persons' (the Chinese term equivalent to unemployment) by their mid-twenties. However, some people in China have started to question the system. As one senior sports official rhetorically asked, 'Do we really need to push children into specialized training at such a young age? They give up their formal education, family life and normal childhood. Only a handful of children can get to the top and many cannot. So what can they do? They are ruined. They don't have education and they cannot even finish their primary school education. When they are 25 years old most of their sporting life is over and what can they do? No education, no qualification, no skill to earn their living, nothing. They are ruined!'[22]

Research conducted in 2002 by Deng Yaping, a former table tennis world and Olympic champion, provided an interesting case study. She concluded that it is not good for those children who started from a very young age to play table tennis and aim to become professional players in the future. They spent their first 15 years doing nothing but playing table tennis. They dreamed of becoming world table tennis champions. However, there were nearly 1,000 professional table tennis players in China, but only 20 of them could join the national team and have the opportunity to reach to the top. The majority had to retire at the age of 25. Deng argued that because of their early professional training the players spent years and put all their concentration on table tennis. As a result table tennis players could do nothing, but play table tennis. When they left their small table tennis world and entered the society they found that nobody wanted them and they were useless. This has adversely affected these young men and women's self-esteem and self-confidence.[23]

Although the sports system has ruined so many young athletes' hopes and lives it has survived for 55 years without any challenge. The reasons are arguably deeply rooted in the Chinese sports culture consisting of sports patriotism, hero worship, the sense of shame and pride, and the sprit of single-mindedness.

Sports Patriotism

Possibly the most severe constraint on the flexibility of Chinese sports culture is the passion of patriotism. Ever since the beginning of the twentieth century athletes have operated in an atmosphere of pervasive nationalism. From the 1980s onwards those who have wanted China to gain the admiration of the West, have believed that although China lost some years on the international sports stage, it can still catch up, move to the top, and become a sports superpower. Sports patriotism unites the whole nation.

Thus the sports culture itself can produce a spirit of passive acceptance in those who are qualified to appraise what is being proposed. The very people who might be expected to suggest improvements or alternatives to official policies feel inhibited for fear of not appearing properly patriotic. For example, Zhao Yu, who was famous for his critical articles on Chinese sports policy, was jailed for several months after the Tiananmen massacre. However, when interviewed in 1993 at the height of 'sports medalism' and on the eve of China's bid for the 2000 Olympic Games, he claimed that he supported the bid. For him it was a matter of patriotism.[24]

Chinese sporting intellectuals are not only powerless in criticizing policies; they also seem unable to engage in the usual intellectual activity of pointing up weaknesses and flaws in the sports culture. They produced a theory called 'juguo tizhi' to support the government's medalism. It claimed that if the whole country channelled its energy and resources into this one channel, sport could succeed quicker than any other social sector. The success of sport could quickly restore the confidence of the nation, bringing Chinese people new satisfactions and new aspirations. More importantly, it could deliver the new image of China to the world.[25]

Patriotism, furthermore, seems to gag the voice of Chinese athletes themselves and leaves them mute because they are so easily overwhelmed with the fear that anything they might say will bring discredit to China's international reputation. It is not surprising that almost all famous athletes when they received their awards repeat the same words: 'The honour belongs to the Party, the Country and the People.'

The leaders themselves are also hostages to the conformity of patriotism. That is, in advancing policies they have to make it appear that what is being proposed is vital to the national interest. The only faults they can expose are the trivial ones, the failings of individuals. There can be no serious analysis of the failings of the system as a whole. As a consequence, in 1988 when the Chinese athletes failed to repeat the successes of the 1984 Olympics, the Sports Minister Li Meng Hua was sacked. A new minister Wu Shaozu from the army was appointed to improve the system in order to once more bring glory to China. Therefore, a new Olympic Strategy was produced in 1990. Its aim was for China to become a leading sports power by the end of the twentieth century. The new minister claimed: 'The highest goal of Chinese sport is success in the Olympic Games. We must concentrate our resources on it. To raise the flag at the Olympics is our major task.'[26]

Hero Worship

The Chinese have a propensity for explanations, due to the persistence of the Confucian belief that people are prone to emulate the good and the successful. It is believed that if proper models are held up to the public, there will be widespread imitation. Chinese culture concentrates on positive rather than negative examples. After the Cultural Revolution almost all institutions fell behind with the exception of one – sport. In 1978 China attended the Asian Games and won 151 medals – second on the medal list. In 1984 China attended the Olympic Games in Los Angeles and won 15 gold medals – fourth on the medal list. Asian and Olympic victories brought hope to the Chinese after their long history of humiliation by Western powers and their Eastern neighbours. Athletes have become icons of modernization and an inspiration for all walks of life.[27] Thus, national sports teams replaced Dazhai and Daqin, the ideologues' models of commune and industry, respectively, in providing inspiration for other sectors of China. Sports heroes and heroines, like Xu Haifeng a shooter, the first Chinese Olympic gold medallist, Li Ling, a gymnast, who won four Olympic gold medals, Ma Yanhong, a gymnast, the first Chinese female to win an Olympic gold medal in 1984, replaced Lei Feng, the ideologues' model, a soldier famous for serving the people selflessly.

    The new sport culture of the post-Mao period advocates competitiveness. As Wang Meng, the Culture Minister, claimed in 1984: 'In the past few years there has been a lot of discussion in society about the reason for the successful development of sport. Many comrades felt that the mechanism of competition in sport is comparatively well developed, that the competition is fierce, moreover that the results cannot be disputed. Competition, therefore, is the spirit of our reform movement.'[28] The result was that sports heroes and heroines, most of them child athletes, have become models for economic reforms intended to make the Chinese society and economy openly competitive.

Pride and Shame

To understand Chinese child athletes we have to understand their cultural roots. In Chinese culture, steeped in Confucianism, a sense of pride and shame is of the utmost importance. Geoffrey Gorer argued that a sense of pride is a desire to increase one's renown in the eyes of one's fellows; a sense of

shame is a fear of losing one's renown in the eyes of one's fellows.[29]
This 'pride–shame' culture relies on external sanctions and rewards for good
behaviour and good performance. For the Chinese, shame means 'losing face'
and loss of pride. For a person to 'know no shame' is equivalent to saying that
he has no decency. In Chinese sport, results must satisfy the requirements of
collective pride. It must make others respect and admire China. Chinese sport
is concerned with the 'best' because, above all, it increases renown – the sense
of pride – and avoids loss of face which the Chinese feel acutely. A concern
for renown, the hope of heroic stature, and a duty to wipe out the shames of
past history are the mission of sport and the young athletes.

   As Lucian Pye has pointed out: 'The secret of the survivability of Chinese
culture lies in the intense self-consciousness of the socialisation processes by
which young Chinese are brought up by their families and guardians. Little is
left to chance as Chinese children are taught correct behaviour and the
importance of loyalty to the group.'[30] This analysis can be comfortably applied
to Chinese athletes. They are brought up with the desire to achieve something
and to let their parents, coaches and the whole nation have something to be
proud of. They fear failure because it brings shame to their family, their
country and even their peers. Li Ling, the outstanding gymnast, the winner of
four gold medals in the 1984 Olympics, decided to retire after the Games.
However, the national team needed him to perform in 1988 even though he
knew that he was not at his best, but he agreed for the sake of the team.
He performed and failed in the 1988 Olympics. As soon as he finished his
performance and retired to the changing room he cried, not for himself but for
his peers. He said: 'I am sorry, my friends. I am ashamed for you.'[31]

   It is also important to remember that, for most athletes, behind the feeling of
shame stands the fear of contempt. The modern selective sports system brings
even more fear of rejection and abandonment. A young person is sent to a sports
school at the age of six or seven and is expected to become a star and not to fail.
Take Lu Li for example. Lu Li became a gymnast champion in the 1992
Olympics when she was 13. She went to Hunan provincial sports school at the
age of six. Her parents were both workers in a local factory. It was a long way
from her home to the sports school. Every day, after her normal school hours, her
mother or father would take her by bike to the sports school – in the cold of
winter and the heat of summer. Sometimes, when her parents were not available,
Coach Zhou would take her into her home and look after her as if she was her own
daughter. When she was ten years old she became a residential pupil in a sports
school where she had to look after herself. She and her school mates got up at
6:00 a.m. for two hours training. After her breakfast she went to a normal primary
school. She came back at noon and received training for the whole afternoon.
Life was not easy for a little girl but she never thought that she could go back,
neither did her peers. She learned her social role in this collective structure.

Lu Li succeeded at the age of 13. As soon as the television showed her perfect performance in Barcelona, the leaders of the factory, city and province came to her parents' home with congratulations and rewards: her family moved into a newly furnished, three bedroom new flat, her father was promoted from factory floor worker to office clerk, her coach Zhou was promoted, Lu Li herself received reward money of more than 30,000 RMB from the Sports Ministry, various sponsors in the form of rich and patriotic Hong Kong businessmen, and advertising. She was caught in a trap when she was injured at 14 and wished to retire.[32] It was impossible. The loss of face of so many was impossible to accept. She was pressured on all sides to continue.

It is crucial to recognize that China has its cultural distinctiveness. There is a fundamental sense of belonging to the superior Chinese civilisation and the Chinese values that are precious to them. They believe China will become a strong nation again in the twenty-first century. They believe that this goal can be achieved because they tend to place great store in what can be accomplished by human effort. At present, sport offers the best example and sports heroes and heroines are inspirational icons. China was full of joy and pride when the women's volleyball team beat the teams from the, Russia and Japan to become the Olympic champions, and when China won 32 gold medals and came second (behind the USA) in the medals table at the 2004 Athens Olympics. The slogan was 'March out of Asia and into the world'.[33] The ambition now is 'Beat the USA and become the No. 1 Superpower at the 2008 Beijing Olympic Games'.

Single-mindedness

Chinese culture highly values single-mindedness. It believes that success in almost any endeavour calls for total concentration and the focusing of all energies on the task at hand. It is taken for granted that anyone who has achieved greatness in any activity has done so because of their complete devotion.

However, the tension between the ideals of sacrifice and the benefits of personal reward is central to Chinese sports culture in large measure because for the Chinese, the self is essentially defined by the individual's sense of belonging to some large group, in particular the family, by extension the Chinese race and nation. The individual sense of self arises almost totally from his group identity. More precisely, the Chinese sense of identity comes from the notion of great self, and from the necessity of 'sacrificing the smaller self to fulfil the greater self'.[34]

This concept of greater self also means that the whole nation should focus its energies into sports excellence. It is assumed that all attention should be focused on competitive sport, especially the medals of the Olympics and

Asian Games (it is important to show Asian neighbours that China is still a powerful country). Any attempt to expand the boundaries of this focus can be easily treated as not just diluting policy priorities but actually subverting national effort, for to compromise single-mindedness is essentially an immoral, irresponsible act. The debate in 1989 on whether attention should be focused on gold medals or on mass sports and national health stirred a storm in the normally tranquil building of the Sports Ministry. It ended with the national Olympic Strategy which called for attention to the medals. Anything that reduced single-mindedness and caused distraction is an abomination. Therefore, in the 1980s and 1990s China became a sport feverish and medal-crazy country that did not consider protection of the young athletes' rights.

Human Rights and Child Athletes' Rights

Barnes argued that, 'A "right" is a just a claim or recognized interest; it is a moral or legal entitlement that others are duty-bound to respect.'[35] Donnelly claimed that 'Human rights are literally the rights one has because one is a human being' and human rights are needed because they are 'not for life, but for life of dignity'.[36]

In the West, the rights of individual and freedom are based on philosophical tradition from classic Greek through to the European Enlightenment. The legal systems are designed to protect it, such as the English Petition of Rights (1627); the French Declaration of the Rights of Women and Citizens (1791) and the American Bill of Rights (1791). Law stands above individual officeholders as a neutral arbiter to which disputes are referred and on the basis of which are resolved. Therefore, the Western political tradition of the modern nation-state is rooted in the concept of the rule of law.[37]

In contrast, the Chinese political system is rooted in the concept of men. The individual officeholders stand above the law and serve as arbiter to whom disputes are referred. This is because the concepts of Chinese culture are based on Confucian ethics. Confucianism is too large a doctrine to discuss in detail here. However, what is immediately relevant is that under Confucianism there were three bonds: absolute loyalty and obedience were due from ministers to emperor, from son to father and from wife to husband.[38] These bonds may be seen as the essence of Confucianism. These imperatives formed the very foundation of monarchical despotism and social inequality, dividing people into rigid status groups with different rights and duties not only according to social custom but also in law. It was this stable core of Confucian doctrine that, for almost 2,000 years, ensured that it served as an official creed.

The chief precept of Confucian ethics was filial piety. This was the basis of the monarchical as well as the family system. Filial piety and loyalty to the ruler/emperor were twinned concepts in Confucianism, for the emperor was regarded as the father of the people, and a man's 'filial' obligations were fulfilled only when he extended his loyalty unreservedly to the ruler/emperor. The rationale for 'piety' was social order at all levels.[39] It was inflexible. It defined privileges and obligations in accordance with the individual's status. It ran directly contrary to modern ideals of liberty and equality.

The Chinese Government learned from the Soviet Union to set up new legal institutions in the 1960s: the Ministry of Public Security, which was responsible for police work; a 'procuracy' at each level of government, which investigated and prosecuted crimes and reported to the supreme People's Procuracy; and courts at each level of government, headed by the Supreme People's Court, which heard and decided cases and set punishment. However, the political system is rooted in the Confucian concept: the conformity to the ruler, not the law.[40] The Chinese Communist Party and the Chairman of the Party are above the law. For example, in the anti-rightist campaign in 1957, Mao's revenge against intellectuals' criticism put five million intellectuals into jail and hard labour or even death without reference either to laws or the legal system. In the Cultural Revolution from 1966 to 1976, Mao's idea to purify his ideology and destroy his opponents had brought political, economic and cultural disaster to the Chinese society for ten years without any reference either to laws or the league system. Ba Jin, one of the most famous writers of modern Chinese literature, pointed out repeatedly in the 1990s that 'the urgent focus is not to fight against Western bourgeois/capitalist ideology but our feudal ideology. Our society, on the surface, is very modern, but underneath, the Confucian concept of men, not law, still dominates people's thinking and action.'[41] Li Shengzhi, an influential sociologist, argued: 'China has experienced more than one hundred year's struggle for modernity, however, the dominant ideologies in China are still Confucianism, feudalism and totalitarianism in which the three obedience are still the corn: absolute obedience to the ruler/emperor, the father and the husband.'[42]

Therefore, in a society where the parents, the coaches and teachers, and above all, the party and the government, believe that they all have absolute authority over children and where the progress of the children is essential to the greater good, children's rights will hardly become a priority. Modern high-performance sport demands more talented young athletes and the government, businessmen, sports authorities and agents, coaches, educators, sports scientists, medical staff and parents are working together to supply the demand. Consequently, young children are encouraged to involve in sport. They are systematically selected, trained and competed under highly work-like conditions for long hours and under enormous pressure. Although there are some arguments on whether child athletes could be considered as child labour, the characteristics of child labour identified in the World Labour Report in 1992 do match those Chinese child athletes: working too young, working long hours, working under strain, working on very little pay, taking too much responsibility and subject to intimidation.[43] The question is, who ultimately has the responsibility for welfare of those child athletes in China?

In 1993, the Children's Rights Approach, which was grounded in the United Nations Convention on the Rights of the Child, stated that there are five specific rights: the right to do as one chooses with one's body; the right to be consulted; the right to physical and psychological integrity; the right to associate freely with whom one chooses; the right to education. The Convention also makes specific provision in respect of two situations in which children's rights require optimal surveillance and protection. This includes children exploitation through sport and the traffic and sale of champions.[44] However, this voice has not reached China yet.

Doping

An urgent issue of the protection of child athletes in China is doping. In the medal-crazy atmosphere that has existed since the 1980s, the rights of athletes in general and the rights of child athletes in particular are ignored. Coaches and sports authority figures forced young athletes to take drugs in order to get medals at national and international competitions. For example, at the athletics of the National Games in 1997 in Shanghai 19 athletes had surpassed the level of the gold medalists and 39 athletes had reached the level of the bronze medalists in 2000 Sydney Olympics three years later.[45] However, the Chinese athletes only got, in total, one gold medal, one seventh place and one sixth place in athletics at the Sydney games. Luo Xuejuan, the Olympic Swimming gold medallist in 2004 claimed at the Ninth National Games in 2001 in Guangzhou: 'the water of the swimming pool is dirty (meaning: most of the swimmers take drugs), but I am clean'.[46] A head coach of the national athletics team stated: 'I am very disappointed by the current situation. Many coaches now don't pay attention to how to enhance their athletes' performance by scientific and hard training but by taking drugs. They spend a lot of time to learn which drug is more effective for their athletes.' Some companies and some individuals even come to the training centres and teams to sell drugs to coaches and athletes in the open. They give the people who buy their drugs a large commission. There are stories of the drug salesmen and the people who buy the drugs both become millionaires in a short time.[47] The national athletic coach pointed out: 'The doping issue is not just one of taking drugs but an issue of corruption!'[48]

In 2000, at the National Junior Sports Championships, 25 per cent of athletes tested positive. Xie Yalong, the Director of the National Athletics Management Centre cried: 'This situation is frightening! Doping has destroyed our athletes and our coaches. They don't concentrate on their hard and scientific training but on scientifically taking drugs.'[49] Yuang Weiming, the Sports Minister, has acknowledged that doping has destroyed China's young athletes.[50] Furthermore, there is no law to protect young athletes who are forced to take drugs. Neither are there advisory bodies to advise Chinese athletes about their rights of defence and appeal when they are found positive. Fifteen athletes were accused of taking drugs at the Ninth National Games in Guangzhou in 2001 and they were punished by losing their titles and banned from competitions for several years. However, not a single athlete was advised that he/she had the right to defend himself/herself. In short, China has not prepared a place to listen to the voices of athletes. A senior Chinese sports official pointed out in 2001 that the research on protection of young athletes should become a major agenda of Chinese sport. However, since human rights are always a sensitive topic in China the rights of young athletes are sensitive too. Years passed and nothing has been done.[51]

Conclusion

Under the control of the communist authority, the education of Confucian culture and the influence of the global commercialism the system, which developed during the last 55 years, continues to produce more and younger sports stars for national pride, ideological superiority, social conformity and economic advance. Child athletes' civil rights, legal rights and above all, their human rights are ignored in China. They are children, but they have lost their innocent childhood.

NOTES

1. Wu Shaozu, Xiong Xiaozheng and Tan Hua, (eds.), *Zhonghua renmin gongheguo tiyushi* [Sports History of the People's Republic of China] (Beijing: Zhongguo shuju chubanshe, 1999) pp.74–83.
2. Wu (note 1) pp.112–13; 'Fan Hong, Two Roads to China: the Inadequate and the Adequate', *The International Journal of the History of Sport* 18 (2001) 156–17.
3. Wu (note 1).171–200.
4. Fan Hong, 'Not all Bad! Communism, Society and Sport in the Great Proletarian Cultural Revolution', *The International Journal of the History of Sport*, 3 (1999) 47–71; Qian Jiang, *Ping pong waijiao shimu* [The Beginning and the End of the Ping Pong Diplomacy] (Beijing: Renming tiyu chubanshe, 1987) Fu Lianglong, 'Wenge zhong nongcun tiyu xinsheng de sikao' [Sports in rural areas during the Cultural Revolution], *Tiyu shi wenji*, 6 (1989) 108–10; Xi Jie, 'Wenge qijian shanxi qunzhong tiyu chutan [On the Mass Sport in Shanxi province during the Cultural Revolution]', *Tiyushi lunwen ji*, 6 (1989) 119–25.
5. Fan Hong, 'The Olympic Movement in China: Ideals, Realities and Ambitions', *Culture, Sport, Society*, 1 (1998) 149–168.
6. Cited in *Xin tiyu* [New Sport], 2 (1962) 4.
7. When I was ten years old I was selected to attend a provisional training camp. I was required to swim 10,000 m in the morning and 10,000 m in the afternoon. After the day training finished I was too tired to get out of the water and my coach has to pull me out. I lay at the bank

of the pool for half an hour to get my strength back to go to her dormitory and was too tired to eat anything. All I wanted was to lie down. This intensive training lasted for three months. Sometimes I just wanted to quit and to go home but my parents were so proud when I was selected and I could not let them down.

 8. A BBC documentary film crew visited the school in July 1995.
 9. Cited in Peter Donnelly, 'Child Labour, Sport Labour', *International Review for the Sociology of Sport*, 32:4 (1997), 395.
10. Christiane Sanderson, *The Seduction of Children* (London: Jessica Kingsley, 2004) pp.34–5.
11. See Celia Brackenridge's contribution in this issue.
12. Celia Brackenridge and Sandra Kirby, 'Playing Safe', *International Review for the Sociology of Sport*, 32:4 (1997), 412.
13. Zhao Yu, *Majiajun diaocha* [The Investigation of the Ma's Army], (Beijing: Renming wenxue chubanshe, 1998) pp.92 and 161.
14. Zhao Yu (note 13) pp.154–60.
15. Zhao Yu (note 13) pp.127–59.
16. Zhao Yu (note 13).
17. Interview in the football school by Fan Hong in Northern China in July 2002.
18. S. Kirby and L. Greaves, 'Le jeu interdit: Le harcelement: sexuel dans le sport', *Recheches Feminises*, 10 (1997) 5–33; Celia Brackenridge, *Spoilsport* (London: Routledge, 2001) p.18.
19. K. Young, 'Tort and Criminal Liability in Sport: the Conundrums of Workplace Hazards vs Masculinist Consent', paper presented at the Olympic Scientific Congress, Malaga, Spain, 15–20 July 1992.
20. Peter Donnelly (note 9) p.395.
21. Wu (note 1) p. 565.
22. Interview in the Sports Ministry by Fan Hong in Beijing in July 2001.
23. Deng Yaping, 'From Boundfeet to Olympic Gold in China: The Case of Women's Chinese Table Tennis', MA thesis, Nottingham University (2002) pp.110–11.
24. Interview with Zhao Yu by Fan Hong in July 1993.
25. Wu (note 1) pp.17–18, 288–351.
26. See his opening address at the Congress of Olympic Movement Studies in Beijing, 1993. The extract was published under the title 'The Olympic Strategy and Sport Reform in China', Xie Yalong (ed.), *Aolinpike yanjiu* [Olympic Studies] (Beijing: Renming tiyu chubanshe, 1993) p.402; see also Fan Hong, 'Making Sporting Heroines in Modern China: A Cultural Explanation', *Stadion* XXVI, I (2000), 120–1.
27. Rong Gaotang, Zhang Caizhen, and Bi Shiming (eds), *Dangdai Zhongguo tiyu* [Contemporary Chinese Sport] (Beijing: baikequanshu chubanshe, 1987), p.13; Fan Hong, *Footbinding, Feminism and Freedom: The Liberation of Women's Bodies in Modern China* (London and Portland, OR: Frank Cass, 1997) pp.302–06.
28. Wang Meng, 'Jinji jizhi' [On the Mechanism of Competition], *Zhonhguo tiyu bao* [*Chinese Spot Daily*], 20 August 1988.
29. G. Gorge, 'The Concept of National Character' in G. Gorge (ed.) *The Danger of Equality and Other Essays* (New York: The Free Press, 1966) p.22.
30. Lucian W. Pye, *The Mandarin and the Cadre: China's Political Culture* (Ann Arbor, 1988), p.4.
31. Xing Xing, 'Ticao wangzhi Li Ling de gushi [The Story of the Prince of Gymnastics, Li Ling] *Nanning ribao*, 13 November (1988).
32. Interview with Lu Li in Beijing by Fan Hong in July 1993.
33. Rong (note 27) p.428.
34. R. W. Wilson, *The Moral State: A Study of the Political Socialization of Chinese and American Children* (New York: Interscience Publishers, 1974), p.35.
35. J. Barnes, *Sports and the Law in Canada* (Toronto: Butterworth, 1996) p.47; Bruce Kidd and Peter Donnelly, 'Human Rights in Sport', *International Review of the Sociology of Sport* 35 (2000), 131–48.
36. I. Donnelly, *Universal Human Rights in Theory and Practice* (Ithaca, NY: Cornell University Press, 1989) pp.9, 17; Kidd and Donnelly (note 35) p.132.
37. Kidd and Donnelly (note 35) p.133.

38. Fan Hong (note 27) p.18.
39. Fan Hong (note 27).
40. Li Shengzhi, *Fengyu changhuang 50 nian* [The Collection of the Essays of Fifty Years] 4th edition (Hong Kong: Mingbao chubanshe, 2004) pp.4–14.
41. Ba Jin, *Shuixiang lu* [The Collection of My Thoughts] (Beijing: Sanlian shudian, 1999) pp.135, 224, 285.
42. Li (note 40) pp.334–36 and 343–57.
43. See Donnelly (note 36) pp. 391, 395.
44. Ibid. p.401; Kidd and Donnelly (note 35) pp.141–42.
45. Wu Ping, 'Zhongguo tiyu buwang zuogui' [Chinese Sport and Anti-doping] *Titan zhoubao* [*Sports Weekly*] 10 February 2001.
46. Cited in Wu Ping, 'Fang Luo Xuejuan' [Interview with Luo Xuejuan], *Titan zhoubao*, 15 October 2001.
47. Wu Ping (note 46).
48. Cited in Wu Ping (note 46).
49. Cited in Wu Ping, 'Zhongguo tianjing pitai jinlou' [Current Situation of the Chinese Athletics] *Titan zhoubao*, 22 October 2000.
50. Wu Ping (note 46).
51. Interview in the Sports Ministry in Beijing by Fan Hong in July 2000.

Human Rights, Globalization and Sentimental Education: The Case of Sport

RICHARD GIULIANOTTI

In February 2003, the United Nations, the Swiss Agency for Development and Cooperation, and the Swiss Federal Office of Sports, convened an international conference on 'Sport and Development' that was held in Magglingen, Switzerland. Over 380 conference delegates from 55 nations were in attendance, representing governmental bodies, the United Nations system, athletes, sports organizations, non-governmental organizations (NGOs), scientific research institutes, and media corporations. The conference followed at least two others that had spotlighted sport, human rights and development issues.[1] The Magglingen convention, however, brought a fresh political impetus to the sports–human rights relationship. The chairpersons of the various conference sessions reported the conclusions that had emerged; these points were incorporated within the 'Magglingen Declaration and Recommendations', a document that was submitted in turn to the United Nations for implementation.

The hosting of these conventions has certainly been inspired by the belief of international organizations that sport may be utilized to achieve positive social outcomes. According to the Red Cross in Indo-China, 'Sport transforms men and women by endowing them with strength, endurance, vivacity and courage'. For the United Nations High Commission for Refugees (UNHCR), Sadako Ogata said, 'Sports and recreation are vital for all children. For a refugee child they are irreplaceable in helping rebuild a destroyed world.' The Secretary-General of the United Nations now has a Special Adviser on Sport for Development and Peace. According to the current incumbent, Adolf Ogi, a former President of Switzerland:

> Sport teaches life skills. Sport remains the best school of life. With sport, young people learn: to manage victory; to overcome defeat; to become team players and to be reliable and gain the other team members' confidence; respect for opponents and the rules; that for good results regular training is needed; and, to know their limits and themselves better. The positive lessons and values of sport are essential for life.[2]

Driven by these convictions, numerous international organizations have introduced various forms of sport-related work to promote peace, development and human dignity. Here are some examples of that work:

1. The International Commission for the Red Cross (ICRC) has employed sports stars to publicise its anti-personnel mines campaign.
2. The ICRC, the International Olympic Committee (IOC), and other international federations have assisted victims of genocide in Rwanda.
3. The International Labour Organization launched its 'Red Card to Child Labour' campaign at the 2002 African Nations Cup finals. In December 2002, the campaign was adopted by Real Madrid, notably for the club's centennial exhibition fixture, generating extensive coverage in the Spanish media.
4. Red Deporte y Cooperación was established in 1999, with headquarters in Madrid and the United States, with the aim of 'educating values and promoting physical, intellectual and psychomotor skills and development amongst underprivileged youth through organized sport activities'.[3] The main beneficiaries of the eight programmes that it runs in South America and sub-Saharan Africa are low income and high risk children and youths as well as specific groups of young women.
5. In Colombia, the *Fútbol por la Paz* project was established through local sports associations to rehabilitate and reintegrate drug-addicted young people and those caught up in drug trafficking.
6. Partnerships have been established between international federations and humanitarian NGOs, e.g. the IOC and the UNHCR, Fédération Internationale de Football Association (FIFA) and SOS-Children's Villages.

Now, there is no question that some remarkable sports-focused work is being done by NGOs in regard to reconciliation, peace-building, and rehabilitation work. The football schools in the Balkans are a particularly strong illustration.[4] However, there are some significant problems in any argument that considers sport *a priori* to be a force for human goodness.

First, the position taken by those such as Adolf Ogi is essentially a functionalist one, in that it assumes that sport meets crucial social needs and is a powerful and positive force for social integration. Of course, there is much historical counter-evidence to suggest that sport can just as easily prove far more dysfunctional than functional to social order, in dramatizing or intensifying sources of social conflict, as expressed, for example, through nationalism, sexism, racism and other strains of xenophobia.

Second, in their development and peace work the shift of 'sport evangelists' to locations outside the West may constitute a form of neo-colonial repositioning. Through the twentieth century, sports evangelism at home had sought to promote organized sporting activities to dissipate the lower orders' dangerous energies and to divert them from 'licentious' social practices (such as drinking, gambling, casual sex, and the following of youth subcultural styles). There is little convincing evidence to suggest that such evangelism has proved wholly successful among young people in the West over the years. However, it appears to be assumed, the young people in the old colonies may be more readily organized to receive and internalize the tendentious, self-controlling messages buried within sports.

Third, even if we accept for argument's sake that sport is a force for positive transformation, the focus of sporting humanitarianism tends to be heavily skewed towards meeting the needs of young people. My concern is that such prioritization, not least in the allocation of sport resources, is unnecessarily exclusionary towards other social cleavages, notably women and the old.

Fourth, underlying all of these concerns are more fundamental questions regarding the cross-cultural politics of sport humanitarianism. Is there sufficient dialogue between the donors and recipients before sports-related aid is offered? Are recipients sufficiently empowered to claim ownership over these projects? Ultimately, what are the complex dynamics of power and meaning behind cross-cultural 'cooperation' between donor and recipient groups?

These problems were uppermost in our minds when we presented our paper to the Magglingen conference.[5] In line with the conference's remit, our discussion concluded in strongly practical mode by advancing recommendations for the deployment of sport in facilitating peaceful solutions within contexts of war, violence and social crisis. With a few minor emendations, these recommendations were adopted by conference delegates and included within the final declaration.

To summarize these recommendations, we argued for

- The expansion of sport programmes in conflict zones, to promote rehabilitation and reconciliation.
- Dialogue between the donors and recipients of aid. Donors must receive the informed consent of recipients, whose members should include women, adults, the old and the disabled.
- Reflection on the role of sports bodies and NGOs in promoting sport's internationalism and humanitarian ethos, and its possible contributions to development. Ties between specific athletes and particular regions should be strengthened.
- Sports bodies and other NGOs to evaluate projects before implementation, and to explore their sustainability and clarify long-term ownership.
- The expansion of connections between NGOs and sports federations.

But all of this required to take place alongside more direct strategies for alleviating famine, warfare, poverty and forced migration.

In this brief discussion of issues relating to sport, human rights and development, I seek to build on these arguments by probing more deeply the kind of concerns raised in the fourth criticism, relating to the political and cross-cultural dimensions of sports projects. The discussion is divided into three main parts.

I open by outlining how sport's governing bodies relate to the 1948 Universal Declaration of Human Rights and the rise of a 'culture of rights'. Second, I address the question of cross-cultural difficulties in establishing human rights cultures with reference to critical analysts of globalization. Third, I turn to conceptualize the interrelations between human rights, globalization and humankind with reference to the work of Robertson and Rorty.

Sport, Human Rights and the 1948 Declaration

The cornerstone of any discussion of human rights must be the 1948 Universal Declaration of Human Rights. The Declaration itself is couched in the highly individualistic terms that are hegemonic within Western liberal democracies. With the very partial exception of Articles 28 and 29, the 30 articles say hardly anything on collective rights, whether in regard to nation-states, international society or humankind. Explicit mention of sport is absent, although Article 24 does insist that 'everyone has the right to rest and leisure', while Article 27 highlights the individual's 'right freely to participate in the cultural life of the community'.

For developing nations particularly, there is a grim irony in the historical processes that underlie the Declaration. The Western powers 'discovered' these other cultures, enslaved the peoples, expropriated their natural and human resources, and then, once such exploitation had proved too exhausting to maintain, the colonists introduced the colonized to notions of nationhood, political independence, free-market international trading, and human rights. Such hopeful guarantees of human dignity would have been perfectly unnecessary if this cycle of colonization and decolonization had never started in the first place.

A more specific irony lies in sport's historical contribution to the colonial subjugation of non-Western cultures. Western sports institutions have been directly implicated in acts of cultural genocide. I mean this not only in the more general sense that Western sports were constituent parts of the colonial military–industrial complexes that enslaved or proletarianized whole societies. Rather, and more specifically, cultural genocide arose in the deliberate supplanting of non-Western body cultures with imperial games.[6] In British imperial outposts, sport was utilized particularly by Christian missionaries and other imperial pedagogues to crush indigenous cultural identities and practices, to set about creating 'a universal Tom Brown: loyal, brave, truthful, a gentleman and, if at all possible, a Christian'.[7]

As one would expect, official institutional discourses within sports organizations rarely encroach upon this dubious (and largely hidden) history. Rather, the official discourses prefer to recognize only those moments of sports-related violence that have been produced by 'enemies' of Western states, such as the Nazis (the 1936 Olympics), Arab terrorists (the 1972 Olympics), or football hooligans (1985 Heysel disaster).[8]

However, far more deadly and far more frequent have been those instances of terrorism or the infringement of fundamental human rights that have been initiated by states which are members of international sports federations and which are at least recognized, if not supported, by the United States and its allies. For example, it is estimated that over 500 demonstrators were murdered by Mexican 'security' forces in what became known as the Tlatelolco Massacre in Mexico City, ten days before the city was permitted to host the Olympic Games. Ten years later, FIFA gifted the World Cup finals to the junta that ruled Argentina, despite the fact that this 'bulwark against regional communism' was proceeding to murder 30,000 people (mainly its own citizens), and to detain and torture tens of thousands more, between 1976 and 1983.[9] Nor are the developed nations free from critical scrutiny. Prior to the 1982 Commonwealth Games in Brisbane, the Queensland legislature passed an Act that effectively cleared aboriginals from the streets. These few points, and countless others summarized elsewhere, paint a picture of strong cohabitation between international sports movements and states that have systematically impugned the human rights of their citizens.

The extent to which contemporary sport federations emphasize an actively humanitarian mission may be tested in economic and organizational terms. First, there is an obvious danger that sports governing bodies will hide behind the rhetoric of 'human rights', 'peace' and 'development', rather than prioritize these missions in hard cash. Comparisons of internal sports budgets are instructive. For example, FIFA's 'humanitarian support fund' has an annual budget of two million Swiss francs (around £907,000) which is distributed to projects selected by the FIFA Finance Committee, chaired by Julio Grondona of Argentina. Among the monies disbursed in 2003 was approximately £30,000 allocated to HIV/AIDS prevention campaigns at the fifth African under-17 championships in Swaziland. Compare that budget to the £5 million spent by FIFA's inner circle over six weeks in Paris during the 1998 World Cup finals; or, to the further £1.6 million ear-marked for official 'presents' such as watches and pendants. According to the investigative journalist David Yallop, who unearthed these figures, such profligate sums might be better spent elsewhere:

> Imagine an injection of that money into the work being done by an organisation like SOS Children's Villages–a non-denominational organisation founded 45 years ago and now caring directly for some 200,000 disadvantaged children in 125 countries. In 1994 Havelange created a FIFA Youth Fund to help this organisation. Perhaps Sepp Blatter can be publicly shamed into matching the disgusting excesses of Paris with an equivalent amount donated to SOS Children's Villages.[10]

Second, if we turn the spotlight more closely on international sports governing bodies such as the IOC and FIFA, they do not fare particularly well in terms of observing the Declaration through their principles and procedures. For example:

- Article 1 emphasizes that 'all human beings are born free and equal in dignity and rights'. Sports governing bodies tend to ignore egalitarianism by prioritizing elite athletes in resource allocation or bowing to elite interests in the largest sporting nations or institutions.
- Article 3 insists *inter alia* that all have the right to 'security of person'. Sports clubs and governing bodies have tended to place too little emphasis on protecting the long-term physical wellbeing of athletes.
- Article 4 insists that 'no one shall be held in slavery or servitude', but sports governing bodies offer little protection to young athletes, especially those in the developing world, who are signed to professional contracts that provide for little more than indentured labour.
- Article 10 states that 'everyone is entitled in full equality to a fair and public hearing by an independent and impartial tribunal', but sport's 'disciplinary procedures' against athletes are often adjudicated on by officials in private.
- Article 18 insists that 'everyone has the right to freedom of thought, conscience and religion', but sports governing bodies traditionally take a harsh stand on those athletes who are deemed to 'bring politics into the stadium'.
- Articles 19–21 relate to the rights of people to express opinions openly, to receive and impart information through any media freely, to associate without hindrance, and to participate in government and other public services. As Chomsky points out, safeguarding these articles is crucial for the full and effective implementation of the Declaration.[11] However, sports governing bodies habitually restrict freedom of expression by disciplining those who criticize officials and procedures. They restrict mediation of sports to a cartel of broadcasting Trans National Corporations (TNCs). They employ some oppressive crowd control techniques at major sports venues. They countermand participation in the governance of sport, in part through their well-documented, secretive control of information and clientelist political relations.
- Article 23 seeks to protect the working rights of individuals, including membership of trade unions. Sports governing bodies do little at grassroots level to protect the representative rights of professional athletes.
- Article 25 states that all have rights to a 'basic standard of living', including health care and security during unemployment, sickness or old age. Sports governing bodies take no effective institutional steps to protect their professional athletes in this sense.
- Article 26 stipulates that 'everyone has the right to education', which 'shall be directed to the full development of the human personality'. Historically,

among young athletes, specialization in sports disciplines with a view towards entering elite levels has invariably led to a serious deficit in other forms of education that would otherwise promote their personal and social development.

• Article 27 entitles all authors of 'artistic production' to have their 'moral and material interests' protected. More commonly, the practices and images of elite athletes have been commodified with comparatively little or no recompense to the sports 'artists' themselves.

These observations would suggest that international sports federations require to go beyond the vague idealism of their mission statements, and to consider more precisely how their various constitutions and internal procedures accord with the Declaration.

International sports governing bodies must confront the genesis of a 'culture of rights' that operates at popular and legal levels.[12] This culture is represented institutionally through the growth of critical NGOs, legally through the advent of human rights conventions and charters, informed globally through the Internet, and committed politically to challenging the cultures of secrecy and democratic exclusion within different systems of governance. More broadly, discourses and movements that pursue the globalizing of rights often connect their struggles to the direct challenging of the Western-driven hegemony of neo-liberal globalization. Currently, international sports governing bodies may feel relatively insulated from the concerted criticisms and protests directed by diverse 'anti-globalization' movements towards the World Trade Organization (WTO), the G8, and TNCs (such as sport merchandise companies like Nike and Reebok). However, if one aim of these movements is to institutionalize human rights through sport, then it is a small step politically to refocus these campaigns at the very heart of sports governance. Sports federations that are popularly perceived as corrupt, unaccountable and undemocratic are easy targets for those embodying the new culture of rights.

At a juridical level, as the culture of rights spreads into legal statutes and diplomatic charters, so claims to the autonomy or 'exceptionalism' of sport lose their footing. Already, international sporting bodies have come under pressures from national and international legal systems on the matters of labour markets, illicit drug use, and interpersonal violence. Sports federations might at least anticipate any future moves to enforce human rights conventions more fully by systematic reflection on their own procedures.

Universalism, Relativism and Human Rights

While it is important to explore the empirical and ethical disjuncture between humanitarian discourses and practices within international sports federations, our discussion still requires to theorize the conception of human rights in more critical terms, with reference to the complex questions of power and meaning. Are seemingly altruistic beliefs in human rights and development merely the velvet gloves that soften the double whammy of Western colonialism and neo-colonialism? Is it possible that 'human rights' is an essentially Western cultural conception that, in truth, carries no universal reach?

Serge Latouche provides one of the most polemical analyses of how development, human rights and globalization have driven the Westernization of the world. Latouche argues that the Western model is a 'techno-economic machine' that is 'impersonal, soulless, and nowadays masterless'; having 'impressed mankind into its service', it has 'shaken off all human attempts to stop it and now roves the planet'. 'Development' involves simply 'aspiring to the Western model of consumption, the magical power of the white man, the status which went with that way of living'. Thus, the Western 'anti-culture' destroys cultural difference, imposing a triptych of development procedures, namely industrialization, urbanization, and 'nationalitarianism' (the imposition of the nation state as the only acceptable political form in world affairs). NGOs are part of the same 'game', pursuing 'some kind of world domination' by reaching the furthest corners. Latouche does claim that 'uniformity has its limits': other cultures can resist Westernization by retaining 'their own ways of spending leisure time, and their own foods – even in the great metropolises of Africa, Asia or Latin America'. With regard to 'human rights', Latouche falls back on a cultural relativism argument. The West has no *universal*, rational grounds for challenging or preventing practices in other cultures that it deems to be 'uncivilized' or inhumane. The old and extreme illustration (Western horror of cannibalism) is trotted out to argue that Western rationalism is really founded upon ethnocentricity.[13]

Sport, for Latouche, can only be implicated in this violent invention of the 'Third World'. Sport promotes forms of international record-setting that can entail cultural annexation – for example, no Tibetan ever attempted to climb Everest, but the societies around the Himalayas have since become reorganized to facilitate Western competitors. Sport advocates the performance-directed freedom of individuals to participate, to possibly win, thereby nourishing hopes of deliverance from poverty, but of course, as in the capitalist marketplace, only a handful of participants really succeed.[14]

International sport bodies, as NGOs, may be considered to be involved in building 'world domination' through pushing their little sporting flags into new territories, for example through funding development projects in war-torn African regions where states exist only in theory. Some Third World cultures might produce alternative, more fraternal sporting practices that stand in marked contrast to the aggressive nationalism stoked in Western contexts.

But it remains highly problematic to construct categorically different forms of body culture to those institutionalized and inculcated by Western organizations like the IOC or FIFA.

Post-modern social theorists agree with these arguments on fundamental cultural differences, but can identify greater cultural agency in non-Western societies. Baudrillard, for example, makes an important analytical differentiation between three contemporary global forces: 'globalization' that relates mainly to neo-liberal exchange relations; 'universality' that relates to Enlightenment values such as democracy, human rights and liberty; and 'singularity' that relates to 'languages, cultures, individuals and characters, but also chance, accident, etc. – all that the universal, in keeping with its law, impugns as an exception or anomaly'. Characteristically, Baudrillard reckons that universality has come off worst: 'the concepts of liberty, democracy and human rights cut a very pale figure indeed, being merely the phantoms of a vanished universe'. While globalization is strongly placed, it is not certain to be the winner; singularity provides regular irruptions of conflict and challenge through 'forces which are not only different, but antagonistic and irreducible'.[15]

There are obvious benefits in these general critiques of the inter-relations between human rights, development and cultural 'singularity'. They draw potent historical connections between political economic exploitation and specific cultural practices within sports. They help us to maintain a self-critical reflexivity towards the apparent altruism and declared universal benefits of specific aspects of our culture, particularly in relation to human rights and sport.

However, I am concerned that these kinds of cultural relativism regarding human rights harbour three core weaknesses that carry strong practical consequences.

First, in *political* terms these arguments fail to consider how claims to 'radical cultural difference' may by forwarded by non-Western elites to justify their oppressive powers. For example, are we to ignore the prohibitions, violence and killings surrounding women's football teams in Algeria, on the grounds of 'radical cultural difference'?[16]

Second, in *anthropological* terms these arguments freeze, in time and space, other cultures as 'authentic', rather than seeing such cultures as essentially fluid, hybrid and inherently dynamic matrices of meaning. In turn, the culturally relativist arguments imply that, in rejecting the 'development' path, we should return to some notional cultural arrangement without explaining either the social system to be founded as substitute or how future relations with developed nations can be managed. Hence, the harassment of Algerian women's football teams represents one of many cultural and political responses within a dynamic socio-cultural context. If Western development workers and sports-centred NGOs step back from this context, they privilege de facto one set of arguments (opposition to women in sport and public life) over other positions.

Third, in *analytical* terms relativist arguments may be advanced to protect the interests of Western elites as well as non-Western autocrats. As Chomsky indicates, there is an odious 'relativism' in the opposition of the United States, for example, towards the full implementation of the Declaration or to the progressive egalitarianism of the United Nations, Educational, Scientific and Cultural Organization (UNESCO).[17] Similarly, in sport, we need to oppose those Western federations that consider the issue of rights to be more important for 'civilizing' non-Western societies rather than looking more closely at their own backyard.

This is not to deny that there is a real tension between universalism and rights-protection in the codes of human rights. On one hand, human rights standards may enshrine trans-cultural respect for difference, providing a shelter for minority peoples and practices. On the other hand, more weightily, human rights provide for a selective critique of cultural difference on the basis of 'antirelativist standards'.[18] Non-Western peoples are clearly cognizant of this dilemma. The most successful strategy towards dealing with the dilemma is not to insist upon the cross-cultural unintelligibility of 'human rights', or to permit elite groups to rebuff enlightened overtures. Instead, indigenous peoples adopt a more practical strategy, in terms of probing human rights standards and international state conventions, to explore spaces that facilitate reform. From the Western perspective, we are still left with the question of how we should articulate clearer sociological and political-philosophical perspectives for relating human rights to senses of cultural difference.

Human Rights, Globalization and Sentimental Education

To develop a path out of these problems, I think it is helpful to relocate our concern with human rights and 'humankind' more sociologically, before exploring a political-philosophical response to cross-cultural communication. What I propose is to consider Robertson's theorization of human rights relative to globalization, in conjunction with Rorty's conception of Western 'sentimental education'.[19]

Robertson has argued that, despite its language of individualism, the political rise of human rights reflects a stronger 'thematization of humanity' as part of the globalization processes of recent years. For Robertson, 'humankind' is one of four 'elemental reference points', the other three being the individual, the nation-state, and international society. Since the 1870s, the interplay of these reference points has increasingly determined the shape and texture of globalization. Our sharpened understanding of humankind is reflected in contemporary debates regarding not only collective human rights, but also the future of the human species and its relationships to the environment. It is further indicated in the thematization of the possibility that the world may somehow be made 'for-itself', rather than simply 'in itself'.[20]

This vision is challenged by rival discourses and processes that emphasize untrammelled individual agency in the marketplace, the inalienable sovereignty of nation-states, and the *Realpolitik* of international diplomacy. Consequently, Robertson identifies four visions of world order that correspond respectively with each of these reference points. Humankind is at the heart of what Robertson classifies as the 'global *gemeinschaft* 2' model, and this considers global order as achievable only through establishing 'a fully globewide community' that is underpinned by a 'commitment to the communal unity of the human species'. There are two versions of the 'global *gemeinschaft* 2' model: the first, *centralized* version advocates the creation of a 'global village' with a 'globewide Durkheimian conscience collective'; the second, *decentralized* version anticipates a more pluralistic form of world community.[21]

In a prior paper, we have sought to explore how this thematization of humankind may be concretized within the sport of football.[22] Now, as we have indicated already, there are more than enough counter-examples to show that sport connects to other world visions dominated alternatively by freewheeling individualism, Machiavellian statecraft or turbulent international affairs. Yet we may also note that elements in sport carry both the centralized and decentralized visions of the humankind (global *gemeinschaft* 2) model. Centrally, the 'global village' is most potently represented through globe-wide mass media coverage of tournaments such as the Olympic Games; and, the 'conscience collective' is envisaged by global sports federations that endeavour to have all competing nations recognize and embody the official rules and ethics within sports. De-centrally, the notion of a 'pluralistic world community' is surely the logical culmination of the 'sincere internationalism' identified by Morgan in the Olympism of Coubertin. For Morgan, Coubertin's goals were akin to those of liberals like Rorty, namely to have people 'soften, but, per impossible, not nullify their ethnocentrism by enlarging their range of acquaintance ... to get them to see that their cherished beliefs and ways of life are only one among many other such beliefs and ways of life'.[23]

The reference to Rorty here is opportune, since his more specific reflections on human rights help us, in my view, to clarify the inter-relations between human rights, cross-cultural dialogue and sport. According to Rorty, we should embrace neither 'cultural relativism' nor its universalist opponent (a pro-Western 'foundationalism'). Rather, in a point that I consider highly compatible with Robertson's view, Rorty insists that we should accept that ours *is* a 'human rights culture'. Rorty insists that it is better to be born into this human rights culture rather than somewhere more 'deprived'. Even the most detestable characters (such as ethnic cleansers or gang rapists) must be viewed as deprived, wherein deprivation is defined by the absence, of Western conditions that enable a sufficiently risk-free existence, and of the adequate thematization of human suffering that we take for granted in the media and the arts.

Our task is generally to make the human rights culture 'more self-conscious and more powerful' by producing 'generations of nice, tolerant, well-off, secure, other-respecting students'. Rorty recommends that these students receive a 'sentimental education', which involves 'manipulating their sentiments in such a way that they imagine themselves in the shoes of the despised and oppressed'. Rorty recognizes that sentimental education has problems in Western culture. We presume that reason is a more powerful force than sentiment. We fear that privileging sentiment politically will entail pinning our hopes on the condescension of 'rich bleeding hearts' like Bill Gates. More practically, 'sentimental education only works on people who can relax long enough to listen'.[24]

Yet, it is the 'long, sad, sentimental story' that works best to convince others that we should care about strangers, even those whose practices are strikingly alien to our own. We must put our cultural sceptics into the shoes of the stranger, to explain how it is 'to be in her situation – to be far from home, among strangers'. Or we might imagine the stranger as within our kin and kind, to suggest she 'might become your daughter-in-law'.[25]

Rorty's argument is not without weaknesses. It does not provide the most systematically reasoned account of how the foundationalism–cultural relativism debate can be concluded rather than evaded. More sociologically, he does not have an adequate account of how 'sentimental education' can co-habit with pre-existing geometries of power. Are not our children, for example, encouraged to become more sentimental towards distant peoples whose religious and diplomatic ties are close to the West? Nevertheless, as Brown notes, Rorty does present the understanding of rights as intrinsic to 'a functioning ethical community' alongside the problems connected to any universalist application of human rights.[26]

I consider Rorty's argument to be particularly worthy of elaboration in the case of sport. Sport arguably provides for cross-cultural encounters with the other, forcing us into bodily and normative dialogue with those that we might find 'irrational' or culturally abominable. Playing sport competitively forces us to think ourselves into the shoes of the opponent. Sport opens domains for advanced forms of sentimental education in regard to human rights. The global institutions of sport and their universal legal frameworks allow for the strengthening of our 'shared moral identity which brings us together in a moral community'.[27] As part of the recreational realm, sport operates in the main within the 'relaxation time' in which sentimental education may work. The pre-event biopics and short documentaries on North African female runners or Middle East football teams should contribute to the establishment of sympathy among those in the West who would otherwise miss thematizations of deprivation.

There are potential problems, of course. Sentimental education might be refracted through mediation to become another form of condescension: that is, the hypostatized melodrama of deprivation, the playing upon sentimentality to narrate 'remarkable' and 'exceptional' stories of individual achievement to the detriment of context and an ethical education. Moreover, the thinking of ourselves into the shoes of others should not be dazzled by commodity fetishism, as we buy ourselves literally into their Nikes or Reeboks. Despite these problems, sport still provides perhaps the most culturally popular medium through which senses of moral obligation towards absolute strangers might be communicated through imagined belonging. We might suggest to our cultural fellows that caring for others is required since they might join our family; more likely, we could suggest that they or their friends might one day join our other cherished institutions, namely our sports teams.

Conclusion

To sum up, I accept that a significant role has been carved out for sport to play in promoting peace and enhancing human dignity. This does not, however, entail that we must subscribe to the more naïve or evangelical arguments regarding sport's *innate* goodness. Rather, we must bear in mind the historical relationship of sport to forms of colonialism and neo-colonialism. We must also continue to make critical sociological analyses and judgements regarding the actual 'function' (or otherwise) of sport in achieving societal objectives, such as conflict resolution or social rehabilitation of the traumatized within particular circumstances. Sport can have significant benefits within especially difficult contexts, but only when the 'development' projects are rooted in meaningful dialogue with recipient groups, and when such programmes are accompanied by more direct policies to alleviate disease, hunger, war and forced migration. The governing bodies of the most popular sports can make significant headway by recognizing the rising 'culture of rights', and by seeking to ensure that their own procedures accord closely with human rights standards.

If we examine the question of human rights and sport at a more theoretical level, then we must turn to discuss the universalism–relativism debate. I have sought to indicate that a cultural relativist approach towards reading human rights has the virtue of highlighting the interconnections between Western imperialism and cultural values. In this context, given some of the weaknesses that are set out above (and these are not exhaustive), I would suggest that the cultural relativism argument is best used heuristically, in exposing each element in the cross-cultural transmission of 'rights' discourses and procedures within sport to questions of systematic doubt.

The advanced realities of globalization are such that non-Western cultures have themselves turned to pursuing advantageous spaces within the context of rights discourses. In the globalization process set out by Robertson, the rise of human rights and thematization of 'humankind' gives rise to two particular visions of global community in contrast to other forms of global arrangement. Such particular visions are themselves rather particular to the West. Developing this point, through Rorty, we might consider the West to be the 'human rights culture', still heavily influenced by Enlightenment values, yet most capable of communicating these mores, not simply through reason, but 'sentimental education'.

Rorty's points therefore remind us that there is much to do at home in strengthening the status of human rights, to educate future generations into recognizing the everyday social significance of these values. The rapid mobility of elite sports athletes, and in particular their transfer across Western sports clubs and nations, has the capacity to demonstrate to us how fateful our membership is of any 'community of fate', whether this relates to a club allegiance or to nationality. In sport, therefore, we must avoid the reduction of 'human rights' to pure sentimentalism, empty rhetoric, and anodyne photo-shoots. Taking human rights seriously necessitates the internal transformation of Western societies and the sports institutions themselves, as well as engaging empathetically, dialogically, with non-Western cultures.

NOTES

1. The two conferences are *Sport en Ontwikkelingssamenwerking*, University of Utrecht/Dutch Foreign Affairs Ministry, Utrecht (16 January 1998); and *How You Play The Game: Sport and Human Rights*, The Human Rights Council of Australia, Bondi, Sydney (1–3 September 1999).
2. A. Ogi, 'Conference Address', Sport and Development International Conference, Magglingen, Switzerland (16–18 February 2003).
3. See ⟨www.redoporte.org⟩.
4. See Gasser and Levinsen, this issue.
5. R. Giulianotti with G. Armstrong and H. Hognestad, 'Sport and Peace: Playing the Game', paper to the Sport and Development International Conference, Magglingen, Switzerland (16–18 February 2003).
6. See J. Bale and J. Sang, *Kenyan Running* (London: Frank Cass, 1994).
7. J. A. Mangan, *The Games Ethic and Imperialism* (London and Portland, OR: Frank Cass, 1998) p.18.
8. See S. Lambrinidis, 'Sport in Conflict Prevention and Peace Promotion', paper to the Sport and Development International Conference, Magglingen, Switzerland (16–18 February 2003).
9. On the complex relations between the military junta and sport inside Argentina, see E. Archetti, 'Argentina 1978 and After: Military Nationalism, Football Essentialism, and Moral Ambivalence' (unpublished paper, 2003).
10. See D. Yallop, *How They Stole the Game* (London: Poetic Products, 1999) pp.295, 296, 311.
11. See N. Chomsky, 'Recovering Rights: A Crooked Path', in M. J. Gibney (ed.) *Globalizing Rights* (Oxford: Oxford University Press, 2003) p.76.

12. On this matter, see the collection M. J. Gibney (ed.) *Globalizing Rights* (Oxford: Oxford University Press, 2003).
13. See S. Latouche, *The Westernization of the World* (Cambridge: Polety Press, 1996) pp. 3, 20, 31, 105.
14. Latouche (note 13) pp.129–130n; p.45.
15. J. Baudrillard, *Screened Out*, (London: Verso, 2002) pp.158–59.
16. On women's football in Algeria, see the *Guardian* (6 November 1999). On women's sport and human rights in Islamic societies see, in particular, A. E. Mayer, *Islam and Human Rights: Tradition and Politics*, 3rd edn (Boulder, CO: Westview 1999) pp.115–16.
17. N. Chomsky (note 11) p.55.
18. R. Niezen, *The Origins of Indigenism: Human Rights and the Politics of Identity* (Berkeley, CA: University of California Press, 2003) p.143.
19. See R. Robertson, *Globalization: Social Theory and Global Culture* (London, 1992); R. Rorty, 'Human Rights, Rationality, and Sentimentality' in S. Shute and S. Hurley (eds.) *On Human Rights: The Oxford Amnesty Lectures 1993* (London: Basic Books, 1993).
20. See R. Robertson (note 19) pp.183, 184.
21. See R. Robertson (note 19) pp. 78–79. Similarly, Scholte locates the rise of human rights in the wider envisioning of a 'cosmopolitan community'. Echoing Robertson, Scholte suggests that international indications of rising 'universalism' include the greater relevance of 'global village' metaphors. Other trends towards cosmopolitan communitarianism include the Universal Declaration of Human Rights which is adhered to by most states, the establishment of other rights charters by regional bodies in Africa and Europe, the establishment of the International Criminal Court, the success of NGOs such as Amnesty International, the growth of international environmental movements, and the advance of 'cosmopolitan solidarity' on the right of Third World societies to certain levels of 'humane development'. See J. A. Scholte, *Globalization: A Critical Introduction* (Basingstoke: Palgrave, 2000) pp.178–79.
22. R. Giulianotti and Roland Robertson, 'Die Globalisierung des Fußballs: 'Glokalisierung', transnationale Konzerne und demokratische Regulierung', in P. Lösche, U. Ruge and K. Stolz (eds.) *Fussballwelten: Zum Verhältnis von Sport, Politik, Ökonomie und Gesellschaft* (Opladen: Leske and Budrich, 2002).
23. W. J. Morgan, 'Cosmopolitanism, Olympism, and Nationalism: A Critical Interpretation of Coubertin's Ideal of International Sporting Life', *Olympika* IV, 88–89.
24. R. Rorty (note 19) pp.127, 128.
25. Ibid. pp.133–34.
26. C. Brown, 'Universal Human Rights: A Critique', in T. Dunne and N. J. Wheeler (eds.) *Human Rights in Global Politics* (Cambridge: Cambridge University Press, 1999) p.120.
27. R. Rorty (note 19) p.117.

The Olympic Industry and Civil Liberties: The Threat to Free Speech and Freedom of Assembly

HELEN JEFFERSON LENSKYJ

Free speech and freedom of assembly are two key components of the social conditions that people in democratic societies typically refer to as *human rights* or *civil liberties*. In this article, I will examine the threats to free speech, in the form of a free press, and to freedom of assembly, in the form of peaceful protest, posed by the Olympic industry. As I have explained in two critical Olympic books, I use the term Olympic *industry* to indicate that the International Olympic Committee (IOC), the national Olympic committees of its member countries, and its global corporate sponsors are primarily concerned with profit.[1] Thus, I problematize fuzzy concepts such as 'Olympic movement', 'Olympic family', and 'Olympic spirit' that deliberately cloak the Olympic industry's profit motive in pseudo-religious rhetoric. I examine how the mass media and Olympic boosters, including elected representatives, bow to Olympic industry pressure to suppress critical voices and to criminalize peaceful protest in Olympic host cities.

A Free Press in Olympic Bid and Host Cities?

Universality of information freedom – a free press – constitutes a basic human right. Three factors are identified in the Freedom House *Press Freedom Survey* as threats to a free press: social structures (laws and administrative decisions that influence content); the degree of political influence or control over content; and economic influences of government or private entrepreneurs. 'Political power, even in the most democratic nations, always seeks to manage the news. Democratic systems, however, create checks and balances to minimize state domination of the news media.'[2]

With recent developments in the Olympic industry requiring guaranteed financial support from governments, and escalating costs necessitating private-sector investment if a city is to host the event, there are ample opportunities and motives for governments and private entrepreneurs to attempt to control Olympic-related news. Canadian writer June Callwood's comments on responsible journalism are particularly pertinent:

> A journalist's mandate. . .is to rock the boat. This is done by seeing what is in the spaces between received wisdom and reality, and by putting into public view hard-won information that authorities would prefer to hide. If journalists don't do that, who will?. . .when corruption or bad ideas invade legislatures, a free press assuredly is the public's first line of defence.[3]

In light of the fact that the majority of summer and winter Olympics of the last two decades have been hosted by democratic countries, it seems reasonable (although admittedly naive) to expect that local media would report details of host cities' bids and preparations in a comprehensive and objective manner. Following the United Nations (UN) Universal Declaration of Human Rights, this analysis of Olympic reporting will be based on the assumption that freedom 'to seek, receive and impart information and ideas through any media' is, in fact, a human right.[4]

The Allure of the 'Olympic Gravy Train'

With the resounding financial and media success of the 1984 Olympics in Los Angeles, covering biennial summer and winter Olympic competition quickly became a coveted assignment for the international press. As members of this exclusive club, Olympic journalists soon came to expect a wide array of fringe benefits in exchange for giving favourable treatment to all things Olympic. The 'Olympic gravy train', as some critics called it, posed a serious threat to media objectivity, accuracy and autonomy. On a bigger scale, as sport sociologist Varda Burstyn has argued, the US National Broadcasting Company's (NBC's) $US3.4 billion investment in the Olympics between 1988 and 2008 in effect transformed its staff from independent journalists into 'employees of the investors/owners of the Olympics'.[5]

In 1999, pioneering Olympic whistleblower and journalist Andrew Jennings alleged that 'too many sportswriters in Britain and abroad have accepted money and 'freebies'' from Olympic officials, and noted that one senior British sports writer had been forced to resign because of undisclosed links to the IOC.[6] In his earlier Olympic critique, Jennings investigated the Berlin 2000 bid committee's elaborate media 'friendship' campaign – wining, dining, and gift-giving – designed to ensure that media coverage was seamlessly supportive. He concluded that, 'With a few exceptions, the [Berlin] media was bound into the bid machinery – or bought off.' For example, some local journalists were paid to prepare 'sympathetic articles' for the mainstream press and for the bid committee's magazine, while one newspaper sports editor, who also happened to be a member of Germany's national Olympic committee, was paid to help write the bid book.[7]

In the United States and Canada, also, journalists reaped the benefits of Olympic assignments, including invitations to lavish parties held by bid committees.[8] As *Toronto Star* columnist Jim Coyle observed, it was 'a lot easier, and lots more fun, to collect all the trinkets and make all the trips than to offend those who might turn off the access and the perks'.[9] Rick Hall, Olympic editor for the Salt Lake City newspaper, *Deseret News*, confirmed that editors and journalists avoided producing negative Olympic stories in the hope that the IOC would grant their staff a sufficient number of Olympic credentials, a worthwhile goal from a corporate media perspective since journalists, particularly in television, were seriously disadvantaged in terms of access to venues, athletes, and media centre facilities, if they were denied accreditation.[10]

In an interesting development before the Sydney 2000 Olympics, Tourism New South Wales provided the expected 15,000 unaccredited print media with their own fully equipped media centre in Sydney's central business district. This was not simply an altruistic move; like the Australian Tourist Commission's Visiting Journalists' Programme, established in 1989, the aim was to generate favourable publicity for Australia as a tourist destination. In the case of the unaccredited journalists, it was important, from an Olympic industry point of view, to control the flow of information within one central location, rather than letting them wander off in search of human interest stories that would reflect badly on Australia – for example, in the area of race relations, where horror stories illustrating 200 years of colonialist oppression of Indigenous peoples were not hard to find.[11]

Productive Partnerships: The Media and the Olympic Industry

Olympic industry power extends beyond the top level of the hierarchy – the IOC – to its myriad branches, including national Olympic committees, and local bid and organizing committees, and at all these levels, there is ample evidence of successful attempts to control the mainstream media. With the summer or winter Olympic Games, as well as bid city contests, taking place every two years, and full sessions of the IOC held annually, it is possible to find an Olympic story somewhere in the world almost every day of the year, as even a cursory search of the Internet will confirm. These are not necessarily news articles; many are simply Olympic-related filler items strategically released during the bid process or in the lead-up to the Games, in order to keep the Olympics in the public consciousness, particularly in cities eager to become future hosts.

For their part, the mainstream media have a long history of providing value-in-kind donations to Olympic bid and organizing committees.

One obvious example, in the age of the Internet, is the helpful provision of hyperlinks from major newspaper websites to Olympic industry sources. At the time of writing, with Vancouver/Whistler (Canada) bidding for the 2010 Winter Games, and New York City for the 2012 Summer Games, one can readily find links from the *Vancouver Sun*, *Vancouver Province*, and *New York Times* to their respective bid committee websites. In the 1990s, the *Toronto Sun* and *Sydney Morning Herald* provided a similar function. Needless to say, newspapers and bid committees never provided hyperlinks to community-based Olympic watchdog organizations such as Toronto's Bread Not Circuses Coalition (described below).

For big business, of course, more is at stake than the 'value-in-kind' privileges enjoyed by bid committee members and a band of tame journalists. Huge financial benefits accrue to multinational corporations, national broadcasting companies, developers, hotel and resort owners, the high end of the hospitality, tourism and entertainment industries, and advertising and public relations organizations, while the poor disproportionately bear the financial burden.[12]

Television and newspaper managements negotiate with Olympic officials for exclusive rights not only to cover Olympic sporting events but also to market various 'Olympic properties'. In the case of the Sydney 2000 Olympics, for example, these included the right to publish information on ticketing, the torch relay, and Olympic employment. In theory, there is a 'firewall' between management and editorial departments of media companies, in order to ensure that Olympic or other business deals pose no threat to a free press.

However, as Callwood aptly observed, management can influence content in more subtle ways, as 'ambitious editors and editorial writers and columnists and commentators run interference for them'.[13] She explained that the news staff know what the owner thinks – which perspectives are 'not popular upstairs' – and act accordingly out of 'a healthy sense of self-preservation'. And so, in practice, these 'firewalls' are rather porous, as revealed in the following examples from Salt Lake City and Sydney, cities that mounted successful Olympic bids, from New York, a new entrant in the 2012 race, and from Toronto, a city with two unsuccessful bids to its credit, and a third attempt in process.

The Eye of the Storm: The Salt Lake City Press

As early as 1988, Salt Lake City television journalist John Harrington had been attempting to blow the whistle on questionable aspects of that city's previous Olympic bids. Areas of concern included the unethical business practices of bid leaders Tom Welch and Dave Johnson, as documented in a Utah state auditor's report obtained by Harrington. For their part, television station management bowed to pressure from Welch to suppress Harrington's negative stories, and threatened him with dismissal if he carried out his intention of showing the auditor's report to the United States Olympic Committee.

In 1997, a year before the full extent of the Olympic bribery scandal came to light, Harrington publicly alleged that Welch indulged in 'expense-paid, worldwide, glitzy Olympic schmooze-fests', and was merely 'a pampered figurehead who got to know Olympic delegates at lavish parties, buying them off with first-class travel and expensive gifts, even medical treatment, paid for by others'. In Harrington's view, many of the journalists who ignored the clear evidence of scandal were 'living off the unspoken Olympic-beat quid pro quo', while the few who attempted to blow the whistle found that their careers were in jeopardy. Speaking on the Canadian Broadcasting Corporation (CBC) radio show, *Sportsworld*, in 1999, Harrington explained that, after his *Salt Lake Weekly* exposé of the environmental controversy at the ski-jump site was published in 1994, he was marginalized in local sport media circles and labelled 'a liar', with the result that his independent sports video business was irreparably damaged.[14]

Three years after the IOC bribery scandal, and a few weeks before the 2002 Winter Olympics, the *Salt Lake Tribune* carried an illuminating story on local newspapers' conflict-of-interest policies. Noting that the Salt Lake news media had been criticized for ignoring early evidence of bribery and corruption, one of the *Tribune*'s Olympic journalists, Glen Warchol, examined the ethical dilemma journalists face when they occupy two roles: as objective reporters of the Olympic Games, and as participants in 'Olympic spirit' promotional events. Similar conflicts exist when major television networks, newspapers and sports magazines pay millions of dollars for the honour of calling themselves Olympic suppliers/donors/sponsors/rights-holders, and then receive offers of 'complimentary' tickets and guaranteed positions on the torch relay teams for their staff. The *Tribune* enforced a strict conflict-of-interest policy during the Games, one that forbade 'participating in an event on which you are reporting or directly editing', but *Deseret News* and KSL News, following the national examples of NBC and ABC, saw no conflict-of-interest problem, and allowed their staff both to cover the event and to participate in the torch relay. As Warchol correctly observed, partaking of the 'intoxicating Olympic spirit' may compromise a journalist's credibility in terms of covering controversial Olympic stories fairly.[15]

Taming the Mass Media in Sydney

From the early to mid-1990s, the *Sydney Morning Herald*, with a few exceptions, played the role of cheerleader for the Sydney 2000 bid committee.

During this period, there were reports of freelance whistleblowers whose articles were rejected by major newspapers.[16] Rumours of state government and bid committee pressure on the mainstream media abounded, and by 1993, a *Herald* editorial, 'The media and the Olympic bid', was strenuously objecting to these 'straitjacketing' attempts.[17] In 1994, it became clear that freedom of the press had been in jeopardy since 1990. In the late 1990s, however, the *Herald*'s investigative journalists played a critical whistle-blowing role.[18]

In 1994, former New South Wales (NSW) premier, Nick Greiner, reviewed *The Bid*, a book by written Sydney bid chief Rod McGeoch (with the help of *Herald* journalist Glenda Korporaal), in the *Herald*. Greiner alleged that McGeoch had overlooked what he considered his own 'important' role in ensuring the bid's success. Greiner not only admitted, but appeared proud of the fact, that he had pressured senior media representatives to guarantee their support for the bid, without which, he said, he would not commit taxpayers' money. He said he was pleased to see that several papers had given the bid 'fair, perhaps even favorable treatment', and that most had 'joined in the sense of *community* purpose' (emphasis added).[19] Greiner's disclosures, which were arguably an admission that he had demanded positive media coverage and the suppression of critical stories – in other words censorship – sparked no public outcry in 1994, the year after Sydney was named the host city for the 2000 Games.

In 1999, the *Herald* published a series called 'Breaking China', which focused on McGeoch's plot to discredit the Beijing bid for the 2000 Olympics by producing a research report on China's poor human rights record. His proposal (later voted down) had been to publish the report in London to ensure that it could not to be linked to the Sydney bid committee. The 'Breaking China' story also made reference to the committee's interest in pre-empting criticism from Australian media sources that opposed the Sydney bid.[20]

Also in 1999, the former NSW Minister for the Olympics, Bruce Baird, reported that he had negotiated deals with three major Sydney media companies so that they would not carry stories about the bid committee's 'duchessing' (currying favour with) IOC members during their visits, in part because any accounts of fawning and obsequious behaviour would not sit well with Australians. Baird's claims were vigorously denied by all three companies.[21]

Suppressing Olympic Resistance in Toronto

One of Baird's advisors was Paul Henderson, Toronto's (failed) 1996 bid committee head. Baird claimed that Henderson had warned him about the dangers of negative publicity, pointing to the fact that Toronto's 1996 bid had been destroyed by local reporting of opposition mounted by Bread Not Circuses (BNC), a coalition of community-based Olympic watchdog groups concerned about housing and homelessness, environmental damage, redevelopment, and other harmful social impacts. Some Olympic boosters also believed that Toronto's bid was damaged by a series of articles about BNC written by *Atlanta Journal Constitution* reporter Bert Roughton, although evidence from the subsequent bribery investigations suggested that Atlanta did not need to rely too heavily on such indirect methods when direct gift-giving achieved better results.[22]

Interestingly, when it served Olympic industry purposes, the actions of local anti-Olympic groups, like BNC, were routinely dismissed as ineffective, 'lunatic fringe', and so on. In short, protesters could expect to take the blame (or credit, depending on one's political location) for failed bids, and to be discounted as merely 'a small group of naysayers' when a bid succeeded. But bid committees and their boosters were well aware that the IOC selection committee monitored local opposition and local media coverage, as well as conducting its own independent opinion poll, and so bid supporters faced the challenge of appearing to be open and transparent, while at the same time suppressing negative media coverage. Obviously, from the Olympic industry perspective, it is easier to prevent public relations disasters that to try to control press coverage after the fact. Some examples of the Toronto 2008 bid committee's treatment of BNC members demonstrate this 'preventive' strategy.

In October 1999, I received a phone-call from Canadian Broadcasting Corporation (CBC) inviting me to join a televised panel discussion on Toronto's 2008 Olympic bid. The CBC employee who spoke to me was fully aware that I was a member of Bread Not Circuses, as well as an academic and Olympic critic. When I asked who the other panellists were (explaining that I would not participate on such a panel if I were the *only* critic), the following names were provided: Andrew Jennings, Michael Shapcott, a founder of the BNC Coalition, David Hulchanski, a University of Toronto professor specializing in housing and homelessness issues, Michael Walker, a Toronto councillor and critic of the bid, David Crombie, bid committee chair, and/or John Bitove, its CEO.

In a phone-call I received six days before the show, the original invitation was withdrawn, and I was asked to sit in the audience and offered the chance to ask *one* question. All the prominent Olympic critics, except Walker, had been dropped, and Shapcott, Hulchanski and I had been downgraded to the audience. After first offering the lame excuse that there was not enough room on the platform, the CBC employee admitted that Crombie and Bitove had refused to take part if Shapcott, Hulchanski and I were on the panel, and that the Toronto bid committee was, in effect, dictating to the CBC who would participate in this television programme, in order to present the bid in the best possible light. The three of us subsequently refused to attend, and issued a press statement giving our reasons. When the show aired, it was clear that the Olympic industry had won this particular fight: only one well-informed local critic, Michael Walker, succeeded in gaining sufficient airtime to present his views fully, while the moderator allowed Bitove to dominate the show.

Shapcott, Hulchanski and I subsequently retained legal counsel to lodge complaints with the CBC ombudsperson, the Canadian Radio-Television and Telecommunications Commission, and the IOC's and Toronto bid's ethics commissioners, all to no avail. One *Toronto Star* sports journalist, however, published a critical account of the event: Dave Perkins noted that the bid 'won't take much scrutiny' and that bid committee leaders were 'threatening the CBC with non-participation if certain unfriendly individuals were included on yesterday's panel'.[23]

A similar situation occurred a few weeks later, when City TV host Anne Mroczkowski, in the role of 'moderator' during a phone-in show on the Olympic bid, unequivocally supported bid committee member Jeff Evenson, and joined forces with him to attack BNC representative Richard Milgrom at every opportunity.

There was further evidence of Olympic industry suppression of dissent when BNC asked the bid committee for the opportunity to meet with the IOC inspection team during its visit to Toronto in March 2001. We had communicated this request to the bid committee several weeks earlier, and had been told that the IOC team scheduled its own itinerary. However, in a conversation with a television journalist shortly before the visit, I learned that the press had received detailed itineraries from the bid committee; in fact, BNC received a copy from a sympathetic journalist later that week.

When a BNC member finally made a phone-call to IOC headquarters in Lausanne to request a meeting time, she was told (as we had suspected) that the local bid committee was responsible for planning the inspection team's itinerary. A meeting time was eventually agreed upon, but when around a dozen BNC members arrived at the hotel lobby, the bid committee's public relations person informed us that the IOC team would only meet with four BNC representatives, that the room was too small for more, and so on. When we objected to these terms, security guards ejected the entire group. After more time-consuming negotiations, the large group was permitted to enter, on the understanding that only four would speak. We were escorted by the guards in a locked elevator to the designated meeting room (where there was, not too surprisingly, ample room), and the IOC members listened politely. But this was a hollow victory. The bid representative's time-wasting strategies reduced each speaker's time to less than five minutes; members of the inspection team, quoted in the next day's *Toronto Star*, dismissed the entire presentation as irrelevant; *Star* journalists failed to contact BNC for a balanced report of the meeting; and BNC's subsequent complaints were ignored.

Also in March 2001, during the inspection visit, Toronto bid boosters publicly claimed that the Air Canada Center (the city's major professional basketball and ice hockey venue, and a model for future Olympic construction) was built 'on budget and on time'. In reality, costs rose 50 per cent over a four-year period, and construction was two years late, thereby incurring fines of about $CAN 640,000. All of these developments had been thoroughly covered at the time in Toronto's major newspaper, the *Toronto Star* (for example, in September and November 1996, and February 1999.) Yet, when a BNC member wrote to the *Star*'s editor and ombudsperson, pointing out that the Toronto bid committee's claims (as reported in that newspaper) were contradicted by the *Star*'s own earlier coverage, her letter was neither acknowledged nor published. Clearly, the *Star*, as an official Toronto bid sponsor, did not welcome negative letters.

A few months earlier, after I had managed to get a critical Olympic-related letter published, a senior *Star* reporter, in a phone conversation with another BNC member, alleged that I had misrepresented myself as a 'citizen' when I was really a BNC member – and, apparently, *persona non grata*. I had provided my residential address and phone number, in accordance with the *Star*'s policy, as well as my university affiliation, which they did not publish. Interestingly, soon after this incident, one of my colleagues was identified as a University of Toronto professor when his letter to the editor was published – significantly, on a *non*-Olympic issue. I could only conclude that the editor did not wish to give any extra weight to my contribution by identifying me as a university professor. Other BNC members with identifiable names had similar difficulties, while a few members not known to the *Star* staff managed to get critical letters in print.

These patterns confirm Callwood's analysis of the blurred lines between media management and editorial staff, and cast serious doubt over the *Star*'s objectivity in reporting bid-related news. There were, as noted, some exceptions to this practice. As Michael Shapcott observed, 'It is an interesting world when political journalists treat the Olympic bid as a sporting event, and cheer on the home team; while sports journalists such as Perkins ... treat the bid as a political event and provide some critical scrutiny'.[24]

On that note, in the earlier days of the bid, a *Star* editorial had engaged in what media critic Noam Chomsky called the 'necessary illusion' of self-monitoring: occasional self-criticism or publication of selected dissenting voices in order to create the illusion of a free press.[25] In this example, the editorial questioned that paper's uncritical publication of an unscientific self-selecting opinion poll, known in reputable opinion research circles as a SLOP (self-selected listener oriented poll). 'Should Toronto bid for the 2008 Games?' was the SLOP question published in an August edition of the paper. On 14 August, the *Star* reported 'a little breathlessly' that 'the majority of *Star* readers' supported the bid, with 62 per cent of *self-selected* readers registering a Yes vote on the Starphone line. But, as the editorial pointed out, the paper's policy manual required that news stories incorporating SLOP results should make it clear that they are unscientific.[26]

New York City Joins the Race

In a New York City example that took place in September 2002, two months before the US Olympic Committee selected it as the American contender for the 2012 Summer Olympics, *Newsday* columnist Kathleen Brady wrote one of the few critical pieces to appear in that city's newspapers.[27] Not coincidentally, *Newsday*'s contribution to the bid amounted to only $US 55,000 in contrast to the *New York Times*'s more generous gift, in the $300,000 and above category. Media giant America Online (AOL) Time Warner, whose operations included Cable News Network (CNN) News, gave over $500,000.[28]

In an article titled 'Torch the Olympics and build housing instead', Brady questioned the spending priorities of the mayor and other elected representatives, and the promised solutions to unemployment and the housing crisis that would allegedly flow from hosting the Olympics. Two weeks later, NY bid committee head Jay Kriegel phoned Brady at her home to demand a retraction.[29] These examples are significant for the blatant sense of entitlement displayed by the bid committee leader, who, it appears, was not concerned that his actions would be perceived as interference with the First Amendment right to free speech cherished by Americans.

Freedom of Assembly: A Victim of Sydney's Olympics

Soon after the IOC's 1993 announcement that Sydney would host the 2000 Olympics, NSW legislators sprang into action to pass a comprehensive set of regulations controlling public behaviour, and giving police and private security personnel unprecedented powers, all in the name of 'unobtrusive' Olympic security measures.[30]

The process of privatization and gentrification of formerly public space in the central business district and the harbour foreshores had begun in the 1980s with the redevelopment of the Darling Harbour area, adjacent to the city centre. The Darling Harbour Act criminalized a wide range of public behaviours – in fact, almost every non-consumerist or non-tourist act – in an area that soon became a lucrative tourist attraction. Michael Hall's term 'bourgeois playground' is a particularly appropriate label for this area.[31]

Subsequent Olympic legislation, following the Darling Harbour model, blanketed city parks, plazas, harbour foreshores, stadiums, sporting venues, and the entire Homebush Bay Olympic site with prohibitions against such serious security threats as distributing political leaflets or making speeches – in other words, engaging in peaceful protest. Of course, with the IOC Charter requiring the host city to guarantee that there would be no political protest in or near Olympic venues, politicians could argue that this legislation was essential. Moreover, with elected representatives subject to the NSW government's demand that they suspend partisan politics on all Olympic matters in the interests of meeting inflexible Olympic deadlines, much of the legislation passed without serious debate, and citizens were virtually disenfranchised when these attacks on freedom of assembly were launched. The few exceptions were members of the Green Party – Bob Brown, Ian Cohen and Lee Rhiannon – and a small number of other left-leaning representatives. Dr Peter Wong, for example, targeted the government's hypocrisy in sweeping social problems under the carpet while the eyes of the world (particularly the world media) were on Sydney during the Olympic year. Referring to provisions of the Olympic Arrangements Act, he asked rhetorically:

> What is the motive for this regulation? Is it to show the world during the Olympic, and very likely afterwards, how successful, harmonious and organized a society we are that we do not have social problems that leave thousands of people homeless on the streets? Is it to show that we are a successful economy that can employ everyone, so that there are no beggars on the street? Or is it to show that we can engage our young people and artists in meaningful and fulfilling activities so that they do not have to be a nuisance to the general public? If this is what we want to achieve, this regulation is not the way.[32]

In other attacks on civil liberties, the Homebush Bay Operations Regulation 1999 allowed police and private security guards to use 'reasonable force' to remove individuals they considered to be causing 'annoyance or inconvenience'; a person who objected could also be charged with resisting arrest. Grounds for removal included: 'Damage/ destroy/ remove tree/ plant/ vegetation', 'leave rubbish/ litter', 'use indecent/ obscene/ insulting/ threatening language', 'behave in offensive/ indecent manner', and 'cause serious alarm/ affront'. Olympic protesters were concerned, probably with good reason, that anti-Olympic messages on T-shirts would be viewed as 'insulting' if worn within hallowed Olympic grounds.

Most Olympic regulations were only in force until the Games were over, but several city and harbour areas were covered by restrictions lasting an additional four years or longer. Lee Rhiannon expressed concern that peaceful protests and free expression of political views were now prohibited in the Domain, an area dedicated to public recreation in 1810, and the traditional home of soap-box speakers for decades. This 'symbolic home of free expression and association in Australia' was now aggressively policed by 'a private army answerable only to the [Olympic Coordination Authority] bureaucrats'.[33]

Policing Sydney Sports Grounds – Overzealously

The Sydney Cricket and Sports Ground Act 1978 paved the way for future crackdowns on civil liberties in Sydney area sports grounds. Prompted by the increasing rowdiness of Sydney's cricket and football fans (although not approaching the same scale of violence as European soccer hooliganism), the act empowered stadium staff to call for police aid 'for the removal, by force if necessary, of any person who is found committing a breach of any by-law, or who by disorderly or insulting conduct on the trust lands or on any public place causes annoyance or inconvenience to persons on the trust lands', with particular attention to the ban on bringing in alcohol or other intoxicants.[34] The wording of the 1978 act appears relatively mild when contrasted with the 1999 amendments, enacted at a time when harsh measures regarding public behaviour in areas in or near Olympic venues passed with little debate. Moreover, the amendments were open to a wide range of interpretation on the part of police and security staff.

14. Personal conduct within Ground

A person must not do any of the following within the Ground:

(a) use indecent, obscene, insulting or threatening language,

(b) behave in an offensive or indecent manner,

(c) by disorderly conduct cause serious alarm or affront to a person,

(d) obstruct a person in the performance of that person's work or duties,

(e) fail to comply with a reasonable request or direction made or given by a member of the Trust, a police officer or an authorized person for the purpose of securing good order and management and enjoyment of the Ground.

[...]

16. Removal from scheduled lands

(1) A person who contravenes any provision of this Part .... or who trespasses or causes annoyance or inconvenience on any part of the scheduled lands, may be removed from the scheduled lands or any relevant part of the scheduled lands by a member of the Trust, a police officer or an authorized person.

(2) A member of the Trust or an authorized person acting in accordance with this clause may use such force as is reasonable in the circumstances for the purpose of discharging his or her duty under this clause.[35]

One spectator's recent experience will demonstrate the potential abuse of this act by police and security personnel. Dr John Johnson (not his real name) is an Associate Professor at a NSW university. As a sociologist, his research includes police and private security guards' work practices in public places, and so he has a particular interest in observing their behaviour in sports grounds (although his purpose was not to test the limits of police powers).

Attending a cricket match with friends early in 2002, Johnson was on his way from the refreshments bar where he had purchased beer, when he noticed an interaction between two men, and paused to watch. One of the men (who wore no visible identification as a private security guard) had apparently asked a spectator to leave because he was suspected of having brought alcohol into the grounds. When the security guard told Johnson to go away, he replied, 'In a minute; I'm just watching'; the guard repeated the order, but at no time identified himself as either a security guard or a police officer. Johnson continued to state that his watching did not interfere with anyone. Two uniformed police officers approached him and repeated the command to return to his seat, and again Johnson politely asked why, and pointed out that he was only watching. Because the guard and officers would not identify themselves by name, Johnson also refused to give his name.

The officers suddenly grabbed Johnson from behind, 'frogmarched' him to a garbage bin and forced the beer out of his hands, forcibly turned him around and led him to a holding area and later to a police van, with one officer applying pressure to his wrist to force him to comply, even though he was not resisting. He was eventually taken to a police station, where he was charged with failing to obey a direction, resisting arrest, and not giving his name and address. In the words of one officer (as quoted in Johnson's notes), 'I've had trouble before with loudmouthed smartarses like you standing behind me putting me in danger when I'm doing my job.' Johnson's legal counsel advised him to plead guilty to the first charge, and police dropped the other two. The magistrate found Johnson guilty, with 'no conviction recorded' under a first offence provision, but observed that 'blowing your nose' could be considered an offence under the sports ground legislation.[36]

It is important to note here that Johnson did not display any of the stereotypical physical or behavioural attributes of a 'rowdy' spectator who was likely to cause trouble for stadium security or police. He was not an adolescent or a young adult, his skin was not black or brown, he was not long-haired or unkempt, he was not intoxicated, and he did not speak a 'foreign' language – all characteristics that criminologists have identified in relation to targeted policing by the NSW police service.[37] It appears that Johnson's main 'crime' was to question the mindless directives of security personnel and police, whose primary motivation seems to have been muscle-flexing in a locale where spectators were automatically treated as law-breakers unless they complied to any and every order.

Conclusion

This analysis reveals patterns of Olympic industry threats to civil liberties – most notably, to a free press and to freedom of assembly – in recent bid and host cities in Europe, Canada, the United States and Australia. It is particularly alarming to note that the everyday practices of Olympic industry officials – their cynical 'management' of Olympic news, their cooptation of elected representatives, the sense of entitlement with which they conduct their business, and the 'legacies' of harsh law-and-order legislation – prompt relatively little public concern or outrage. Moreover, from a research perspective, it is disturbing to see how little documentation of Olympic resisters and resistance has appeared in academic publications.

Of course, this is how the Olympic (or any other) hegemonic system operates: coercive tactics are not necessary when the institution has sufficient resources to generate public consensus by shaping ideologies, particularly through control of the mass media. As I noted earlier, pseudo-religious terms like 'Olympic movement' and 'Olympic spirit' are carefully selected to evoke feelings of universal excitement and belonging, while the less savoury profit-making motive is concealed. Activists who attempt to uncover this hypocrisy often find themselves silenced, as the mass media and local politicians capitulate to Olympic industry pressure to censor critical voices and to criminalize peaceful protest in Olympic host cities. Finally, the Olympic industry's generously funded public relations machinery has little difficulty generating brand loyalty – after all, the Olympics *are* 'the only game in town'.

NOTES

1. H. Lenskyj, *The Best Olympics Ever? Social Impacts of Sydney 2000* (Albany, NY: SUNY Press, 2002); H. Lenskyj, *Inside the Olympic Industry: Power, Politics and Activism* (Albany, NY: SUNY Press, 2000).
2. Freedom House, *Press Freedom Survey* (2000) (www.freedomhouse.org/pfs200/method/html).
3. J. Callwood, Dalton Camp Lecture in Journalism, St Thomas University, NB, Canada (23 October 2002).
4. Freedom House, Press Freedom Survey.
5. V. Burstyn, *The Rites of Men: Manhood, Politics and the Culture of Sport* (Toronto: University of Toronto Press, 1999), p.231.

6. A. Jennings, quoted in J. Calvert, D. Connett, M. Gillard and D. Mackay, 'Games up for sale to Highest Bidder', *Guardian Weekly* (31 January 1999), p.23.
7. A. Jennings, *The New Lords of the Rings: Olympic Corruption and How to Buy Gold Medals* (London: Simon & Shuster, 1996), p.188.
8. J. Harrington, Transcript, *CBC Sportsworld* (5 May 1999).
9. J. Coyle, 'Olympic Critic Finally Gets to Say "I Told You So"', *Toronto Star* (30 January 1999) ⟨www.thestar.ca⟩.
10. R. Hall, Transcript, *CBC Sportsworld* (12 May 1999).
11. H. Lenskyj, *Best Olympics Ever?* (note 1) Chapter 3.
12. H. Lenskyj, *Best Olympics Ever?* (note 1); H. Lenskyj, *Inside the Olympic Industry* (note 1).
13. Callwood, Dalton Camp Lecture.
14. J. Harrington, 'Capitol of Hypocrisy', *Salt Lake City Weekly* (7 August 1997); Harrington, Transcript, *CBC Sportsworld*.
15. G. Warchol, 'Journalists Face Ethical challenge of Balancing Olympic Coverage, Participation', *Salt Lake Tribune* (10 January 2002) ⟨www.sltrib.com⟩.
16. W. Bacon, 'Media's Role Questioned', *Reportage* (September 1993), p.6.
17. 'The Media and the Olympic Bid' (Editorial), *Sydney Morning Herald* (15 July 1993) ⟨www.smh.com.au⟩.
18. H. Lenskyj, *Best Olympics Ever?* (note 1).
19. R. McGeoch with G. Korporaal, *The Bid* (Melbourne: 1994); N. Greiner, 'Inside Running on Olympic Bid', *The Australian* (19 October 1994), p.7.
20. G. Ryle and G. Hughes, 'Breaking China: How Sydney Stole the Games', *Sydney Morning Herald* (6 March 1999).
21. 'Media Companies Deny Deal', *ABC News* (19 February 1999) ⟨www.abc.net.au⟩.
22. H. Lenskyj, *Inside the Olympic Industry* (note 1) Chapter 3.
23. D. Perkins, 'Still Talking Road Apples and Oranges', *Toronto Star* (12 January 2000).
24. M. Shapcott, 'CBC Forgets to Tell Viewers that it Dumped Experts From the Panel', Bread Not Circuses website ⟨www.breadnotcircuses.org⟩. (13 January 2000).
25. N. Chomsky, *Necessary Illusions: Thought Control in Democratic Societies* (Toronto: CBC Massey Lectures, 1989).
26. 'Toronto Olympics "SLOP" was Misleading' (Editorial), *Toronto Star* (21 August 1999).
27. K. Brady, 'Torch the Olympics and Build Housing', *Newsday* (17 September 2002) ⟨www.newsday.com⟩.
28. New York City 2012 website (2002) ⟨www.nyc2012.com⟩.
29. K. Brady, Personal communication (7 December 2002).
30. H. Lenskyj, *Best Olympics Ever?* (note 1) Chapter 2.
31. M. Hall, 'The Politics of Hallmark Events', in G. Syme, B. Shaw, M. Fenton and W. Mueller (eds.), *The Planning and Evaluation of Hallmark Events* (VT: Avebury 1989), pp.219–41.
32. P. Wong, Olympic Arrangements Bill, second reading, *Hansard* (12 April 2000).
33. L. Rhiannon, Olympic Arrangements Bill, second reading, *Hansard* (14 April 2000).
34. Sydney Cricket and Sports Ground Act 1978 ⟨www.austlii.edu.au⟩. see also R. Lynch, 'Disorder on the Sidelines of Australian Sport', *Sporting Traditions* 16/1, (1991), 50–75.
35. Sydney Cricket Ground and Sydney Football Stadium By-law 1999 under the Sydney Cricket and Sports Ground Act 1978 (updated September 1999) ⟨www.austlii.edu.au⟩.
36. J. Johnson, Contemporaneous Notes (3 January 2002).
37. D. Dixon (ed.), *A Culture of Corruption* (Leichhardt, NSW: Hawkins Press, 1999); Public Interest Advocacy Centre, *Olympics Liberty and Security Issues: A Briefing Paper* (February 2000); Public Interest Advocacy Centre, *Liberty in the Olympic City: A Briefing Paper* (August 2000).

Watching Brief: Cultural Citizenship and Viewing Rights

DAVID ROWE

Introduction

As sport has become an ever more prominent feature of contemporary cultures, the sites of contestation surrounding it have proliferated.[1] In particular, the outcome of the most important change in the institution of sport over the last century – its convergence with another socio-cultural institution, the media, and the consequent creation of the 'media sports cultural complex'[2] – has meant that questions of civil liberties in sport must be addressed at a wide range of discursive sites. Questions of access and equity in sports participation have been historically and continually prominent, but the profound importance of the media has now also placed the related but distinct matter of representation at the heart of the cultural politics of sport.[3] Much of the concern here has been, quite correctly, with issues of equity (for example, the under-representation of women's sport in the media), ideology (such as the reproduction of class inequality in television sport commentary) and identity (including racial, ethnic and sexual stereotyping of athletes) in the media.[4] However, this mostly textualist focus must be matched, in an age of commodification and globalization of sport, with analytical approaches that are more institutional in nature.

It is important, then, to analyse the mechanisms by which sports texts are brought to their publics in the first place and, once created, to track their passage through a shifting range of viewing sites. Of particular interest to this essay is the rather neglected issue of contestation over access to television sports texts. It is easy, given the vast expansion of the sports media, to assess prevailing circumstances as one of surfeit rather than of shortage. This is certainly the case, in affluent zones of the West and East at least, when all the sports media, including newspaper sports pages, magazines, literature, film, advertisements, television, radio, Internet and even sports apparel, are taken into account. This plenitude, however, may mask the strategic rationing of access to key sports texts in their most valorized form – 'live' television broadcasts. Restricted access – actual or potential – to these most economically valuable and culturally significant of media sports texts inevitably raises issues of citizenship and civil liberties.

Clearly, these developments and issues in the institutions of the sports media are not operating in isolation. Sport is subject to related and unevenly developed processes of globalization, governmentalization, Americanization, televisualization, and commodification[5] that are, simultaneously, re-configuring patterns of sports production (including the labour of athletes) and of its consumption (including the activity of television viewing). In this article I will concentrate on the first and the last two of these processes in a predominantly European context, arguing that their interconnection raises important questions for the relationship between media sport and civil liberties that threaten to expropriate public investment for privately profitable purposes, and progressively to introduce an abundance of provision for the relatively affluent while imposing paucity on those of lesser wealth.

My argument is that televisualization is a process that is integral to any contemporary analysis of sport and should be embraced in any consideration of cultural citizenship. The reproduction of material disadvantage in cultural form is considered here in relation to its negative impact on established and developing rights of cultural citizenship in that key form of popular culture where national public provision meets, most comprehensively, national cultural affect and identity – sport. It is occurring on the media terrain most perfectly suited to the carriage of sport as a national cultural emblem – television. In order to analyse this nexus it is necessary, first, to gain a sense of its history of gathering institutional interpenetration, a process in which the nation state has acted as instigator or, at the very least, as contributor.

Sport and Television

In very broad terms, the history in Europe (and in countries like Australia, Canada and New Zealand with British-influenced television systems) of sports television has been one of pioneering involvement by free-to-air (terrestrial) public broadcasters. There followed the gradual introduction of a public–private mixed sports cultural economy of free-to-air broadcasting.[6] This binary arrangement has been superseded, in turn, by a tripartite system (audio-visual online sport having yet to significantly challenge traditional broadcasting) of public broadcasters, commercial free-to-air broadcasters, and subscription/pay-per-view television sport providers. In the process, television sport has moved significantly from periodic nation-building communications of major sports events to the staple fare of public and commercial broadcasters (for the latter representing a key means of capturing audiences and so of advertising revenue). It has now become the most prized content for the attraction of subscription revenue.

This expansion is tracked by Raymond Boyle and Richard Haynes[7] in the British context, with 2,800 hours of television sport produced by four free-to-air networks in 1989, whereas by 1999 'total sports television output closer to 25,000 [hours] a year' could be watched on five free-to-air channels and various forms of pay TV, including satellite, cable, pay-per-view and dedicated sports channels. Joseph Maguire[8] similarly, notes that 'between 1989 and 1995, European sport coverage increased from 24,000 hours to some 58,000 hours annually'. This growth has occurred in the context of a general expansion of television and other media, of which sport has constituted a major (and almost certainly disproportionate) element. In this way, the commodification of television sport has been significantly enhanced as public monopoly has given way to public regulation, and in so doing presented a third and troubling prospect – the complete commodification of sport on television such that it is governed only by a market that is, in turn, substantially controlled by large, multi- or transnational media corporations.

This trend towards full marketization has problematized the politico-cultural status of sport on television. It concerns whether there is a cultural right of all citizens (or at least those living in societies like Britain and France where 99 per cent of households contain at least one television) to have access to the most important sports presented in the best possible way – predominantly, 'live-to-air' shown where possible in prime time, and presented in a critically informative and incisive manner. Production values, including the number, positioning and type of camera, are also expected to be of a high order, and not reserved only for those watching on a subscription or per-view basis. The opposing rhetorical alternative to this position is to conceive of this issue principally in market terms as one of consumer access to goods and services under the rubric of commodity exchange in the context of the sport, leisure and televisual sectors of the cultural marketplace.

Association football in England is a conspicuous case of this public regulation versus full commodification problematic. As various analysts[9] have noted, the foundation of the English Premier League in 1992 involved a huge injection of media capital into a more hierarchical football structure by means of a lucrative contract with satellite broadcaster BSkyB. Half of the £304 million broadcast rights deal went to 22 (now 20) Premier League clubs,[10] which were in turn well positioned to derive additional income from sponsorship, merchandizing, and so on. While this arrangement meant that rather more television money was available to all English league clubs than before,[11] the other 70 (now 72) clubs received a much smaller proportion under conditions where they were required by law to invest large sums of money in stadium safety improvements.[12] This exchange had a further Faustian dimension in that it 'sacrificed' televised football viewers who had not hitherto subscribed to BSkyB (and perhaps never would because of their financial circumstances) in the interests of enriching Premier League clubs (with a small but patently inadequate 'trickle down' to clubs in lower divisions).

This development, along with the 1995 'Bosman ruling' in the European Court of Justice that ushered in freedom of soccer labour movement within the European Union, and the listing of several clubs on the stock exchange, created a massive boom at the upper end of English football. The result was the enormous enrichment of some clubs, administrators, shareholders, agents and players. For example, Jon Magee[13] points out that, by the turn of the millennium, the club contract alone of the Manchester United captain Roy Keane (that is, excluding income from product endorsements and other sources) was so generous that he became a pound sterling millionaire anew every fifth month. Such extravagant remuneration sharply contrasts with the straitened financial circumstances of the majority of clubs[14] benefiting little from the media-fuelled football boom.

A parallel cleavage opened up between those viewers willing and able to subscribe to satellite and cable television, and those who were required to accept, in all cases except where there had been anti-siphoning protection (for example, of matches involving the national team), far inferior football programming in their homes.[15] It is such emergent forms of cultural stratification that require to be assessed against a tenable model of cultural citizenship.

Cultural Citizenship Rights and Broadcast Sport

Notions of access to, and equity in, television sport as constituting significant elements of citizenship and civil liberty are, perhaps, novel. As Peter Dahlgren[16] has noted, in coming to terms with contemporary citizenship the subjective identities of citizens have increasingly come to the fore, yet 'Just which attributes are relevant is a question that has become more and more complicated'. Debates about civil liberties traditionally tend to pivot on the power of the state over individual citizens in such matters as detention or punishment, and the obligations of citizens towards established social institutions and to fellow citizens. These basic protections and responsibilities have been progressively extended to the legitimate entitlements of the citizen – for example, first to state-guaranteed food and shelter, then to a good education, health care and so on.[17] A developed conception of citizenship is enabling and empowering rather than solely protective, emphasizing not just the material foundations of a viable human life but also the social and cultural dimensions essential to guarantee full participation in the life of the nation (and, by extension, the world of global citizens). Here the media – incorporating genres of news, information, culture, entertainment and their various hybrids – are of especial significance given their consummate capacity to take citizens beyond personal experience limited by space and sensory perception into that collective realm conventionally referred to, after Jurgen Habermas,[18] as the 'public sphere'. Habermas sees the public sphere as a site of fairly conventional political debate, but in an increasingly 'mediatized' world it has mutated into less easily categorized ground where formerly discrete public and private matters collide and intermingle.[19] Media space, correspondingly, becomes of greater importance in assessing issues of distributive equality, especially as culture becomes more systematically integrated into commodity-based systems.[20]

The accelerating 'culturalization' of society, in which symbols, images, languages, and media technologies become progressively pivotal across the panoply of social, political and economic institutions,[21] intensifies and extends the capacity to exercise power in the cultural domain. Cultural exclusion, therefore, is an even more potent weapon of oppression in a culturalized world. Television has emerged as a key medium within that world, to the extent that it may be said to have significantly shaped it. Access to television in domestic households is close to universal in the developed world, with multiple access to television sets now the norm. The capital cost of free-to-air television is modest, involving only basic, mass-produced reception equipment and electrical power. In some countries (like the UK) a television licence is required to underwrite public broadcasting, the cost of which is relatively modest (at time of writing £112 for a colour TV) and with some concessions (a 50 per cent reduction for the registered blind) and exemptions (for viewers of 75 years and over). The availability of public broadcasting (matched only by rare cases of advertisement-free pay and commercial free-to-air TV programmes) also enhances the broadcasting environment by enabling viewers to avoid often-annoying commercials.

Television equipment, of course, has also been much developed in terms of screen size and type, sound, and so on, and with additional programming available for purchase from satellite and cable platforms. While matters of relative deprivation in terms of infrastructure are important (as they were in previous generations with, say, the shift from black-and-white to colour television), there is more concern here with content issues, and so with what appears on screen and when, rather than the technical quality of the broadcast received.

As Peter Golding and Graham Murdock[22] state in considering changes to the structure of television in the UK:

> ... a shift in the provision and distribution of cultural goods from being public services to private commodities signals a substantial change in the opportunity for different groups to have access to them ... By imposing the discipline of price on cultural goods they acquire an artificial scarcity that makes them akin to other goods of considerably greater scarcity. It is for this reason that the political economy of cultural consumption has to be especially concerned with material inequalities.

Within relatively affluent societies it is important, therefore, to ameliorate the social exclusionism that can be systematically generated by a primary reliance on capital accumulation and an assumed collective ability to exercise the power of consumer sovereignty. Maurice Roche[23] notes how, in relation to participation in sport among the general population, a policy under the slogan 'sport for all' was devised in the 1960s in the UK because the desired outcome of mass sporting participation could not be safely left to the commercial sport and leisure markets. By the 1990s, he argues, a policy of 'TV sport for all' that introduced listed events guaranteeing free-to-air transmission was required because, 'Just as the former promoted sport as a cultural right of citizenship, so the latter does the same in relation to TV sport'. This state intervention was a response to the 'clear threat to public access on 'free-to-air' terrestrial TV' [24] presented by large commercial media organizations developing restrictive pay TV platforms. That professional politicians in liberal democracies would risk the ire of such powerful media owners as Rupert Murdoch in this way is an indication that the political consequences of infringing popular rights of cultural citizenship are viewed as particularly perilous.[25]

To return to the case of football, fully unleashing capital logic would, according to John Sugden,[26] 'be seriously damaging to the quality of life for people today, and for unborn generations' because 'In Europe, South America and Africa, football, perhaps more than any other area of popular culture, captures the collective imagination and animates the discourse of citizenship.' This football–citizenship nexus (where the latter relates principally to a sense of collective identity) has, he says, to be 'protected from the more avaricious and predatory ways of unregulated global capitalism'.[27] The extent to which global capitalism can be said to have a coherent logic and to have been empirically established is the subject of sustained, keen debate no less within the sociology of sport than in any other sociological sub-discipline.[28] In the area of media sport, the 'project' of globalization can be said to be, at the very least, incomplete. One example of resistance to 'unregulated global capitalism' is the failure in the late 1990s of the Rupert Murdoch-controlled BSkyB to take over Manchester United Football Club in a bid worth £625 million.[29]

This deal would have seen the most powerful British football broadcaster acquire the most powerful British football club, but British regulatory authority (the then Monopolies and Mergers Commission) refused to approve the takeover on two grounds. The first was straightforwardly economic in rejecting further concentration of oligopolistic power in television, not to mention concerns about the horizontal integration involved in one economic entity (the football club) 'selling', by a process of collective bargaining (that may in the future be replaced by individual broadcaster–club contracts), one of its most valuable 'products' to itself (the media company). The second ground could also be interpreted as economic in that further concentration of wealth in the football industry would exacerbate the current trend of smaller clubs becoming financially unviable,[30] so creating further barriers to market entry. Particular sensitivity to the industrial structure of football resulted from clubs like Tottenham Hotspur, Newcastle, Leicester City, Nottingham Forest and Millwall becoming publicly listed companies.

Yet this was also an obviously social and political decision, with the Monopolies and Mergers Commission required to take into account public interest issues, including the desirability of maintaining 92 professional football clubs around the country rather than a reduced number of clubs concentrated in a small number of large cities, with many current full-time professional players consequently forced into part-time or amateur status.[31] This consideration engages with debates concerning a sports club's contribution to local community life and neo-classical economic critiques of 'unsustainable' sports[32] that cannot be discussed in detail here. In the case of the BSkyB bid, more lavish media funding and coverage for a small number of clubs like Manchester United were not seen to be in the public interest, despite arguments that this would weaken the competitive position of English football vis-à-vis clubs in Europe, such as A.C. Milan, owned by Italian Prime Minister and media entrepreneur Silvio Berlusconi, and in the face of threats to establish a European 'Super League'.[33]

Here the regulatory framework of the nation state intervened in the (converging) broadcast and sport markets in the public interest. The conception of cultural citizenship in this case is broader and deeper than the right of access to quality free-to-air television sport. It embraces the necessary preconditions for sport to be brought to the screen at all, and includes, as noted above, the maintenance of diversity and geographical dispersal within English football.[34] The nation state, however, cannot, in the contemporary world of trade blocs and multilateral agreements, operate in isolation, as was revealed in the case of the aforementioned Bosman Ruling in the European Court of Human Rights that re-drew the division of footballing labour in the European Union. The collective bargaining and sale on an exclusive basis of Premier League broadcast rights may itself breach European Union law. Nation states may, though, also cooperate through their representative entities to intervene in market processes deemed not to be in the interests of cultural citizenship.

For this reason, the same European Union that has created an open labour market and a system of transfrontier television has also allowed a degree of national cultural protectionism by empowering its Member States to proscribe the complete capture of events of national cultural significance (mostly sporting) for restricted access TV platforms by gazetting listed events.[35] Thus, the European Convention on Transfrontier Television incorporates a provision that:

> Each party retains the right to take measures to ensure that a broadcaster within its jurisdiction does not broadcast on an exclusive basis events which are regarded by that Party as being of major importance for society in such a way as to deprive a substantial proportion of the public in that Party of the possibility of following such events by live coverage or deferred coverage on free television.[36]

In practice, this protocol has meant that global mega-media sports events like the Olympics and the World Cup, and summer and winter sports of longstanding importance to a single country or to a smaller number of countries (such as skiing or distance skating), remain widely available to viewers. This arrangement has been supported by the permissibility of collective bargaining for broadcast rights to major events by the European Broadcast Union (EBU), an industry association of mainly public broadcasters whose membership also includes some North African and Middle Eastern broadcasters. The combination of listed events provisions, the desire of peak sport organizations, like the International Olympic Committee, to maximize their audiences, and cooperation between the members of the EBU have prevented a Premier-League style capture of many international sports events by a global pay TV provider, thus retarding the full commodification of TV sport in the name of cultural citizenship rights.[37]

Nonetheless, the power of the globalizing impulse should not be under-estimated. As Hans Magnus Enzensberger[38] argues:

> Capital tears down national barriers. It can make tactical use of patriotic and racist impulses, but disregards them strategically because the commercial interest can have no particular concerns. The free movement of capital tends to draw that of labour behind it, without regard for race or nationality.

In the case of sport, capital can be safely relied upon to 'disembed' continually national sports systems and industries through its relentless and restless quest to uncover new and to reconfigure old markets.[39] Thus, state intervention in broadcast sport might be viewed as swimming against the economic tide, and as obstructing the development of the media sector in the burgeoning 'information age'. Rather than automatically rejecting such innovations it is necessary to examine more closely the competing rationale for deregulation and state intervention in broadcast sport.

Pro and Con: Broadcast Sport and Citizenship Debates

There is a danger that, in defending citizens' access to televised sport, advocates can seem to glorify and mythologize it. As noted in the introduction, there is much for which contemporary sport can be criticized, including its patently unequal gender order,[40] propensity for reproducing racial ideologies,[41] and sometimes-rampant commercial exploitation.[42] Given the flawed nature of the social institution of sport, it is certainly not proposed to make watching it on television a compulsory civil duty. It also needs to be recognized that supporting public access to television sport entails a value judgement, inevitably disputed by those who believe that sport is already over-represented in the media and unduly promoted by government and business to the detriment of other worthy cultural forms and institutions. In other words, sport might already be regarded as culturally hegemonic and arguments for it as aiding and abetting the rise of a 'sportified' monoculture.

In response to such objections to the already existing place of sport in contemporary societies, it is necessary to make a distinction between the institution itself and the ways in which it may collude in the reproduction of social inequalities and formations of power.[43] In this regard sport is no different from other social and cultural institutions, with its media prominence perhaps making it a more visible target for social and cultural critics. While sport is an important and legitimate subject of critique, many attacks on it are barely disguised *bourgeois* expressions of cultural distaste by those who seek to impose hierarchies of taste and discrimination on other citizens that affirm their own, class-inflected positions of power. These responses to sport may involve its rejection *in toto*, the celebration of 'refined' sports (like cricket and baseball) and denigration of its *lumpen* forms (such as rugby league and gridiron), or attempts to reform and poeticize it from the inside (like association football and rugby union).[44] The appropriate critical response, therefore, is not to repudiate sport and lament its popularity with large numbers of citizens (somehow believing that they have been 'duped' into following it through the administration of a cultural narcotic), but to find ways in which sport can most effectively contribute to the realization of a more developed framework of cultural citizenship. Of necessity, this project requires intervention in the media form that is the bearer of sport to most members of the population – television.

It is axiomatic, therefore, that sport, via the electronic media, has become a major social institution in most 'advanced' societies. This social status, as noted above, is in many cases a direct result of very substantial public investment through state-funded or subsidized educational and health systems, the diversion of taxation (or public lottery) funding into sports programmes and organizations, and the development of technologies, techniques and audiences by public broadcasters that have been adopted or appropriated by private, profit-oriented entities. Thus, all citizens have, willingly or otherwise, a stake in the institution of sport and an interest (which they may or may not wish to exercise) in its public communication through publicly regulated (though not necessarily controlled) media channels. The assiduous cultivation of sport by media corporations and other commercial entities is testimony to its social significance,[45] such that television sport can be said to have achieved the status of a public good or service to which all citizens can expect reasonable access.

The level of that access is, of course, contestable. A minimalist approach would see the provision of delayed telecasts and highlights packages of major sports contests and tournaments, or of 'live' broadcasts of 'lower order' sport, as sufficient to meet civil obligations. In countries that have permitted the 'siphoning' of sport from free-to-air to pay television, this is precisely what has been provided. A maximalist position would insist, somewhat improbably, that there should be no difference between offerings on free-to-air and pay television. It is in this discursive space between historically inherited television sport provision and emerging broadcast technologies and platforms that cultural policy formation and implementation takes place. In so doing, it is necessary to avoid conjuring up a 'golden age' of sports television that only exists in the nostalgic imagination. Anthony King,[46] for example, notes that criticism in newspapers like the *Guardian* at the time of the aforementioned 1992 pay TV broadcast agreement between BSkyB and the newly formed Premier League:

> Exaggerates the extent of live television coverage of football in the 1980s. The first League game to be transmitted live was in 1983, and even after that date the number of games transmitted live was restricted.

It would be foolish and self-defeating to seek to return to the levels of TV sport of two decades ago, and to the rather patrician and condescending control of television content in pursuit of edification that it sometimes displayed.[47] The BBC's founding Reithian philosophy was in part committed to 'civilizing' the proletarian element, a broadcasting ideology that was diminished but nonetheless survived the introduction of commercial television in 1955. State broadcasting monopolies and their culturally prescriptive practices survived much longer in most other European countries – in Italy it was not broken until the 1970s, in France and Germany the 1980s, and in 'most of the rest of Europe it came even later'.[48] But, as David Hesmondhalgh[49] notes, the progressive transfer of broadcast sport rights from television stations with a public service remit to those with a profit ethic raises important equity questions:

> This has meant enhanced, more detailed coverage of sport, but it has also meant that, in the UK, football matches between leading domestic teams are rarely shown live on free-to-air television. Fans must pay a subscription of about GB£35 (US$50) a month for a package which includes live Premiership football, or find a pub showing the match . . . . The costs of subscription and pay-per-view means that television may become increasingly vulnerable to the inequalities of access apparent in other media, such as the internet.

For many citizens, the outlay on pay TV sport – which also includes additional infrastructure such as satellite dishes and, when encoded digitally, new televisions or set-top boxes – may be quite reasonable in terms of their discretionary leisure income. For others, however, it will be prohibitive and, as has been noted above, additional features (including pay-per-view, telephony and interactive services) will present opportunities for much more, perhaps imprudent consumption. Satellite dishes and cable links have proliferated in some of the less affluent neighbourhoods, and this is not altogether a surprising phenomenon given the popularity of sport, the paucity of leisure opportunities in many areas, and the persuasive inducements to purchase discounted reception equipment and 'bundled' service packages.

But these may constitute the distortion of expenditure priorities of people of insubstantial means, and require them to pay individually for services that, under a more 'civilly-sympathetic' converged communication regime, they may have received free or at below-market cost. The commercial 'battering ram' of pay TV sport, as famously described by Rupert Murdoch to News Corporation shareholders in 1996, may demolish the 'rough' democracy that free-to-air television had created in its sphere of culture in the late twentieth century.

There are, it can be seen, competing diagnoses of present circumstances, including claims of the arrival of a more progressive post-broadcast era, with new media technologies and viewer expectations of greater choice, and the accompanying flexibility and interactivity that enables them to become 'co-producers' rather than passive receivers of broadcasts.[50] Less dramatic is an assessment of the arrival of 'post-Fordism', whereby there is much greater customization of knowledge-intensive goods and services for discerning and demanding consumers in sport, television and related markets, such as fashion.[51] While elements of these developments are in evidence, they are incompletely and unevenly realized, with traditional broadcasting remaining of paramount importance, especially in the representation of sport.

But there are many uncertainties about changes within the marketplace of television sport.[52] There is pressure to accelerate the uptake of new forms of marketized television delivery 'bundled' with other services produced by the convergence of computing, broadcasting and telecommunications in order to 'add value' to existing media and information services. Customers, therefore, are 'encouraged' to take up these new services (for which they will have to pay) by a 'carrot-and-stick' combination of inducement and compulsion. The inducement is the availability of new content and uses. In the case of sport, this includes more 'live' television sports contests, with viewer choice of camera angles and the instantaneous ability to 'call up' sports data, opportunities to purchase tickets and merchandising, order fast-food without interrupting the viewing experience, networked computer communication with other sports fans, and so on.[53]

Yet, as Raymond Williams[54] argued in his seminal analysis, through a case study of television, of the relationship between developments in technology and culture, technological capability necessarily precedes its use, and the specific framework for its introduction and implementation is the product of the balance of forces of social institutions. Thus, there is no determining logic of use that can be derived from a self-evident hierarchy of technological capacities and cultural needs. For commercial media organizations to minimize risk in this environment there must be more than a simple reliance on assumed product appeal. The commercial media require expensive product and market development under circumstances where consumer preferences can be unpredictable and volatile. For this reason, there is a temptation to use an element of compulsion to supplement product appeal by withdrawing previously available goods and services, by degrading access to them, or by withholding the benefits of new technologies, techniques, forms and uses.

Historical examples include the market defeat of the Beta video format to VHS (video home system) engineered by the superior licensing and distribution of an inferior technology; reductions in the production of vinyl records and analogue audiotapes when compact discs and players were introduced to the market; the reduction of the number of properly maintained public telephones following the introduction of mobile telephones; and the phasing out of analogue telephony and broadcasting in order to promote digitization. Pay television perpetuates this pattern by implementing or threatening 'content starvation'. A classic instance of this practice, as noted earlier, is the siphoning of key sports events from open to restricted-access television platforms.

Again, it could be objected that this is an inevitable and efficient process according to the principle of 'stratified diffusion', whereby goods and services spread in an ordered pattern from an affluent elite to the broad mass of members of a society. As Young and Willmott[55] argue, stratified diffusion presents an image of:

> A marching column with the people at the head of it usually being the first to wheel in a new direction. The last rank keeps its distance from the first, and the distance between them does not lessen. But as the column advances, the last rank does eventually reach and pass the point which the first rank had passed some time before. In other words, the egalitarian tendency works with a time lag.

Young and Willmott argue that this principle works best for possessions, especially consumer durables. The pattern involves newly developed, expensive items becoming mass commodities through the economies of scale deriving from the production of cheap imitations (especially from countries outside the core 'Triad' of the USA, Europe and Japan) and high-volume consumption. The principle holds that, eventually, the wider population will gain access to the telephones, televisions, refrigerators, and washing machines that were once the preserve of the few, but by which time those further up the class structure will have commenced a new minority cycle of consumption, to be emulated later by those without the necessary resources to command them at that time. In the case of television sport, this principle may be applied to hardware, software and service (subscription) costs.

The most benign interpretation of this commodity diffusion cycle is that the rich are product testers for the poor, affirming their status through 'conspicuous consumption'[56] or 'distinction'.[57] However, it also embraces a conservative functionalist assumption that there will always be an unequal class structure in which material wealth and cultural leadership remain concentrated in the hands of a few. Furthermore, it is silent on the question of the degree to which this is an artificially stimulated process of consumption capitalism, imposing a perpetually burdensome level of rising expectations for goods and services that may be superfluous, and encouraging 'wasteful' discretionary expenditure when divorced from goods and services with a high level of 'use value'.

It would obviously be undesirable to seek to block all product innovations and to deny them to the majority of citizens, but it is equally dubious to assume, a priori, that whatever becomes available on the market is transformed into a need or entitlement. A key role of the state in this area is to protect the citizenry from the worst forms of capital exploitation by managing the framework of production and consumption in such a way as to ameliorate rather than exacerbate social inequalities. This means using its strategic power to maintain previous access to desirable goods and services, and to enable less affluent citizens to take advantage of beneficial innovations without excessive (such as multi-generational) time lags.

Thus, in the case of televised sport, in which there has been very considerable public investment and a publicly approved framework for its distribution, it is important to find ways that enable public free-to-air broadcasting to improve its provision of sport by taking advantages of new technologies and advanced techniques. This does not require the wholesale '(re)nationalization' of broadcasting. The consumption of broadcast sport can hardly expect to be exempted from the wider apparatus of commercial leisure. Necessary, instead, is public intervention in the sports media marketplace to secure already-established rights of cultural citizenship and, where appropriate, to extend them. This could take the form of a charter that requires, in exchange for the use of restricted public resources such as broadcast spectrum, and in recognition of the pioneering role of the public sector in the development of broadcast sport, that all citizens are able to participate in and have access to television sport in recognition of its standing within public culture.

As noted above, these deliberations are likely to be complex and controversial, given the levels of economic and affective investment in TV sport. But the shift in the nature of exchange for TV sports broadcasting from publicly collected licence fees and/or taxation revenue, to 'consent' to be exposed to advertising in exchange for desirable content, to the direct purchase of broadcast services or individual transmissions, demands that rights pertaining to watching sport on television cannot be left entirely to the market to determine. Recent decades have seen the ascendancy of neoclassical (or, if preferred, neoliberal) economics and the progressive 'rolling back' of the state.[58] But political resistance has been evident in those zones where citizens can clearly discern that their established or implied rights are being infringed. Access to key television sports events is one such ground upon which such 'civil defence' can be speedily and energetically mobilized.[59] This is why television is a prime site for contestation in contemporary sport.

Conclusion

The argument contained within this article is founded on two principal propositions: that television is a vital component of any current conception of sport, and that television sport is a key component of any consideration of the rights pertaining to contemporary cultural citizenship. Acceptance of these two propositions leads inevitably to the position that the analysis of the relationship between sport and civil liberties must encompass, systematically, issues of access and equity in the watching of sport on television. In order to safeguard what are now taken to be established cultural rights of citizens, and to enable the citizenry at large to benefit from technological innovations and new forms of media use, the state must be vigilant and willing to intervene in the field of broadcasting. This will mean slowing and even reversing the deregulatory trend of the last two decades, a response made necessary by the accelerating and intensifying marketization of the broadcast sector, especially given the gathering strength of digitization and media convergence.

Given the capacity of pay television to provide several 24-hour sports channels, it is highly unlikely and probably undesirable that free-to-air television should seek to match this density of sports coverage. This is because free-to-air broadcasters have a more wide-ranging programming remit and have a much more limited range of channels. It would be unreasonable to impose wall-to-wall sport on all free-to-air viewers. Digitization and its attendant proliferation of television channels makes possible the introduction of pay TV-style 24-hour sports channels on public free-to-air television, a development that would certainly meet massive objections from subscription and pay-per-view broadcasters who are deeply reliant on sport to attract customers. This article assumes that the current rationing of free-to-air television channels will persist for the foreseeable future and that, as has already occurred, where public and commercial free-to-air broadcasters branch out into more specialized programming, this will be on a restricted platform, fee-paying basis.

The key institution in this process of broadcast development and regulation is the nation state, an entity that is widely believed to be, perhaps, in terminal decline[60] – although this trend is not universally regarded as negative.[61] Without uncritically supporting the preservation and resuscitation of the nation state, it can nonetheless be argued that pronouncements of its death and transcendence by globalization, in sport and in other socio-cultural fields, are premature.[62] Indeed, as noted above, it is essential for nation states to cooperate, either through multilateral cooperation or by means of more comprehensive supra-state political entities, like the European Union, in order to be able to counter the power of transnational capital. This requires an analytical approach that is appreciative of the relationship between material and cultural inequality, which is sceptical of claims that privatization and marketization inevitably create greater freedom and choice, and can 'help formulate feasible projects for intervention and change that move beyond paternalism and state control'.[63]

Television sport requires the state to exercise determination in defending and extending the rights of the cultural citizenship associated with it. At the same time, the state must display appropriate restraint in resisting the temptation to prescribe, as it once did, what it believes to be in the interests of the citizenry to see, and to proscribe the rest. It is through engagement with this dynamic that the cultural politics of television sport will be played out.

NOTES

1. I would like to thank the editors, David McArdle and Richard Giulianotti, and anonymous reviewers for exacting but constructive feedback on the first draft of this article.
2. D. Rowe, *Sport, Culture and the Media: The Unruly Trinity* (Buckingham: Open University Press, 1999).
3. S. Birrell and M.G. McDonald (eds.) *Reading Sport: Critical Essays on Power and Representation* (Boston: Northeastern University Press, 2000).
4. A. Baker and T. Boyd (eds.) *Sports, Media, and the Politics of Identity* (Bloomington: Indiana Universtiy Press, 1997); K. Schaffer and S. Smith (eds.) *The Olympics at the Millennium: Power, Politics, and the Games* (New Brunswick and London: Rutgers University Press, 2000); D. L. Andrews and S. J. Jackson (eds.) *Sport Stars: The Cultural Politics of Sporting Celebrity* (London and New York: Routledge, 2001).
5. T. Miller, G. Lawrence, J. McKay and D. Rowe, *Globalization and Sport: Playing the World* (London: Sage, 2001).
6. G. Whannel, *Fields in Vision: Television Sport and Cultural Transformation* (London: Routledge, 1992); P. Goodwin, *Television under the Tories: Broadcasting Policy 1979–1997* (London, British Film Institute, 1998). The public sector has been similarly crucial to the development of the institution of sport in Europe through the educational system and allocation of public funds to peak sports organizations and sports infrastructure. In the United States, where 'the tempo of industrialization was quicker', bringing about 'a similar acceleration in the evolution of American sports', see A. Guttmann, *Games and Empires: Modern Sports and Cultural Imperialism* (New York: Columbia University Press, 1994) pp.74–75, the public contribution to sport has been somewhat occluded. However, the hidden public subsidies for sport in the USA are significant, including exemption from anti-trust legislation. In addition, there is a well-established pattern of publicly-funded inducements to retain or attract sports franchises, and substantial infrastructural support for major sports events (including facilities, transport and security) has been provided by local and national state entities. See S. Nunn and M.S Rosentraub, 'Sports Wars: Suburbs and Center Cities in a Zero-Sum Game', *Journal of Sport and Social Issues*, 21 (1997) pp.65–82; and D. Whitson, and D. Macintosh, 'The Global Circus: International Sport, Tourism, and the Marketing of Cities', *Journal of Sport and Social*

Issues, 20 (1996) pp.278–95. In other words, whatever might be argued in favour of the cultural importance of sport in the USA, its citizens have unquestionably supported that institution as public citizens and not, simply, as consumers purchasing cultural goods and services in the context of a free, privatized leisure market.

7. R. Boyle and R. Haynes, *Power Play: Sport, the Media & Popular Culture* (Harlow: Pearson Education, 2000).
8. J. Maguire, *Global Sport: Identities, Societies, Civilizations* (Cambridge: Polity, 1999).
9. A. King, *The End of the Terraces: The Transformation of English Football in the 1990s* (London and New York: Leicester University Press, 1998) R. Giulianotti, *Football: A Sociology of the Global Game* (Cambridge: Polity, 1999); D. Rowe, 'No Gain, No Game? Media and Sport', in J. Curran and M. Gurevitch (eds.) *Mass Media and Society* (3rd edition) (London: Edward Arnold, 2000) pp.346–61; J. Magee 'Shifting Balances of Power in the New Football Economy', in J. Sugden and A. Tomlinson (eds.) *Power Games: A Critical Sociology of Sport* (London: Routledge, 2002) p.221.
10. King (note 9) p.111.
11. Giulianotti (note 9) p.92.
12. S. Lee, 'The Political Economy of English Football', in A. Brown (ed.) *Fanatics! Power, Identity and Fandom in Football* (London: Routledge, 1998) pp.32–49.
13. J. Magee (note 9) p.221.
14. King (note 9); J. Sugden and A. Tomlinson, *Great Balls of Fire: How Big Money is Hijacking World Football* (Edinburgh and London: Edinburgh, 1999).
15. An alternative is to visit pubs, clubs and sports bars that subscribe to BSkyB. Watching live football in these establishments has become a new and, for many, highly enjoyable form of leisure in the UK (although not for D. Hesmondhalgh, *The Cultural Industries* (London: Sage, 2002) p.226). However, any personal funds saved by not subscribing to BSkyB would perforce be partially or fully expended (or even exceeded) in these non-domestic, commercial premises. Additional cost in such cases could include beverages, transport and food, as well as heightened exposure to gambling and other leisure pursuits with a high potential to absorb both discretionary and, in 'problem' cases, non-discretionary income.
    Of course, this inequality is intensified beyond affluent societies in those countries where a combination of poverty and poor access to communications technology has severely limited exposure of and to sport. John Sugden (note 9) p.67 has noted further that, with regard to media production rather than consumption, there are analogous divisions in operation on a global scale, with the 'awesome scale of the mediation required for the World Cup' making it 'highly improbable that any other than a handful of rich, first world countries, or conglomerates thereof, will be allowed to host future competitions'.
16. Peter Dahlgren, 'Media, Citizenship and Civic Culture', in Curran and Gurevitch, *Mass Media and Society* (note 9) p.317.
17. G. Shaffir (ed.), *The Citizenship Debates: A Reader* (Minneapolis, MN and London: University of Minnesota Press, 1998).
18. J. Habermas, *The Structural Transformation of the Public Sphere* (Cambridge: Polity Press, 1989).
19. Dahlgren (note 16) pp.310–28.
20. T. Miller, *The Well-Tempered Self: Citizenship, Culture and the Postmodern Subject* (Baltimore and London: The Johns Hopkins University Press, 1993); T. Miller, *Technologies of Truth: Cultural Citizenship and the Popular Media* (Minneapolis, MN and London: University of Minnesota Press, 1998).
21. M. J. Wolf, *The Entertainment Economy: How Mega-media Forces are Transforming Our Lives* (New York: Penguin, 1999); D. Throsby, *Economics and Culture* (Cambridge: Allen & Unwin, 2001).
22. P. Golding and G. Murdock, 'Culture, Communications and Political Economy', in Curran and Gurevitch. *Mass Media and Society* (note 9) pp.88–89.
23. M. Roche, *Mega-Events and Modernity: Olympics and Expos in the Growth of Global Culture* (London and New York: Routledge, 2000), p.176.
24. Roche (note 23) p.177.
25. Rowe (note 9) pp.346–61.

26. Sugden, 'Network Football' (note 15) p.78.
27. Ibid.
28. For example, J. Bale and J. Maguire (eds.) *The Global Sports Arena: Athletic Talent Migration in an Interdependent World* (London: Frank Cass, 1994); R. Giulianotti (note 9); J. Maguire, *Global Sport: Identities, Societies, Civilizations* (Cambridge: Polity, 1999); A. Bairner, *Sport, Nationalism, and Globalization: European and North American Perspectives* (Albany: State University of New York Press, 2001); J. A Hargreaves. 'Globalisation Theory, Global Sport, and Nations and Nationalism', in J. Sugden and A. Tomlinson (eds.) *Power Games: A Critical Sociology of Sport* (London: Routledge, 2002); J. Magee and J. Sugden, 'The World at Their Feet': Professional Football and International Labour Migration', *Journal of Sport & Social Issues*, 26 (2002) pp.421–37; P. McGovern, 'Globalization or Internationalization? Foreign Footballers in the English League, 1946–95', *Sociology*, 36 (2002), pp.23–42; Miller *et al.* (note 5).
29. Roche, *Mega-Events and Modernity* (note 23).
30. Lee, 'The Political Economy of English Football', in Brown (note 12) pp.32–49.
31. E. Dunning, *Sport Matters: Sociological Studies of Sport, Violence and Civilization* (London and New York: Routledge, 1999) p.123.
32. D. Whitson and D. Macintosh 'The Global Circus: International Sport, Tourism, and the Marketing of Cities', *Journal of Sport and Social Issues*, 20 (1996) 278–95; J. Maguire, *Global Sport: Identities, Societies, Civilizations* (Cambridge: Polity, 1999); M. Moller, *Reclaiming the Game: Rugby League, Globalisation and Masculinity* (Unpublished PhD thesis, Sydney, 2002).
33. There is little current evidence that the English football market has suffered severely because of the state's refusal to allow such mergers of television companies and football clubs. Magee's (note 9) pp.216–39, qualitative research reveals, for example, that high levels of remuneration in England are a powerful lure for overseas footballers. It is not possible to deal adequately here with the complex political economy of European football. In broad terms, however, the threat to the economic sustainability of leagues in Italy, Spain, France, Germany and Britain itself is presented by declining revenues from the main source of their expansion – television. This is because a 'softer' advertising market for commercial 'free to air' television has reduced broadcast rights income at a time when the disastrous collapse of pay TV companies (such as ITV Digital in the UK, with particularly severe consequences for smaller clubs) has had a serious negative impact on the financial position of European football clubs. See David Rowe, 'Fulfilling the Cultural Mission: Popular for Genre and Public Remit', *European Journal of Cultural Studies*, 7 (2004) pp.381–99.
34. The Scottish football market has had to confront similar issues, as well as having to counter its much larger neighbour to the south. See R. Boyle, and R. Haynes, '"The Grand Old Game': Football, Media and Identity in Scotland', *Media, Culture & Society*, 18 (1996) pp.549–64; Giulianotti (note 9). A proposal that frequently surfaces is to locate the two clubs that overwhelmingly dominate the game there – Glasgow Celtic and Glasgow Rangers – either in an English League or a new one involving clubs in continental Europe. The consequences for other Scottish clubs, if such moves occurred, would be serious indeed. Even more than in England, the future of the Scottish game as comprehensive, competitive and professional is already seriously in question.
35. Rowe (note 33).
36. Council of Europe, *Protocol Amending the Convention on Transfrontier Television*, ⟨www.conventions.coe.int/Treaty/en/Treaties/Html/171.htm⟩ (1998), p.4.
37. In 2002, this bargaining framework had profound consequences for the cost of broadcasting the Korea-Japan World Cup. The EBU and individual national public broadcasters, like the BBC, resisted the sharp increase in broadcast rights sought by ISL/Kirch, to whom FIFA (football's world governing body) had allocated 'on-selling rights'. As a result, both companies collapsed, threatening the availability of the televised World Cup in some countries. In Germany, for example, the state was required to intervene and 'bail out' World Cup broadcasts by hurriedly underwriting broadcast infrastructure See Rowe (note 33). Indeed, it might be argued that the globalization and commercial development of the media sport market has gone, at least temporarily, into reverse in the context of declining advertising

revenues, falling TV audiences in some sports, and static subscription levels. See T. Miller, D. Rowe, G. Lawrence and J. McKay, 'Globalization, the Over-Production of US Sports, and the New International Division of Cultural Labour', *International Review for the Sociology of Sport* (forthcoming, 2003).

38. H. M. Enzensberger, *Civil Wars: From LA to Bosnia* (New York: The New Press, 1994) p.111.
39. Enzensberger (note 38) p.111, goes on to argue that 'the globalization of the world market' was 'completed only very recently', leading to 'molecular' movement of people across the globe. While there can be little doubt that there has been accentuated economic globalization, as noted above, in sport as in other domains, the evidence of its completion is not only inconclusive but, in several key respects, demonstrably inadequate.
40. J. Benedict, *Public Heroes, Private Felons: Athletes and Crimes Against Women*, (Boston, MA: Northeastern University Press, 1997); J. McKay, M.A. Messner and D. Sabo (eds.), *Masculinities, Gender Relations, and Sport* (Thousand Oaks, CA: Sage, 2000); T. Miller, *Sportsex* (Philadelphia, PA: Temple University Press, 2001).
41. J. Bloom, *To Show What an Indian Can Do: Sports at Native American Boarding Schools* (Minneapolis, MN and London, 2000); B. Carrington and I. McDonald (eds.), *'Race', Sport and British Society* (London and New York: Routledge, 2001).
42. Sugden and Tomlinson (note 14); R. Boyle and R. Haynes, *Power Play: Sport, the Media & Popular Culture* (Harlow: Pearson Education, 2000).
43. Boyle and Haynes (note 42).
44. P. Bourdieu, *Distinction: A Social Critique of the Judgement of Taste* (London: Routledge, 1984); D. Rowe, *Popular Cultures: Rock Music, Sport and the Politics of Pleasure* (London: Sage, 1995); D. McGimpsey, *Imagining Baseball: America's Pastime and Popular Culture* (Bloomington and Indianapolis, IL: Indiana University Press, 2000).
45. Boyle and Haynes (note 7).
46. King (note 9) p.119.
47. G. Whannel *Fields in Vision: Television Sport and Cultural Transformation* (London: Routledge, 1992).
48. Goodwin, *Television under the Tories* (note 6) pp.2–13.
49. D. Hesmondhalgh, *The Cultural Industries* (London: Sage, 2002) pp.225–26.
50. D. Rowe, *Sport, Culture and the Media: The Unruly Trinity* (Buckingham: Open University Press, 1999).
51. Giulianotti (note 9).
52. R. V. Bellamy, 'The Evolving Television Sports Marketplace', in L. Wenner (ed.) *MediaSport* (London and New York: Routledge, 1998), pp.73–87.
53. S. R. McDaniel and C. B. Sullivan, 'Extending the Sports Experience: Mediations in Cyberspace', in L. Wenner (ed.) *MediaSport* (London and New York: Routledge, 1998), pp.266–81.
54. R. Williams, *Television: Technology and Cultural Form* (London: Fontana/Collins, 1974).
55. M. Young and P. Willmott, *The Symmetrical Family: A Study of Work and Leisure in the London Region* (London: Routledge and Kegan Paul, 1973) p.20.
56. T. Veblen, *The Theory of the Leisure Class* (London: Allen and Unwin, 1970).
57. Bourdieu (note 44).
58. Miller *et al.* (note 5).
59. Rowe (note 2); Moller (note 32).
60. D. Held, 'The Decline of the Nation State', in S. Hall and M. Jacques (eds.) *New Times: The Changing Face of Politics in the 1990s* (London: Lawrence & Wishart, 1989) pp.191–204; K. Ohmae, *The Borderless World* (London and New York: Collins, 1990); M. Horsman and A. Marshall, *After the Nation State* (London: Harpercollins, 1994).
61. P. Cheah and B. Robbins (eds.), *Cosmopolitics: Thinking and Feeling Beyond the Nation* (Minneapolis, MN and London: University of Minnesota Press, 1998).
62. Miller *et al.* (note 5).
63. G. Murdock, 'Base Notes: The Conditions of Cultural Practice', in M. Ferguson and P. Golding (eds.), *Cultural Studies in Question* (London: Sage, 1997) p.94.

Beyond *Bosman*: The European Union's Influence upon Professional Athletes' Freedom of Movement

RICHARD PARRISH and DAVID McARDLE

The purpose of this article is to explain how the law of the European Union (EU) has revolutionized the freedom of professional athletes' abilities to move from one club to another, and from one EU member state to another, in order to avail themselves of employment opportunities that come their way. The article also provides an assessment of the ongoing endeavours of sports organizations and the EU to forge a new working relationship in the wake of the *Bosman* ruling. Sports organizations want to establish an arrangement that will protect sport from the full rigours of EU law; but the EU is equally concerned with ensuring that fundamental, immutable principles of EU law are respected by clubs, governing bodies and other sporting organizations. One of the key principles that the EU regards as sacrosanct is the principle of the free movement of workers – the right for people to move from one member state to another in order to work – and it was issue that was at the heart of *Belgian Football Association* v. *Bosman* (hereafter '*Bosman*') ([1996] All ER (EC) 97) Consequently the starting point for this article is the European Court of Justice's ruling in *Bosman*, which heralded the demise of two of European football's sacred cows – the transfer system and the player quota rules – as a consequence of the application of the laws on freedom of movement. At this point it should be stressed that the *Bosman* ruling said nothing new. It did not extend EU law in any way, nor did it represent a novel interpretation of legal principles: it was a straightforward application of existing, well-established legal provisions; that the fundamental principles of EU law were incompatible with player quotas and the transfer system was evident long *Bosman*. Evident to everyone, that is, except those involved in sports management and administration.

The *Bosman* Ruling

In 1986, Jean-Marc Bosman had signed professional forms with Belgian club Standard Liège. Two years later, he joined another, smaller Belgian club (SA Royal Club Liègois) on a two-year contract with a monthly salary of approximately 120,000 Belgian Francs. Shortly before this contract expired, in the spring of 1990, he was offered a new deal: a one-year contract with his wages slashed to 30,000 Belgian Francs – the lowest wage the club could offer under the rules of the Belgian Football Association. Unsurprisingly, Bosman refused to sign the new contract and he was placed on the club's transfer list.

Under the rules of the Belgian Football Association, for one month at the end of the domestic season a player on the transfer list was allowed to move to another club even if his old club objected to the move. The old club could not block the transfer by asking an unreasonable and prohibitive transfer fee because in such cases the Belgian Football Association determined the fee to be paid. They used a complex mathematical formula that involved multiplying the player's annual wage by a figure of between two and fourteen (depending upon the player's age). When this formula was applied to Bosman, the figure reached was almost 12 million Francs.

This was far more than other Belgian clubs were willing to pay, but in May 1990 Bosman negotiated a one-year transfer to a French second division club (US Dunkerque) for a tenth of that figure. Dunkerque also had an option to sign him permanently if they paid another 4,800,000 Belgian Francs by the beginning of August. However, RC Liègois doubted Dunkerque would be able to raise the cash, so did not apply to the Belgian Association for the necessary clearance certificates to allow Bosman to move to France. The deal collapsed. RC Liègois suspended Bosman in accordance with the rules of the Belgian Association (under which he would have been re-classed as an amateur player if the club had not done so).

In late 1990, Bosman started proceedings in the domestic courts. He sought an order that RC Liègois pay him a salary while he found a new club and asked the court to prohibit the club from seeking a transfer fee for him. He also requested that the case be transferred to the European Court of Justice (ECJ) for determination of the ultimate issue – the legality or otherwise of the Belgian transfer system. All three requests were granted at first instance, but on appeal the referral to the ECJ was overturned.

Over the next three years Bosman plied his trade at three lower-division clubs in France and Belgium on a succession of one-year contracts while his legal proceedings dragged on. In August 1991, Union des Associations Européennes de Football (UEFA) was joined as a defendant in his action (which was now an action for damages) against RC Liègois. He also started a separate case in the Belgian courts against UEFA itself, contending that its rules were a breach of the EC Treaty, Article 48 (freedom of movement between member states) and Articles 85 and 86 (imposition of restrictive practices and abuse of a dominant position). In April 1992, he amended his claim so as to seek an order that neither its transfer rules nor the rules concerning overseas player quotas were applicable to him.

In June 1992, the Belgian Court of Appeal restored the court of first instance's decision to make a reference to the European Court of Justice under

EC Treaty, Article 177. The reference sought a preliminary ruling on the compatibility of both the Belgian transfer system and UEFA's rules with the provisions of Articles 48, 85 and 86. The questions that the European Court of Justice was asked to consider were: when a player whose contract with a particular club had expired joins another club, does the EC Treaty prohibit the first club from requiring payment from the club that sign him? Second, do the provisions of the Treaty prohibit a national or international sporting association from restricting the right of foreign players from other countries in the European Community to play in the competitions that association has organized?

The first point to be addressed concerned the extent of the ECJ's jurisdiction over UEFA's rules and regulations. UEFA is a confederation member of the Federation of International Football Associations (FIFA), the game's international governing body, and UEFA's regulations require FIFA's approval. Both UEFA and FIFA are based in Switzerland and are governed by Swiss law. However, 'its members are the national associations of some fifty countries, including in particular those of the [European Community] member states which, under UEFA statutes, have undertaken to comply with those statutes and with the regulations and decisions of UEFA'.[1] To illustrate the extent of UEFA's influence, in the qualifying stages for the 1998 World Cup there were nine European Groups accommodating an unprecedented 51 countries and playing across a geographical area that extended from Iceland to Azerbaijan. Israel is also a member of the UEFA confederation, for obvious political reasons.

So far as the Advocate General was concerned, the fact that UEFA was based in a non-member state, that the majority of countries playing under its auspices were non-members and that the practices complained of had been *formed* in a non-member country (i.e. Switzerland) were all immaterial so far as Community Law was concerned. If a company or other body based in a non-member state engages in practices that affect competition or freedom of movement within the Community, then the provisions of the Treaty will be applicable so long as those practices have been *implemented* within the Community. See, for example, *Ahlstrom Osakyhtio* v. *Commission* where a concerted practice (namely, a cartel among wood-pulp producers), though formed outside the Community, was implemented within it and accordingly fell within the Community's jurisdiction. The 'Switzerland issue' was irrelevant.

Once the jurisdictional issue had been resolved, the next plank of UEFA's and the Belgian Association's defence was the predictable one that recourse to law was not appropriate for dealing with sports issues. However, previous cases, notably *Walrave and Koch* v. *UCF*[2] and *Dona* v. *Mantero*[3] had already established that Community law was applicable to sport if it constituted an economic activity. In summarizing the effect of those two cases, Advocate General Lenz opined that:

> ' ... (i) the rules of private sports associations are also subject to community law. (ii) The field of sport is subject to Community law *in so far as it constitutes an economic activity*. (iii) The activities of professional football players are in the nature of gainful employment and are therefore subject to Community law. (iv) Either Article 48 or Article 59 applies to those activities, with no differences arising therefrom. (v) The Court allows certain exceptions to the prohibitions contained in those provisions.'[4]

UEFA argued that it was only the 'superclubs' of Europe whose activities could possibly be said to 'constitute an economic activity'. The provisions of EC Treaty, Articles 48, 85 and 86 ought not to be extended to the activities of humble little clubs like RC Liègois in any event, for the restrictions were certainly proportionate and appropriate when applied to them. However, the Advocate General's opinion was that once professional football had been deemed to be an economic activity, 'the size of that activity is immaterial, as is the question of to what extent it leads to a profit'.[5] He had sympathy with UEFA's argument that transfers existed in order to subsidize the smaller clubs, and that applying the provisions of EC Treaty, Article 48 would have consequences for the entire organization of football, not just the professional game. But 'that argument relates to the *consequences* of the Court's decision, not the question of the *applicability* of Community law, and thus cannot be an obstacle to that applicability'.[6]

Advocate General Lenz was equally dismissive of two other arguments put forward by UEFA. First, it suggested that even if Community law was applicable to sport, Article 48, in particular, was not appropriate for solving football's specific problems. The Advocate General reiterated that 'professional football is an economic activity and is therefore subject to Community law'.[7] He also dismissed the argument that the case concerned a dispute between a Belgian player and the Belgian Association, and that it was a purely internal situation to which Article 48 was inapplicable. The obvious response to such a suggestion was that 'the main action originates in a failed transfer from a *Belgian* to a *French* club. ... There is thus evidently a situation which extends beyond the frontiers of one member state'.[8]

Having reached the conclusion that Article 48 was applicable, the Advocate General went on to consider whether UEFA's quota rules breached its provisions. 'No deep cogitation is required to reach the conclusion that the rules on foreign players are of a discriminatory nature', he decided. 'They represent an absolutely classic case of discrimination on the ground of nationality. Those rules limit the number of players from other member states whom a club in a particular member state can play in a match. Those players are thereby placed at a disadvantage with respect to access to employment, compared with players who are nationals of that member state.'[9] The rules may have only limited the number of foreigners who could *play* in any match rather than the number of foreigners a club could actually have on its books, but that still amounted to a restriction on freedom of movement. 'Every club which plans and acts in a reasonable manner will take the rules on foreign players into account in its personnel policy. No such club will therefore engage more – or significantly more – foreign players than it may play in a match.'[10] By way of example, the Advocate General cited the two financially strongest clubs in his native Germany, Bayern Munich and Borussia Dortmund, who had just five and six foreign players respectively on their staff in the 1995/96 season out of squads of 21 and 25 players. In the earlier case of *Dona* v. *Mantero* the Court had allowed the imposition of restrictions on the number of foreign players that could play in national leagues. But the justification for those restrictions lay in 'reasons which are not of an economic nature, which relate to the particular nature and context of such matches and are thus of *sporting interest only*, such as, for example, matches between national teams of different countries'.[11]

The Advocate General in *Bosman* was troubled by the ramifications of this decision. 'In view in particular of the fact that matches between national teams – as in the football World Cup – nowadays indeed have considerable financial significance, it is hardly still possible to assume that this is not (or not also) an economic activity.' He was able to avoid the matter 'since the question is not relevant to the present case'.[12] Of more immediate were three other arguments put forward in an attempt to justify the discriminatory provisions:

> First, it is emphasised that the national aspect plays an important part in football; the identification of the spectators with the various teams is guaranteed only if those teams consist, at least as regards the majority of players, of nationals of the relevant member state. Moreover, the teams that are successful in the national leagues represent their country in international competitions. Second, it is argued that the rules are necessary to ensure that enough players are available for the relevant national team; without the rules on foreigners, the development of young players would be affected. Third and finally, it is asserted that the rules on foreigners serve the purpose of ensuring a certain balance between the clubs, since otherwise the big clubs would be able to attract the best players.[13]

All these arguments have traditionally been trotted out by clubs and the various governing bodies when the need to defend quotas or the transfer fee system has arisen and, on this occasion, the 'spectator identification' argument struck the Advocate General as particularly fallacious. 'As to the identification of spectators with the teams, there is... no need for extensive discussion to show the weakness of that argument. ... The great majority of a club's supporters are much more interested in the success of their club that in the composition of the team.' Even if the 'national aspect' arguments did have any merit, 'it could not justify the rules on foreigners. The right to freedom of movement and the prohibition of discrimination ... are among the fundamental principles of the Community order. The rules on foreign players breach those principles in such a blatant and serious manner that any reference to national interests which cannot be based on Article 48(3) must be regarded as inadmissible as against those principles.'[14] The Advocate General was also aware that the way in which young players were developed gave the lie to the argument that youngsters' development, citing Ajax Amsterdam as a rare example of a top club that had invested heavily and consistently in its youth policy. Young players benefit enormously from playing with and against top-quality players of whatever nationality, but 'it is admittedly correct that the number of jobs available to native players decreases the more foreign players are engaged by and play for the clubs. ... That is a consequence that the right to freedom of movement necessarily entails.'[15]

The important point that this part of the judgment established was that professional football had consistently chosen to ignore the fundamental basics of Community law and hoped it would be left alone, rather than work out how it could best comply with its obligations under the EC Treaty. *Bosman* highlighted the need for clubs to develop lawful player development systems rather than rely on quotas and in buying and selling established players among themselves.

The argument that restrictions on foreign players preserved a balance between clubs, because they prevented the biggest sides from swallowing up all the talent and thereby widening the gulf between those clubs and the smaller ones, attracted a degree of sympathy from the Advocate General. But the onus fell on football's authorities to show their significance was so great that they ought to be regarded as an exception to the provisions of EC Treaty, Article 48 under the 'appropriate and proportionate' test. They had failed to discharge that burden. The Advocate General also pointed out that while the rules on foreign players had been worked out with, or approved by, the Commission, this did not give them any particular legal significance or place them in a privileged position. 'The Commission is neither entitled nor in a position to amend the scope or meaning of the provisions of the Treaty by its actions. It is for the Court of Justice alone to give binding interpretations of those provisions.'[16]

Advocate General Lenz went on to say that young players and smaller clubs could be protected by means other than an unlawful restriction on freedom of movement. He suggested that a policy of collective wage capping or the distribution of funds on a more equitable basis might have the desired result while preventing further breaches of the EC Treaty, but having reviewed all the authorities' other points at length, the Advocate General was moved to conclude that 'the transfer rules hitherto in force are not justified by reasons in the general interest'.[17] The problem was that, although the end results of the transfer system might be in the sport's best interests, the means of achieving those ends had to be lawful. Failing that, there had to be sufficiently compelling reasons for maintaining a transfer system that was manifestly incompatible with Article 48. The authorities had failed to satisfy the court on either point.

The Court shared the Advocate General's view that the transfer system was unlawful under Article 48 and held that because this was the case, 'it is not necessary to rule on the interpretation of Articles 85 and 86 of the Treaty'.[18] However, the decision not to rule on Articles 85 and 86 means the legality of transfers that take place between two clubs based in the same state remained unclear. Article 48 only applies to restrictions that prevent free movement between one state and another, but if a domestic system requires the payment of transfer fees while there are no fees payable on cross-border deals, that affects inter-state trade patterns and thus the operation of the wider market. Accordingly, such activity falls within the scope of Article 85(1). While sports authorities knew that, post-*Bosman*, the payment of a fee for an out-of-contract player moving from, say, Brondby to Arsenal was unlawful, it was some time before it became clear that the position was the same in respect of an out-of-contract English-qualified player moving from Portsmouth to Southampton.

Sport and the European Union Post-*Bosman*

Since the ruling in *Bosman*, European sport has found itself operating in a new legal environment. Commenting on the ECJ's disposal of two further sports related cases in 2000, Bell and Turner Kerr observed that 'it seems that the legality of nearly every sports regulation is being called into question'.[19] In the minds of the governing bodies of sport, the blame for this attack on sporting self-regulation lies at the door of the EU and its over-zealous regulators. The EU has, after all, presided over investigations into practically every significant sporting rule. For example, originally assured that the *Bosman* ruling only affected out-of-contract transfer payments, the Commission subsequently questioned the compatibility of in-contract payments with EU competition law.[20] Furthermore, the European Court extended the *Bosman* principles of free movement to non-EU countries with whom the EU had concluded association agreements.[21] Combined with the post-*Bosman* investigations into how sport organizes itself, markets its television rights and even how it sells tickets to events, suspicion grew within the world of sport that the EU had an 'agenda' to ensure that the increasingly commercially successful sports sector was afforded no special treatment.

This analysis is questionable. The existence of a problem with the EU's approach to regulating the professional sports sector is not universally accepted. Arguably, the EU's approach demonstrates remarkable sensitivity to sport. For instance, Weatherill argues that if a problem exists it is that the EU is too generous to sport.[22] Furthermore, the problem is sport's own making. Litigants from within the sports sector have used the EU's public and private enforcement channels to defend their rights and the intransigent governing bodies have been unwilling to meet them halfway – with *Bosman* style consequences. While some governing bodies harboured desires to re-fight the *Bosman* battle over the transfer system and nationality restrictions, most are now resigned to merely plotting how to safeguard what remains of their sporting autonomy. A period of self-reflection on the part of the governing bodies has resulted in the realization that in order to distance themselves from EU law they must paradoxically embrace it.

This conclusion stems from the calculation that the EU's constitutional predisposition for market regulation combined with the lack of a Treaty base for a sports policy has resulted in the economic aspects of the Treaty being applied to the sports sector without a reference to the potentially counterbalancing influence of the social and cultural elements of the Treaty. This has meant that the EU has tended to regulate sport as a business without acknowledging that it is also a socially and culturally significant game which has developed its own internal rule structure indispensable for its proper functioning. In consequence the provisions on freedom of movement and competition policy have dominated the legal environment in which sport operates in Europe. Both these legal avenues have been considered rather blunt instruments in resolving disputes within the sports sector which, it is suggested, operates under different market conditions to other industrial sectors.[23]

After a period of ill-informed criticism of the EU following the *Bosman* ruling, organized sporting interests in Europe embarked on a campaign to more effectively communicate this position to the EU and suggest ways in which EU law may reflect the more broad-based nature of the sports sector. The result has been dubbed the 'Amsterdam process'.

The Amsterdam Process

The *Bosman* ruling not only created tumult within the European sports movement, it also refocused attention on a fundamental problem in EU 'sports policy'. Is sport a business to be regulated in the same way as any other economic activity operating within the single market or is it a game with its own rule structure and a social and cultural activity which could be used to promote European integration? Furthermore, if it combines both features, is EU law sufficiently flexible to accommodate both positions? Prior to *Bosman* such calculations were not necessary. The approach to sports regulation taken by the ECJ in *Walrave* and *Donà*, in which the Court held that sport was subject to Community law whenever practiced as an economic activity, was not fully enforced by an EU disinterested in an activity of marginal economic significance in the 1970s and 1980s.

The *Bosman* ruling took place in a different context to that of *Walrave* and *Donà*. Sport began to practice as a significant economic activity. In addition, the EU had just completed the single market and the ideology of the four freedoms was particularly strong.[24] Arguably, the governing bodies of sport miscalculated this new environment and attempted to maintain a slavish adherence to rules devised in a previous age. Nevertheless, they successfully managed to conflate *Bosman* with wider themes in European integration, particularly the perception that the EU was adept at destroying traditional structures on the altar of market modernity. *Bosman* therefore served their purpose in so far as the ruling managed to re-assert socio-cultural ideas within the EU's sports policy and politicize the regulatory environment in which sport now found itself. Politics became the lever to prise open the insulated world of sports regulation in the EU.

The European Parliament, a traditional supporter of socio-cultural integration, expressed the view in the Pack Report on the Role of the EU in the Field of Sport that sport should be afforded legal status in the forthcoming Amsterdam Treaty.[25] Lobbying by Parliament and the governing bodies took place throughout the Amsterdam intergovernmental conference process to further articulate this goal. The subsequent soft law Amsterdam Declaration on Sport (1997) proved a disappointment for them.[26] However, it did launch a series of politically significant initiatives which reflected the more broad-based approach to sports policy the EU was aspiring to. In particular, the Commission's Helsinki Report on Sport and the member states' update of the Amsterdam Declaration made during the 2000 Nice Treaty deliberations have greatly informed much of the sports related jurisprudence of the ECJ and the Competition Policy Directorate General.[27] The ECJ rulings in *Lehtonen* and *Deliège* in 2000 illustrate the willingness of the Court to respect the Amsterdam process and the specificity of sport even though sport was still legally detached from the Treaty.[28]

The Commission's response to Amsterdam has come in the form of a review of how competition law is applied to sport.[29] The Commission has, in effect, sought to locate different types of sporting agreements within specific regulatory territories. This, it believes, adds clarity to the legal environment in which sport operates. Within this framework, the Commission and Court have located sporting rules within one of three territories. The first is a territory of *sporting autonomy*. Rules located here are deemed to be inherent to sport and as long as they are considered proportionate to the objectives pursued by the governing bodies are deemed to fall outside the scope of EU law or be considered compatible with it. Within the context of labour mobility, selection criteria for sporting events and the use of transfer windows are broadly located within this territory.[30] Nationality restrictions in the composition of national teams are, for now, also located here.[31] A wider range of sporting rules are located within a second territory described by Foster as *supervised* sporting autonomy.[32] Here lies the March 2001 agreement between the European Commission and FIFA/UEFA on the re-modelled transfer system which permits restrictions on an athlete's mobility which would be considered unlawful in other industries.[33] Finally, there exists a third territory of *judicial intervention*. Rules located here are considered unlawful by the EU. The most prominent examples relating to labour mobility are those issues dealt with by the Court in *Bosman*. Hence, out-of-contract transfer payments and nationality restrictions in club football are not permitted.

The construction of this separate territories framework has persuaded some that sufficient flexibility exists within the EU's legal framework for the specificity of sport to be recognized without the need for Treaty reform. The willingness of the Commission to employ a wide definition of the exemption criteria contained within Article 81(3) of the Treaty when disposing of sports-related cases confirms this flexibility.[34] However, while the Amsterdam process has informed the jurisprudence of the Commission and Court and, as such, has delivered a more settled and clarified legal environment for sport to operate within, it is only articulated through soft law (non-legal guidelines). The fear expressed by the European sports movement is that it is not sufficiently legally entrenched to offer long-term stability. Further lobbying has therefore taken place by some governing bodies for a sports article to be added to the EC Treaty thus granting the EU a competence in sports policy.

Sport and the Treaty

The focus of the lobbying was the European Convention on the Future of Europe. This body was established by the December 2001 Laeken European Council. The Convention was requested to conduct a review of the activities of the EU with a view to proposing a new Constitutional Treaty for the Union. Its final report of 18 July 2003 proposed the incorporation of sport into the legal framework of the new Treaty Establishing a Constitution for Europe.[35] During previous intergovernmental conferences (notably Amsterdam and Nice) the member states had not unanimously supported the establishment of a legal base for a sports policy in the Treaty. In June 2004, the member states agreed a final Constitutional text. In it, Article 16 proposes a change in the legal status of sport by defining it as an area for 'supporting, coordinating or complimentary action' within the context of education, youth, sport and vocational training policy. Elaborating this is Article III-182:

Article III-182: Education, Youth, Sport and Vocational Training:

182(1) The Union shall contribute to the promotion of European sporting issues, whilst taking account of its specific nature, its structures based on voluntary activity and its social and educational function.

182(2) Union action shall be aimed at: (g) developing the European dimension in sport, by promoting fairness in competitions and co-operation between bodies responsible for sports and by protecting the physical and moral integrity of sportsmen and sportswomen, especially young sportsmen and sportswomen.

182(3) The Union and its member states shall foster co-operation with third countries and the competent international organisations in the field of education and sport in particular the Council of Europe.

182(4) In order to contribute to the achievement of the objectives referred to in this Article, (a) European laws or framework laws shall establish incentive actions, excluding any harmonisation of the laws and regulations of the Member States. They shall be adopted after consultation of the Committee of the Regions and the Economic and Social Committee (b) the Council of Ministers, on a proposal from the Commission, shall adopt recommendations.

For the sports organizations, the new provisions potentially serve two purposes. First, the International Olympic Committee (IOC), the National Olympic Committees (NOCs) of the 25 member states, the European Non-Governmental Sports Organizations (ENGSOs) and UEFA calculate that an article for sport in the Treaty would place a binding obligation on the Commission and the Court to recognize the specificity and autonomy of sport when deciding sports-related cases. The late inclusion of the phrases 'specific nature' (182(1)) and 'bodies responsible for sports' (182(2)) are important additions in furtherance of these goals as is the reference contained in 182(4) to 'excluding any harmonisation of [the] laws'. Clearly, however, the interpretation of these words by the EU's judicial bodies remains central. Once in force, Article 182 effectively constitutionalizes the Amsterdam process and potentially offers the sports world a more stable and clarified legal environment. While UEFA was party to an IOC proposal sent to the Convention supporting an article for sport in the Treaty, their publicly stated position was to support the adoption of a protocol which would achieve the same result as a Treaty article without the need to grant the EU a competence in sport.[36]

The second purpose of a Treaty article for sport relates to its location within the EU budget. Although Articles 16 and 182 would not entail harmoniszation of national legislations, 'supporting' measures may take the form of financial support, administrative co-operation, pilot projects and guidelines.[37] This means that the EU would be legally able to allocate sports-related budgetary appropriations and thus resolve the legal difficulties encountered thus far in this field following *UK* v. *Commission*, in which the Court held that each budget item must have a legal base.[38] This ruling resulted in the suspension of the EU's sports spending programmes.

While the resolution of sports budgetary status may be considered a positive outcome should Articles 16 and 182 be adopted, the central issue relating to the legal status of sport in the context of labour mobility remains unchanged. The proposed Constitutional Treaty does not offer sport an exemption from the rights of free movement, freedom to provide services and the right of establishment which have already been enshrined in law. Consequently, it does not offer any hope of a retrospective (re)examination of *Bosman*. However, prospectively what it does offer is a legal base for the Court to make expanded use of the so-called 'sporting exception' in EU law. The application of this principle (sometimes known as the 'rule of reason') rests on the assumption that sport operates under different market conditions to other sectors and consequently measures that on first appearance seem anti-competitive actually positively promote competition. The reference to 'specific nature' should be read in this light. Clearly, much uncertainty remains in this field and arguably issues pertaining to the employment relationship between club and player are better addressed not through Constitutional change but through a collective bargaining agreement between the parties which at EU level can be achieved within the EC Treaty's provisions on social dialogue.

The Social Dialogue

A common feature in many industrial sectors is the existence of a social dialogue between organized labour and employers. Such a dialogue has frequently resulted in the establishment of a collective bargaining agreement which regulates the employment relationship between the two parties. In the context of the European sports sector, such a dialogue may be considered preferable to the application of EU labour and competition law which are rather blunt instruments when the complex and unique characteristics of the sports sector are at issue. For instance, while *Bosman* clearly confirmed the relationship between sport and EU labour law, the organic nature of this field of law means that sport must develop a strategy of how to respond to subsequent developments. For example, the relationship between sport and EU labour law has assumed added significance since the passing of EU Directive 1999/70/EC on the protection of workers on fixed-term contracts, a particular feature of the sports sector.[39] This directive introduces a principle of non-discrimination against workers on such contracts vis-à-vis their colleagues on contracts of indefinite length. Rather than dealing with such legal developments reactively and rather than attempting to escape their reach through the construction of an article for sport in the Treaty, European sport may rather seek to embrace European law and shape their future legal environment themselves.

Articles 138 and 139 of the EC Treaty provide the platform through which collective bargaining agreements in European sport can be achieved. Article 138 states that:

(1) the Commission shall have the task of promoting the consultation of management and labour at Community level and shall take any relevant measure to facilitate their dialogue by ensuring balanced support for the parties. (2) To this end, before submitting proposals in the social policy field, the Commission shall consult management and labour on the possible direction of Community action. (3) If, after such consultation, the Commission considers Community action advisable, it shall consult management and labour on the content of the envisaged proposal. Management and labour shall forward to the Commission an opinion or, where appropriate, a recommendation. (4) On the occasion of such consultation, management and labour may inform the Commission of their wish to initiate the process provided for in Article 139. The duration of the procedure shall not exceed nine months, unless the management and labour concerned and the Commission decide jointly to extend it.

Article 139 states that:

should management and labour so desire, the dialogue between them at Community level may lead to contractual relations, including agreements. (2) Agreements concluded at Community level shall be implemented either in accordance with the procedures and practices specific to management and labour and the Member States or, in matters covered by Article 137, at the joint request of the signatory parties, by a Council decision on a proposal from the Commission. The Council shall act by qualified majority, except where the agreement in question contains one or more provisions relating to one of the areas for which unanimity is required pursuant to Article 137(2). In that case, it shall act unanimously.

Consequently, Articles 138 and 139 offer sport at least three opportunities to influence developments in EU social policy and labour law. First, they give sport the right of consultation and opinion over new Commission proposals. These opinions may affect the content of future legislation. Second, they permit interested parties in sport to intervene in the legislative process initiated by the Commission. This means that via the conclusion of a Europe-wide agreement, sport can take its own responsibility in regulating the subject contained in the Commission proposal. Third, Article 139 also allows the 'social partners' in European sport to initiate their own Community-wide agreement independent of a Commission proposal. Such agreements can be implemented in accordance with national practice or via a Council Decision.

The nature of such agreements are potentially very wide. However, an obvious issue likely to be discussed in the context of the social dialogue in the European sports sector are employment rights. Themes such as contractual terms, transfer windows, the transfer system, salary capping, image rights, pension funds and doping rules are issues which could potentially be covered by a collective agreement. Of course, for there to be a 'dialogue' there clearly needs to be two interested parties representing management on the one hand and labour on the other. Translated into the European professional football sector, this means clubs and players. However, the issue of representivity is a complex one for the sports sector and a precondition for involvement in the social dialogue. Guidance on this matter is provided by the Commission. Commenting on the establishment of sectoral dialogue committees, the Commission suggested that they are:...

> to be established in those sectors where the social partners make a joint request to take part in a dialogue at European level and where organizations representing both sides of industry fulfil the following criteria (a) be cross industry or relate to specific sectors or categories and be organized at European level (b) consist of organizations which are themselves an integral and recognised part of member States' social partner structures and have the capacity to negotiate agreements and which are representative of several Member States and (c) have adequate structures to ensure their effective participation in the work of the committees.[40]

The players have had for some time an international union representing their interests. The Fédération Internationale des Associations de Footballeurs Professionels (FIFPRO) came into existence in the mid-1960s as a mechanism to coordinate the activities of national players' associations and represent players' interests in an increasingly international age. FIFPRO has emerged into an important and powerful player regarding dialogue with the EU as witnessed by their involvement in the re-structuring of the international transfer system in Europe throughout 2000/01. They are also supportive of attempts to establish an EU-sponsored social dialogue in football.

Identifying the social partner for FIFPRO is more complex. A number of organizations may lay claim to the role of representing employer (club) interests. FIFA and UEFA provide a platform for clubs to discuss issues of common interest. However, they are not employers and they have a much wider responsibility to the game and as such cannot claim representivity. Similarly, the G-14 group of the most powerful clubs in Europe can only claim to represent the interests of their 18 members. Clearly, the interests of the 18 most powerful clubs in Europe do not necessarily equate with the interests of clubs at all levels of the game. The Association of European Union Premier Professional Leagues (EPFL) is perhaps a better model. The EPFL is a grouping of major European leagues formed in 1998 to represent the interests of clubs throughout Europe. Furthermore, it has acquired experience of dealing with UEFA through participation in UEFA's Professional Football Committee. However, some doubts as to the representivity of the EPFL have been expressed. In particular, it is the leagues and not the clubs that are members of the EPFL. Furthermore, they are not employers and only the top leagues are represented. In addition, the relationship the Association has with players in terms of protecting their interests creates a possible conflict of interest in social dialogue negotiations. For this reason other employer organizations have been mooted.[41]

Conclusions

How should *Bosman* be interpreted? Should it be seen as the birth of a new and aggressive phase of the EU's regulation of the sports sector or did it merely establish minimum employment rights for professional athletes while also signalling the beginning of a policy of non-intervention in sport? Although the Court's conclusions on the use of the transfer system and nationality restrictions are damming, the Court demonstrated sensitivity to the sports sector. In particular the Court argued that '... in view of the considerable social importance of sporting activities and in particular football in the Community, the aims of maintaining a balance between clubs by preserving a certain degree of equality and uncertainty as to results and of encouraging the recruitment and training of young players must be accepted as legitimate'.[42] As the Advocate General commented in his opinion on the *Bosman* proceedings, it was the failure of the governing body to explore less restrictive means of achieving these objectives that would count against them.

Nevertheless, despite their intransigence, all is not lost for the governing bodies. A policy of constructive dialogue with the EU has achieved two significant results. First, the Amsterdam process has delivered a relatively settled and clarified legal environment for sport to operate within. Both the Commission and the Court have demonstrated a willingness to cross-reference their sports-related judgments with the broad thrust of EU 'sports policy' – this despite no legally rooted policy actually existing. Second, the governing bodies have been successful in persuading the member states to define sport as an official competence of the EU through its inclusion in the new Constitutional Treaty. While this cannot be used as a vehicle to insulate sport, both prospectively and retrospectively, from the reach of EU law, it does provide a formal (legal) reference point in the constitution to assist the Commission and Court in the execution of their duties. Nevertheless, despite the reference to 'specific nature' contained with article 182(1), the wording of Articles 16 and 182 are a considerable departure from the very precise proposal submitted by the IOC and UEFA to the Convention. In it both parties sought legal protection for specific sports rules. The Constitutional Treaty does not offer this high level of protection.

For the governing bodies to achieve such status in EU law they must lend their support to a collective bargaining agreement in the sports sector. While UEFA may have originally been fearful of the loss of regulatory control this may have entailed, it has, in fact, much to gain from the legal stability in employment matters the social dialogue offers. Indeed, a slightly more positive view of the social dialogue is emerging within UEFA, a view that will undoubtedly be confirmed once the limitations of the sports article are revealed and if the clubs and players begin negotiations regardless of the support of Europe's governing body. The remaining obstacle therefore concerns the representivity of the employers' union. Once this has been established, Europe's first collective bargaining agreement in professional football should be possible and a new phase in European football labour relations shall begin.

NOTES

1. *Belgian Football Association V. Bosman* [hereafter *Bosman*] [1996] All ER (EC) 145.
2. *Walrave & Koch v. Association Union Cycliste Internationale* [1975] 1 CMLR 320.
3. *Dona v. Mantero* [1976] 2 CMLR 578.
4. *Bosman* (note 1): 104. Emphasis added.
5. Ibid. 104.
6. Ibid. 105.
7. Ibid.
8. Ibid. 105,6. Emphasis in original.
9. Ibid. 106.
10. Ibid. 107.
11. *Dona v. Mantero* [1976] 2 CMLR 578, 582.
12. *Bosman* (note 1) 108

13. Ibid. 109.
14. Ibid.
15. Ibid. 111.
16. Ibid. 112.
17. Ibid. 145.
18. Ibid. 161.
19. A. Bell and P. Turner Kerr, 'The Place of Sport Within the Rules of Community Law: Clarification from the ECJ?, The *Deliège* and *Lehtonen* Cases', *European Competition Law Review*, 23 (2002), 260.
20. For the resolution of this case see DN: IP/02/824, 'Commission closes investigations into FIFA regulations on international football transfers', 05/06/2002. See also Letter from Mario Monti to Joseph S. Blatter, 5.03.01 D/000258.
21. Case C-438/00, *Deutscher Handballbund eV* v. *Kolpak* [2003] ECJ.
22. S. Weatherill, 'Fair Play Please: Recent Developments in the Application of EC Law to Sport', *Common Market Law Review*, 40 (2003) 51–93.
23. For example, unlike in other sectors, monopoly would not serve the interests of sports clubs who rely on competition for their success.
24. The four freedoms are the free movement of labour, goods, services and capital.
25. The Pack Report on the Role of the European Union in the Field of Sport, Document A4-0197/97 (28/5/97).
26. Declaration 29, Treaty of Amsterdam amending the Treaty on European Union, the Treaties Establishing the European Communities and Certain Related Acts (1997).
27. CEC, 'The Helsinki Report on Sport', 1999, 644, Brussels. See also See also 'Declaration on the Specific Characteristics of Sport and its Social Function in Europe, of which Account Should be Taken in Implementing Common Policies', Presidency Conclusions, Nice European Council Meeting, 7, 8, 9 December 2000.
28. Case C-176/96, *Jyri Lehtonen and Castors Canada Dry Namur-Braine* v. *Fédération Royale des Sociétés de Basketball and Ligue Belge-Belgische Liga*, [2000] ECR I-2681. Joined cases C-51/96 & C-191/97, *Deliège* v. *Asbl Ligue Francophone de Judo and others* [2000] ECR I-2549.
29. DN: IP/99/133, 'Commission debates application of its competition rules to sport', 24/02/1999.
30. See *Deliège* and *Lehtonen*.
31. See *Walrave* and *Dona*.
32. K. Foster, 'How can Sport be Regulated?', in S. Greenfield, S. and G. Osborn (eds), *Law and Sport in Contemporary Society* (London and Portland, OR: Frank Cass 2000).
33. DN: IP/02/824, 'Commission closes investigations into FIFA regulations on international football transfers', 05/06/02. See also Letter from Mario Monti to Joseph S. Blatter, 5/03/0, 1D/000258.
34. Article 81(3) empowers the Commission to disapply the provisions on restrictive practices contained within Article 81(1) of the EC Treaty if the offending rule can be justified. However, please note that the Commission's monopoly on the exercise of this judgment ended when Council Regulation No. 17 of 6 Feb. 1962 was replaced by Council Regulation (EC) No. 1/2003 of 16 Dec. 2002 on the implementation of the rules on competition laid down in Articles 81 and 82 of the Treaty, O.J. 2003, L1/1 (entering into force May 2004). National competition authorities are now also empowered to apply Article 81(3).
35. CONV850/03. 18 July 2003. Brussels.
36. Article 311 of the Treaty states 'the protocols annexed to this Treaty by common accord of the member states shall form an integral part thereof'.
37. P.3-4. CONV 375/1/02.
38. Case C-106/96, *UK* v. *Commission* ECR I-02729.
39. In effect from 28 June 2000.
40. COM(1998) 322 final.
41. Anon., 'Promoting the Social Dialogue in European Professional Football', *International Sports Law Journal*, 3 (2003).
42. Para. 106 Case C-415/93.

Civil Rights, Doping Control and the World Anti-doping Code

BARRIE HOULIHAN

There cannot be many occupations where part of the contract requires workers to be observed by a complete stranger, possibly two or three times a year, urinating. Nor can there be many occupations where workers are obliged to notify employers of their location during their free time. For elite athletes, whether adults or minors, such indignities and intrusions are a normal part of their participation in high-performance sport whether they consider themselves to be employees (as would be the case for professional footballers) or club members (as would be the case for most swimmers or track athletes). As the concern to address the issue of doping in sport has intensified over the last four years, there has been a renewed debate regarding the roles, responsibilities and rights of athletes in relation to anti-doping policy and doping control procedures.

The focus for this article is on a range of issues concerning the civil rights of athletes especially in relation to the World Anti-Doping Code. The article begins with a brief examination of the nature of civil rights and political power in sport and then proceeds to consider four overlapping aspects of the contemporary debate about anti-doping policy which have significant implications for the rights of athletes, namely, the World Anti-Doping Code, the operation of the Court of Arbitration for Sport, child athletes' rights in relation to doping control, and genetic engineering.

The renewed efforts to tackle the problem of drug abuse in sport were prompted in large part by the extent of doping uncovered during the 1998 Tour de France and the subsequent anti-doping conference convened by the International Olympic Committee (IOC) in February 1999. The conference led to the establishment of two organizations which have had a substantial impact on debates about anti-doping policy and which have the potential to shape the anti-doping effort over the medium term. The first is the World Anti-Doping Agency (WADA), established in November 1999, whose mission is 'to promote and co-ordinate at international level the fight against doping in sport in all forms'. WADA is governed by a board which includes representatives from the major stakeholders in international sport, such as the IOC, the international federations (IFs) and governments. Not only has WADA funded a considerable increase in the annual number of unannounced, out-of-competition drug tests (about 3,000, conducted on top international athletes) but it has also sought to achieve closer harmonization between sports organizations and public anti-doping authorities in important areas of policy, including the tariff of sanctions, the conduct of hearings in doping violation cases, and doping control management processes. The vehicle for achieving closer harmonization is the World Anti-Doping Code the second draft of which was published in October 2002. The second important new body is the International Intergovernmental Consultative Group on Anti-Doping in Sport (IICGADS) which was formed partly to provide a constituency from which the representatives of public authorities could be selected and partly to provide a forum in which governments and inter-governmental bodies such as the European Union (EU) and the Council of Europe could seek to generate a common response to issues in doping in general, and the funding of WADA in particular, on behalf of public authorities.

Until the formation of WADA and IICGADS the global anti-doping campaign was characterized by fragmentation, especially between the IOC, the major IFs and the relatively small number of governments who took an active interest in the issue. Each of these organizations tended to develop policy in isolation and amidst lingering mutual suspicion. While harmonization was much discussed, little progress was made beyond the efforts of small groups of activist governments (e.g. the International Anti-Doping Arrangement group) and occasional bursts of activity by the IOC (e.g. the publication of the IOC Anti-Doping Code). The generally low levels of trust, co-operation and compatibility between policy makers left loopholes for drug abusing athletes to evade penalties thereby infringing the rights of 'clean' athletes and undermining confidence in the anti-doping regime which was increasingly perceived as poorly managed and reliant upon dubious science. The work of WADA in general, and the drafting of the World Anti-Doping Code in particular, provide important opportunities to regain athletes' confidence through the development of a policy framework which is consistent in its application, effective in its management, and which both respects and promotes the rights of athletes.

Civil Rights, Power and Sport

In relation to both politics and the law, athletes often appear to inhabit a twilight world especially when it comes to issues associated with anti-doping policy. In relation to public policy toward sport in general and doping in particular athletes are routinely relegated to the margins of debate often on the unsubstantiated, if not patently false, assumptions that their interests equate to those of their national governing body (NGB) and that the NGB officers have their best interests at heart. Sport policy is generally made for, or on behalf of, athletes, rarely in consultation with athletes, and almost never in partnership with athletes. In the UK, with the exception of professional football and, to a lesser extent, professional cricket, rugby union and rugby league, there are few sports where athletes have an organized and independent voice. UK Competitors is the only organization in the country which aims to provide elite athletes, outside the major professional sports, with an effective independent voice in the policy process. The few governing bodies of sport that do provide a voice for athletes do so either through limited membership of the body's decision-making forum or through the formation of an 'athletes committee/ commission' linked to the main forum, but safely quarantined from any significant decision-making opportunities.

With very few exceptions, members of athlete committees or commissions are selected by officers rather than elected by their peers and consequently lack the capacity to speak authoritatively on behalf of their fellow athletes and have no obligation to act in an accountable manner. Most athlete representation, where it exists at all, is invariably paternalistic, tokenistic and fulfils purposes associated more with legitimation of NGB decisions than with empowerment and involvement in decision-making processes. Initially funded through a grant from UK Sport, UK Competitors recently had its extension of funding refused by the UK Sport Board. Perhaps even UK Sport prefers athletes to be seen rather than heard and is happy to accept athlete representation through the British Olympic Association as the acceptable voice of the high performance athlete community. The poor representation of athletes within the UK is mirrored at the international level. The IOC is typical, preferring a tightly managed Athletes' Commission, whose member- ship it substantially controls, and token representation on the IOC itself to having to deal with an independent athletes' organization. However, it has to be acknowledged that independent athletes' organizations are rare with the OATH (Olympic Advocates Together Honorably) organization, established in 1999, moving from high-profile campaigning for the rights of athletes to financial collapse in the space of two years.

If athletes are marginalized in the policy-making process relating to doping, is their vulnerability compensated for by effective protection of the law? The answer would appear to be 'No' as courts in many countries are reluctant to intervene in sports disputes and the various human rights conventions provide little obvious support for the position of the athlete. However, before examining the attitude of courts to doping-related sports disputes it is important to note that there are two ways in which the law can be influential in shaping the context in, and processes through which, athletes' civil liberties might be defended. The first is that domestic courts might be encouraged to extend their remit to include the judicial review of the decisions made by sports bodies and the second is that sports bodies, especially their disciplinary tribunals, might adopt and incorporate elements of legal good practice into their procedures. The latter might be the result of NGBs seeking to dissuade the courts from intervening by modelling their processes on the principles and practices of the courts. Certainly in England the courts have generally been reluctant to intervene even when acknowledging, as Lord Justice Hoffman did, that 'power can be private as well as public'. In dismissing a claim for judicial review of a decision of the Jockey Club he went on to argue that 'This does not mean the rules of public law should be available in law for curbing excesses of private power...'. However, the courts have not been consistent as the High Court did accept jurisdiction in the case brought by Sandra Gasser against the International Association of Athletics Federations (IAAF) following its decision to impose a ban on her due to a positive drugs test. However, the decision went in favour of the IAAF and its use of a strict liability definition of doping.

More recently, there has been some debate regarding the extent to which reference to various human rights conventions, most notably that Bill of Rights which forms part of the American constitution and the European Convention on Human Rights which was incorporated into English law in 1998, could be extended to provide protection for the rights of athletes. Civil liberties refer to that 'first dimension' of human rights and include liberty of person, freedom of speech, thought and belief, and the right to own property. Civil liberties have two elements one associated with rights of participation in the political process and the other, more relevant in connection with doping control, which relates to the 'modern liberal concept of achieving individual freedom by creating a private sphere for every human being which is to be protected against any undue interference by the state and *other powerful actors*...'.[1] Only a small number of rights, such as freedom from torture, are considered absolute with all other rights deemed to be capable of limitation by the state in particular circumstances, which the European Court of Human Rights described as 'pressing social need' such as the maintenance of public safety, public order or national security. Given that about 22 countries have publicly funded anti-doping agencies the government would need to demonstrate that there was a 'pressing social need' to be served by the intrusiveness of drug testing in sport.

According to Nowak, the state also has an obligation to protect the individual's enjoyment of civil rights against private interference. 'The obligation to protect thus refers to the so-called "horizontal effects", that is, to legal effects which human rights produce on the horizontal level between private parties.'[2] The extent to which such a 'horizontal effect' exists is unclear as the Human Rights Act 1998 makes no explicit provision regarding relationships between private parties. However, Boyes argues that 'Despite statements made by the Lord Chancellor during the Bill's passage through

Parliament that clearly signal that the enforcement of the rights as between private individuals is not the intention of the Act, there does appear to be an argument that the Act will, even must, impact on purely private relationships.'[3] According to Morris and Little it is likely that the Human Rights Act will add to the 'energetic and imaginative development of natural justice jurisprudence by the courts [and produce] a "kind of code of fair administrative procedure" to be observed by governmental bodies and certain domestic associations'.[4] In a survey, conducted by Morris and Little of ten major UK national governing bodies, they found that, while the pattern was far from consistent, many principles of natural justice had been incorporated into the rules and procedures of most of the NGBs.

Among the civil rights that are particularly relevant to any discussion of doping control are the right to a fair hearing and the right to privacy. In addition, a number of economic and social rights are relevant in relation to doping, in particular those concerning the right to work and those relating to the protection of children in employment. The right to a fair hearing implies an equal opportunity to present one's case, that is to examine witnesses and to be present during all stages of the hearing. Fairness also implies an expeditious hearing, but also time to prepare one's defence, and the right to be represented.

The right to privacy is an extremely complex area of human rights law both in terms of defining the scope of these rights and in determining the grounds on which they might be limited. The right to privacy (for example, to refuse to give a blood sample or to urinate in front of a stranger from the doping control agency) can be overridden if there is a compelling social or national need. Thus, compulsory blood sampling in cases of suspected drunken driving or where there is a need to determine paternity is justified by the need to protect the welfare of others. Whether the need to prevent cheating in a sports competition provides an equally compelling justification is debatable and Boyes notes that the European Court of Human Rights has tended to adopt a very restrictive interpretation of the Convention. However, experience from the United States suggests that challenges to drug testing under the similar privacy provisions of the US Constitution have generally not been successful.

A right associated with that of privacy is the right to individual self-determination (for example, the right to take either recreational or performance-enhancing drugs) which is frequently limited by reference to national interests such as the cost of treatment of drug addiction. The right to work, as embodied in the European Social Charter, requires states to acknowledge that all shall 'have the opportunity to earn their living in an occupation freely entered upon, that all workers shall have the right to just conditions of work, that they shall have the right to safe and healthy working conditions and to fair remuneration sufficient for a decent standard of living'.[5]

However, as should be clear from the foregoing discussion it is often difficult to disentangle the more abstract discussion of athletes' rights from the institutional context of power relations within which such discussions take place. Rights and liberties may be capable of being defined in the abstract but it must be remembered that they are always operationalized in a context of public policy and power relations.

The World Anti-Doping Code

The '[World Anti-Doping] Code is the fundamental and universal document upon which the World Anti-Doping Programme in sport is based. The purpose of the Code is to advance the anti-doping effort through universal harmonization of core anti-doping elements'.[6] The Code provides the foundation for international anti-doping policy and is supported by the adoption of a series of international standards (largely concerned with the management of the doping control process, e.g. sample collection, laboratory analysis and laboratory accreditation) and a series of models of best practice (e.g. model rules for international federations and other signatories). Throughout the preamble and seven main Articles of the Code there is constant reference to athletes, but largely as the object of the Code rather than its subject. The opening statement in the introduction to the second draft of the World Anti-Doping Code sets the paternalistic tone when it identifies as one of its two purposes 'to protect the athletes' fundamental rights to participate in doping-free sport and thus ensure fairness and equality for athletes worldwide'.[7]

Article 1 of the Code details the basis on which acceptance of the Code by athletes is assumed: 'Athletes, including minors, and athlete support personnel are bound by Article 1 by virtue of their membership, or accreditation, or participation in sport or sport organizations' (Article 1.1). The Article is followed by a brief explanatory note which states that 'The Article makes it clear that athletes need not sign any document in order to be bound by the Code. . .'.[8] The note does, however, indicate that sports federations or national anti-doping agencies might want to obtain 'direct confirmation of [the] athlete's. . . acknowledgement of this acceptance' but only for the reason of 'further educating them concerning the Code'.[9] The indirect link between athletes and the Code is in marked contrast to the strict liability rule which is adopted to determine doping rule violations and which states that 'It is each athlete's personal duty to ensure that no prohibited substance enters his or her body. Athletes are responsible for any prohibited substance found to be present in their bodily specimens.'[10] In the explanatory text the drafters note that they are 'aware that arguments have been raised that a strict liability standard is unreasonable and, indeed contrary to natural justice, because it does not permit the accused to establish moral innocence. It has even been argued that it is an excessive restraint of trade. The Panel is unconvinced by such objections... '[11]

The draft Code confirms the athlete's right to a fair hearing and specifies the following principles: a timely hearing; fair and impartial hearing body; the right to be represented by counsel at the person's own expense; the right to be fairly informed of the asserted anti-doping rule violation; the right to respond to the asserted anti-doping rule violation; the right of each party to call, examine, and cross-examine witnesses; the person's right to an interpreter at the hearing; a timely written decision; and right to appeal to the Court of Arbitration for Sport. The draft Code also states that 'the athlete shall also be given, upon request, a copy of the laboratory documentation package...'.[12]

In general, the Code provides a conventional statement of rights which could be found in the rules of procedures of tribunals in many countries. However, there are four areas where it is either silent or vague. First, although the right to see laboratory documentation is specified the right to see evidence in relation to violations of the Code which do not involve an adverse laboratory result is not so clear. If an athlete is accused of tampering with his/her urine sample or refusing a test one would expect that similar access to evidence (e.g. sampling officer's reports and witness statements) would be granted. Second, one aspect of the statement of rights that requires clarification is the right to 'a timely hearing'. The concern among many international federations is that athletes procrastinate and while there should be an effective defence against attempts to undermine anti-doping policy by undue delay on the part of the athlete there also needs to be a guarantee that the athlete has sufficient time in which to prepare his/her defence. Third, the right to be represented by counsel, but at the athlete's own expense, runs counter to accepted practice in many countries where systems of legal aid ensure that professional legal advice is available to poorer defendants. Finally, while many professional bodies hold disciplinary tribunals in private the justification for a similar practice in doping cases needs to be explicit.

The right to a private hearing is only one aspect of the privacy rights that are affected by the Code. One of the rule violations identified in the Code relates to athlete availability and refers to 'failure to provide required whereabouts information'.[13] The explanatory notes justify the rule on the grounds that 'without accurate athlete location information [unannounced out of competition testing] is inefficient and sometimes impossible. This Article, which is not typically found in most existing anti-doping rules, requires athletes to be responsible for providing and updating information on their whereabouts so that they can be located for No Advance Notice Out of Competition testing.'[14]

However, the draft Code states that information regarding the whereabouts information 'shall be maintained in strict confidence at all times and shall be used exclusively for purposes of planning, co-ordinating or conducting testing'.[15] There is a fuller discussion of aspects of confidentiality and privacy in Article 1.11, which states that the names of athletes alleged to have violated anti-doping rules 'shall not be publicly disclosed until completion of the administrative review...'.[16] The administrative review referred to is a process undertaken by the relevant anti-doping organization following allegations of a violation of anti-doping rules designed to determine whether there are grounds for proceeding to a disciplinary hearing. While it is not clear whether the athlete can attend the review he/she will be invited to present a statement.

The draft Code makes a number of specific references to the athlete's right to work especially in Article 1.7.3 which provides guidance to signatories regarding the provisional suspension of an athlete pending the outcome of any hearing. The Code acknowledges that the anti-doping rules of many international federations already allow provisional suspension, but states that suspension should only be imposed if an administrative review has taken place to determine whether there are grounds for a hearing. The Code also makes clear that should an anti-doping violation be established the athlete will lose all medals, points and prizes acquired in the competition at which the violation occurred. However, if the athlete is a member of a team the consequences for the team are to be determined by the relevant international federation. In addition and depending on the seriousness of the violation the athlete may be subject to a period of ineligibility, a two-year period being the norm for a first violation involving steroids.

Two issues arise here in connection with the rights of the athlete, the first of which relates to the justification provided in the Code for treating all sports in the same way with regard to the imposition of sanctions. Three reasons are given for imposing, for example, a two-year period of ineligibility for the use of steroids, the first of which is that 'it is simply not right that two athletes from the same country who test positive for the same prohibited substance under similar circumstances should receive different sanctions only because they participate in different sports'. The second argument is that 'flexibility in sanctioning has often been viewed as an unacceptable opportunity for some sporting bodies to be more lenient with dopers' and the third is that the 'lack of harmonization of sanctions has... frequently been the source of jurisdictional conflicts between international federations and national anti-doping organizations'.[17] The first reason privileges some criteria (nationality, same drug, similar circumstances, e.g. same competition) over others (those associated with the characteristics of the sport and the pattern of the elite sporting career) and is a judgement that should be more strongly supported by reasoned argument rather than broad assertion. The other two reasons, the duplicity of some sporting bodies and the lack of negotiated protocols between anti-doping bodies, imposes consequences on athletes arising from the failure to overcome weaknesses within and among sports organizations.

None of the three reasons is compelling and the differences between sports, in particular, are far from being of secondary importance. The Article on sanctions deliberately provides for a lower sanction, two years, for a first violation, followed by a life ban for a second violation. While allowing an athlete a second chance to compete without drugs is widely accepted, the significance of the two-year ban needs to be seen in relation to the competition structure and career 'life-expectancy' within particular sports. In some gymnastic events, for example, the length of time an athlete could normally expect to remain competing at the highest level is far shorter than that for a rower, middle-distance runner or equestrian eventer. Equally significantly, there may only be one competition for the gymnast, usually the Olympic Games, which offers global media exposure and prestige. There might also be a lack of other means of indicating relative ability, for example the opportunity to set world, continental or national records. For the runner, the IAAF world championships have a status close to that of the Olympic Games and even for athletes who under-perform at both the Olympics and the world championships there is always the possibility of setting a new record at other IAAF recognized events, such as the Grand Prix series of competitions. It is, at the very least, debatable whether the gymnast who, due to the imposition of a two-year ban, misses possibly his/her only chance to compete in the Olympic Games is being treated in an equitable fashion when compared to the 5,000 m runner who has a far greater likelihood of competing in a future Olympic Games as well as having the possibility of a high media profile world championships or securing his/her place in sporting history through record-setting.

A further, but far less significant, difference between sports is the distinction between individual and team sports. During a period of suspension a swimmer or runner or any athletes whose sport relies primarily on individual attributes can continue to train and practice in much the same way as he/she did when eligible for competition. By comparison most team sports require a training regime which involves the practice of set plays or the development of understanding with other members of the team. The team member may therefore have to suffer a further period of de facto ineligibility once the official period has been completed while he/she reintegrates into the team. While a standard period of ineligibility might be administratively convenient it is inequitable and can be justified, if at all, only as an interim arrangement until such time as a sanction tariff can be introduced which is more sensitive to the characteristics of the athlete's sport and working conditions.

The Court of Arbitration for Sport

The Court of Arbitration for Sport (CAS) has emerged in recent years as an increasingly important arbitration body in international sport and is intended to fulfil a crucial appeal function within the World Anti-Doping Code. CAS, which developed from a tribunal established by the IOC in 1983, is an arbitral body concerned with the resolution of sports disputes. Since 1994 CAS has been formally independent of the IOC and was made accountable to the International Council of Arbitration for Sport, a body of 20 high-ranking jurists who sit in an individual capacity and who work within the terms of the Code of Sports-related Arbitration. CAS deals with two types of disputes – commercial and disciplinary. A substantial proportion of the disciplinary disputes are doping-related which arrive at CAS on appeal. In addition to offices in Lausanne, New York and Sydney, CAS also has an ad hoc division which functions during major sports competitions such as the Olympic Games or the Commonwealth Games and aims to resolve disputes within 24 hours. Although the precise role of CAS in relation to the World Anti-Doping Code has yet to be finally agreed it is clear that WADA would like to see CAS fulfilling a central function in the implementation of the Code and be the 'exclusive recourse for challenging... decisions' with the proviso that CAS decisions may be subject, on limited grounds, to judicial review through Swiss law.[18]

Arbitration through bodies such as CAS is often preferred by parties to a dispute for various reasons, not least of which are the lower cost and the greater likelihood of a speedy decision. A third reason for their popularity is that they accumulate a body of expertise which should be sensitive to the peculiarities of high-level sport. However, a key criterion for evaluating the work of CAS is whether it defends effectively, or at least, takes sufficient account of, athletes' rights. Although CAS, its parent Council and its Code, may well bestow a formal equality between the individual athlete and the anti-doping organization this can obscure a continuing imbalance in power relations. The key question is not whether CAS would provide a bulwark against the rich, greedy and vexatious athlete nor whether it would provide a secure foundation for the World Anti-Doping Code, but whether CAS would protect the interests of the generality of athletes in disputes with their international federations. Foster is, quite rightly, sceptical and argues that 'The power relationship between a powerful global international federation, exercising a monopoly over competitive opportunities in the sport, and a single athlete is so unbalanced.... Rather like the employment contract, a formal equality disguises a substantive inequality and a reciprocal form belies an asymmetrical relationship.'[19]

However, the evidence from the Court's relatively brief involvement in hearing appeals against convictions for doping violations indicates that CAS is capable of independent judgement and is neither an agent of the international federations, the IOC or the national Olympic committees nor ideologically predisposed towards the interests of sports organizations. McLaren notes that in a number of cases 'CAS has endeavoured to maintain a balance in the doping offences by not literally applying the strict liability concept in some cases requiring a degree of fault before upholding the imposition of a sanction' and Nafziger notes that in reaching its decisions 'principles of equity seem to play a role'.[20] CAS has also asserted its independence of both major international federations, such as the International Amateur Swimming Federation (FINA), and the IOC in finding in favour of the athlete. McLaren is confident that the growing popularity of CAS as an appellate body is due to its 'jurisprudence approach' and its lack of timidity in overruling or modifying IF or IOC decisions on doping violations. Indeed six of the seven appeals brought before the ad hoc division of CAS at the Atlanta Olympic Games overturned disciplinary action taken against athletes.

Burger shares a similarly positive view of the Court arguing that following the reform of the Court in 1993 the 'independence and impartiality of the CAS has been strengthened to the point of striking a welcome balance between the concerns of sports participants and the logic of the law'.[21] However, Burger does leaven his positive assessment of CAS by pointing out that the mere existence of CAS will not necessarily prevent costly litigation especially from professional athletes who, in the United States in particular, have the necessary financial resources to sustain expensive litigation. One might also add that while taking an appeal to CAS is undoubtedly cheaper than progress through domestic courts it is not cost free and may well prove prohibitively expensive for individual athletes. Burger also notes the lack of capacity within CAS to award compensation as 'the principle deficiency'. Thus the athlete who successfully establishes that a sports organization has wronged him or her in a doping case has no means through CAS of seeking compensation for their loss. Moreover, though the establishment of the ad hoc division of CAS to adjudicate disputes which occur during a major sports competition is welcome, it has, arguably, limited the rights of athletes by requiring them, as a condition of participation in the competition, to accept dispute resolution through CAS. Conferring mandatory jurisdiction on CAS creates a situation where 'athlete's "consent" to CAS jurisdiction at the games was arguably illusory since it was extracted under duress (namely the threat of exclusion from the games)'.[22]

Siekmann and Soek caution against over-optimism regarding the capacity of CAS to promote the rights of athletes as 'The CAS does not adjudge the merits of decisions that are appealed before it, nor does it apply a marginal test to such decisions. As a rule it deals with cases *de novo*'.[23]

Finally, from the standpoint of some governments, mainly in Europe, the draft Code's identification of CAS as the preferred appellate body has three drawbacks: first, its status in the Code appears to rule out access of aggrieved parties to the civil courts; second, the fact that CAS is incorporated under Swiss private law rather than public law is a further source of concern; and third, access to CAS appears to be denied to public authorities as its remit is confined to intra-sport disputes.

Child Athletes' Rights

Until the formulation by the United Nations of the Convention on the Rights of the Child in 1989 most countries treated children as the passive subjects of the law and the objects of protection. Sports organizations have generally been slow to acknowledge their obligations to ensure that the rights of children who take part in their sport are adequately specified and then protected. All too often it has been the scandal of child athlete sexual abuse that has prompted sports organizations to take action rather than a desire to implement the UN Convention. Specifically in relation to doping control and young athletes there are a number of articles in the UN Convention that are directly relevant and which provide a benchmark against which to evaluate the World Anti-Doping Code. Article 3 requires that the best interests of the child should always be the primary consideration while Article 5 states that the child should always be provided with appropriate direction and guidance. Other relevant Articles refer to the right of the child to have his/her opinions taken into account in all decisions affecting him/her (Article 12), to be protected from abuse and neglect (Article 19), to enjoy the right to health (Article 24), to be protected from illegal drugs (Article 33), and to be protected from exploitation (Articles 32, 34 and 36). According to David, 'Following the principle of the cascade the state has the primary responsibility to implement these rights, but also sports federations, especially in countries where they are public or subsidized institutions. . .'.[24]

Consideration of the implications of the UN Convention for anti-doping efforts needs to be set within the context of a substantial number of doping cases involving elite athletes below the age of 18. In 1996 the US swimmer Jessica Foschi tested positive for steroids at the age of 15, at various times throughout the 1990s a number of Chinese swimmers aged under 18 tested positive for prohibited drugs, at the 2000 Sydney Olympic Games the Romanian gymnast Andreea Raducan tested positive for pseudoephedrine at the age of 17, and in 1995 a South African athlete tested positive for steroids in the junior national championships at the age of 14. There is also extensive evidence of widespread use of drugs among non-elite athletes at the high school and higher education levels.[25] More seriously there is evidence, most notably in the former German Democratic Republic, of the systematic abuse of young athletes by coaches and the marked failure of domestic national sports organizations to protect the interests of child athletes.[26]

As regards the protection of the rights of children there are few explicit references to the application of the Code to a minor who is defined as a person 'who has not reached his or her eighteenth birthday'.[27] Article 1 makes it clear that minors are covered by the Code in the same way as adult athletes and athlete's personnel. The only other explicit reference to minors is in the Article dealing with sanctions where it is noted that an 'athlete's age and competitive experience' can be used in mitigation in assessing the degree of fault. The Code is silent in a number of areas concerning the rights of child athletes where one might expect either the provision of guidance or reference to the existing rules and practices of particular international federations. One such area is in relation to the disclosure of names where minors are treated in the same way as adult athletes insofar as their names will be made public following the administrative review by the anti-doping authority where a violation of the Code is alleged. While it would not be feasible to keep confidential the names of violators of the Code there may be a case for delaying disclosure until the case has been proven thus bringing anti-doping hearings closer to conventional practice in domestic courts where the names of child defendants are routinely kept confidential.

A second area concerns the responsibilities that are placed on minors. Article 5.1 (Roles and responsibilities of athletes) makes no distinction between adults and minors, yet imposes substantial responsibilities including 'to be knowledgeable of and comply with all applicable anti-doping policies and rules...' and 'to be available for sample collection' which involves notifying the relevant anti-doping authority of their whereabouts. Given that in some sports, such as gymnastics and swimming, the age at which athletes enter elite development squads can be well below the age of 18, it is quite proper to argue that a minor should not, and indeed cannot, assume the same obligation or bear the same degree of responsibility as an adult. If this argument is accepted then it prompts the question who, rather than the young athlete, should be expected to bear these responsibilities. Although the coach should bear some responsibility, it is impossible to avoid the conclusion that the parents of a young athlete also share responsibility. However, the Code says nothing about the role of parents: they are not mentioned as part of the athlete's 'support personnel'.

A third area of concern is the neglect of any discussion of the possible role of an advocate for young athletes. Although it might be assumed that their national governing body would fulfil this role it would provide greater reassurance that the rights of young athletes are being safeguarded if WADA, for example, were to identify a number of individuals or an organization that could fulfil an advocacy function on behalf of the young athlete in doping cases and thus ensure that they were able to take full advantage of the safeguards of athlete's rights included in the Code.

Genetic Engineering

The mapping of the human genetic code through the human genome project has created the possibility of major advances in the treatment and prevention of many serious diseases and, although the development of therapeutic applications of genetic engineering is still clearly in its infancy, there has already been debate regarding the implications of genetic modification for sport. According to Munthe there are four ways in which the knowledge of the human genome might be used in sport.[28] The first is the capacity to fine tune the chemical composition of a drug to suit better the athlete's genetic make-up or to use knowledge of an athlete's genetic make-up to optimize his/her programme of training and nutrition. While the refinement of drugs through exploiting knowledge of an athlete's genetic makeup might result in increased problems in detection, the practice will not pose problems that are qualitatively different from those currently faced either in relation to the rights of the athlete or the actions of anti-doping authorities referred to in the earlier discussion.

The second way in which knowledge of the human genome might be used is to modify the genome in specific ways, including the use of genetically modified red blood cells or the production of various hormones. Interest has tended to focus on research into the use of genetic therapies to counteract anaemia and to help restore withered muscle, through the stimulation of IGF-1 (insulin-like growth factor-1) production, both of which have potential applications similar to EPO and steroids respectively. In addition to increases in bulk, genetic therapy offers the prospect of inserting genes into a cell to create a faster 'twitch' muscle in sprinters or a stronger take-off leg for high-jumpers. The effective exploitation of this type of 'genetic doping' is still some way in the future but it has the potential to raise significant issues relating to athletes' rights due to the likely procedure for detection.

Although there is no consensus regarding the most reliable means of detection of genetic doping there is a view that the virus used to transport the gene and the DNA within the gene will leave a 'footprint' that will make detection possible, but that it will not be identifiable from a urine or blood sample and only from a tissue sample. At the time when blood sampling was introduced to help in the detection of EPO there were concerns about the invasiveness of the procedure as blood unlike urine was not a waste product.

The concerns were largely allayed by the acknowledgement that blood sampling and analysis was routine for most elite athletes as part of their training regime. However, removing tissue for analysis is not part of normal training regimes, may result in mild tissue damage (bruising) that would impair performance even if only slightly, and heightens a risk of infection. It is likely that there will be far stronger grounds for objecting to random testing than for either blood or urine sample collection on the basis of infringement of an athlete's right to privacy.

Furthermore, it might be deemed necessary by anti-doping authorities to collect information regarding athletes' genetic profile at an early stage in their career in order to be able to identify more accurately later genetic modification. This practice would undoubtedly raise substantial issues regarding the privacy of genetic data given that the collection of similar data, for example by insurance companies and employers has been strongly opposed as an unjustified intrusion into a person's private life.[29]

Munthe's third way in which genetic knowledge might be exploited in sport is where modifications could be made very early in the life of the human organism to the germ-line cells of the newly fertilized egg. Here the rights issues are far more complex.[30] If it is assumed that genetic modification could be achieved in such a way that athletic performance is enhanced the position of both the athlete and the anti-doping authorities are unclear. To what extent could the athlete be held responsible for the decisions of his/her parents to genetically modify the embryo? If one were to argue that the genetic modification was a breach of the rights of the embryo (itself a contentious assertion) then would anti-doping authorities be compounding that injustice by excluding the athlete from competition? In current broadly equivalent cases involving the doping of minors the young athlete is subject to a period of suspension and the coach, or whoever administered the drug, is also sanctioned. However, unlike steroids, the effect of some genetic modification may not be temporary or reversible thus imposing a de facto life ban.

Finally, there is currently the capability to select individuals on the basis of their genetic make-up. Young athletes whose genome suggests they are unlikely to reach the highest levels of performance could be identified before a governing body or sponsor invested too much money in them. A crude form of genetic selection already exists in some sports, such as skating, where athletes need to start training very young. One national skating coach always asks to meet the parents of promising young skaters to see how big the parents are and thus to estimate whether the youngster will be too big to be an elite skater when they have reached maturity. While systems of talent identification based on the analysis of genetic information might be controversial they do not raise significant issues for anti-doping policy.

Although WADA and the IOC have both considered the implications of advances in genetic modification for anti-doping policy the World Anti-Doping Code does not deal with the issue specifically. However, the Code would cover the second and third applications of genetic technology identified by Munthe by the Article (1.2.1.2.1) that refers to prohibited methods. At one level genetic modification is simply one more advance in doping that anti-doping authorities, such as WADA, have to face and could therefore be treated in much the same way as other manipulative practices, such as blood doping through transfusion of blood. At the very least the prospect of genetic modification adds a layer of complexity to existing issues regarding athlete rights but also adds a series of new and less tractable issues.

Conclusion

It is clearly possible to argue that the protection of the rights of the athlete will be significantly strengthened by the World Anti-Doping Code and by the likely central role of the Court of Arbitration for Sport within the appeals framework. As the Code becomes the recognized reference document for anti-doping policy and doping control it will be increasingly difficult for international federations to avoid incorporating into their rules and procedures the principles and models of good practice formulated by WADA. Similarly, CAS already enjoys considerable respect among athletes due to its expertise and its repeated willingness to modify or overrule the decisions of international federations. Perhaps the only major area of concern relates to the treatment of the specific circumstances of child athletes and the lack of a more explicit and comprehensive statement of how their rights as elite athletes will be effectively protected.

However, despite this generally positive assessment, it is difficult to be wholly enthusiastic about a system for the protection of athletes' rights which relegates athletes to the margin of decision making. Discussions of governance in sport emphasize that one mark of 'good governance' is the extent to which primary stakeholders, defined as those without whose continued support the organization could not survive, are involved in the decision processes of the organization.[31] Bestowing rights (even with sincere and benign intent) is not the same as asserting or winning rights as what can be bestowed can easily be removed and the formal bestowal of rights may bear little relation to their subsequent interpretation. As Kidd and Donnelly note 'Rights are inherently political and contingent. That is their articulation, acceptance and realization involves complex, ongoing processes of assertion, struggle and negotiation between competing interests in the context of changing social, economic, political and ideological circumstances.'[32]

Moreover, while the Code provides a significant degree of protection for athletes it is a form of empowerment that emphasizes individual entitlement rather than encourages solidarity and collective voice. Empowerment through the definition and codification of rights is symptomatic of the prevailing dominance of individualism and the decline in the collective response to marginalization and discrimination. The reference to rights in the Code reflects a passive conceptualization of rights. The codification of athletes' rights is as much about setting the limits of action and specifying the responsibilities of the athlete as it is about creating conditions for the effective articulation of individual or collective interests.

The most positive interpretation is that the World Anti-Doping Code secures civil rights but at the expense of political rights, an outcome which is consistent with the comment by Justice Dubin during the hearings into drug use in Canadian sport: 'It is to be observed that an individual's participation in sport is not a right but a privilege, and as such it is subject to the rules governing the sport in which the athlete wishes to participate.'[33] Unless and until athletes gain a collective voice in important areas of sport policy such as doping they will always be expected to be suitably grateful when privileges are granted and rights bestowed. While there is undoubtedly much to applaud in the World Anti-Doping Code, from the athlete's standpoint it is important to acknowledge the fragility of rights which are founded so clearly on the goodwill of powerful policy actors.

NOTES

1. M. Nowak, 'Civil and Political Rights', in J. Symonides (ed.) *Human Rights: Concepts and Standards*, (Aldershot: Ashgate, 2000) p.69.
2. M. Nowak (note 1) p.74.
3. S. Boyes, 'The Legal Regulation of Sports Governing Bodies', Anglia Polytechnic University, paper, (2000).
4. P. Morris and G. Little, 'Challenging Sports Bodies' Determinations', *Civil Justice Quarterly*, 17 (1998) 130, quoting from Wade and Forsyth, *Administrative Law* (Oxford: Oxford University Press, 1994).
5. A. Eide, 'Economic and Social Rights', in J. Symonides (ed.) *Human Rights: Concepts and Standards* (Aldershot: Ashgate, 2000) p.141.
6. World Anti-Doping Agency (WADA), World Anti-Doping Code, 2nd draft, Lausanne, p. 4 (2002).
7. World Anti-Doping Agency (note 5) p.4.
8. World Anti-Doping Agency (note 5) p.7.
9. World Anti-Doping Agency (note 5) p.7.
10. World Anti-Doping Agency (note 5) para. 1.2.1.1.1.
11. World Anti-Doping Agency (note 5) p.9.
12. World Anti-Doping Agency (note 5) paras 1.8.1, 1.10 and 1.7.2.1.1.
13. World Anti-Doping Agency (note 5) para. 1.2.1.4.
14. World Anti-Doping Agency (note 5) pp.10–11.
15. World Anti-Doping Agency (note 5) para. 1.11.4.
16. World Anti-Doping Agency (note 5) para. 1.11.3.

17. World Anti-Doping Agency (note 5) p.23.
18. World Anti-Doping Agency (note 5) para.1.10.
19. K. Foster, 'Is There a Global Sports Law?', International Sports Law seminar paper, Anglia Polytechnic University (November 2001) p.11.
20. R. McLaren, 'A New Order: Athlete's Rights and the Court of Arbitration at the Olympic Games', *Olympika* 7 (1998) pp.5–6; J. A. R. Nafziger, Globalizing Sports Law, *Marquette Sports Law Journal*, 9/2 (1999) p.253.
21. C. J. Burger, 'Taking Sport out of the Courts': Alternative Dispute Resolution and the International Court of Arbitration for Sport, *Journal of Legal Aspects of Sport*, 10/2 (2000) p.126.
22. P. Morris and G. Little (note 4) p.145.
23. R. C. R Siekmann and J. Soek, *Arbitral and Disciplinary Rules of International Sports Organisations* (Cambridge: Cambridge University Press, 2001) p.72.
24. P. David, Children's Rights and Sport, *Olympic Review*, 24 (1999) p.38.
25. See L. Wichstrom and W. Pedersen, Use of Anabolic Steroids in Adolescence: Winning, Looking Good or Being Bad?, *Journal of Studies on Alcohol* January (2001); S. Tanner *et al.* 'Anabolic Steroid Use by Adolescents: Prevalence, Motives and Knowledge of Risks', *Clinical Journal of Sport Medicine*, 5 (1995) pp.108–15.
26. W. W. Franke and F. Berendonke, 'Hormonal Doping and Androgenization of Athletes: A Secret Program of the German Democratic Republic Government', *Clinical Chemistry* 43/7 (1997) pp.1262–79; S. Ungerleider, *Faust's Gold: Inside the East German Doping Machine* (New York: Thomas Dunne Books, 2001).
27. World Anti-Doping Agency (note 1) Appendix 1 p.4.
28. C. Munthe, 'Selected Champions', in T. Tännsjö and C. Tamburrini (eds.) *Values in Sport* (London: Routledge, 2000).
29. A. Miah, 'Genetics, Privacy and Athletes' Rights', *Sports Law Bulletin*, 4/5 (2001).
30. A. Miah, 'The Engineered Athlete: Human Rights in the Genetic Revolution, *Culture, Sport, Society*, 3/3 (2001) pp.25–40.
31. R. Leblanc, 'Governance in International Sport and the IOC: "Best Practice" From the Private Sector', paper to the OATH symposium, New York (1999).
32. B. Kidd and P. Donnelly, 'Human Rights in Sport', *International Review for the Sociology of Sport*, 35/2 (2000) pp.133.
33. Justice C. L. Dubin, *Commission of Inquiry into the Use of Drugs and Banned Practices Intended to Increase Athletic Performance* (Ottawa: Ministry of Supply and Services, 1990) p.491.

Privacy, Confidentiality and Human Rights in Sport

ANGELA J. SCHNEIDER

Since the occurrence of two major doping scandals in international sport – (i) Ben Johnson's positive test for steroid use in the Seoul Olympics in 1988; and (ii) the Tour de France doping scandal in 1998 – we have seen royal commissions, ministerial task forces, parliamentary committees, World Conferences, World Summits and the creation of the new World Anti-doping Agency (WADA).[1] Despite all this activity there still remain some serious unanswered ethical questions, particularly in regard to athletes' rights to privacy and confidentiality.

Doping and anti-doping programmes raise a variety of issues, some of which involve human rights. Anti-doping rules are part of the rest of the rules governing any particular sport. Doping affects the rights of all athletes. While doping rules are part of an overall set of rules for the governance of sport, doping also goes beyond these because – unlike being called for a foul – doping has implications beyond the playing field. The referees on the field do not observe doping and it may involve criminal behaviour.

Doping is therefore viewed as the concern of private sport organizations and public authorities at the same time. An incidence of doping may be both against the rules of sport and contrary to specific anti-doping legislation or general domestic laws. Doping may have consequences for eligibility to participate in sport and it may have civil, professional or even criminal consequences off the playing field. As a result, doping is a particular breach of sporting rules – and other rules – that has, over time, developed a number of characteristics.

This article provides an ethical analysis, particularly from a human rights perspective, of the rules and enforcement of bans on doping substances or practices in sport. The terms 'banned' and 'prohibited' are often used interchangeably in relation to anti-doping in sport. In anti-doping these terms are usually used to describe the substances that are prohibited by anti-doping rules and regulations in sport (i.e. included on the World Anti-Doping Code list of prohibited substances and methods or lists compiled by other relevant anti-doping authorities). The consequences of doping control programmes that will be examined are related primarily to: (i) the content of the banned list; and (ii) the management of the results of the testing process. In other words, just what it is we are testing for, the methods used for testing and the process for levying penalties in the event of a positive test and a doping infraction.

Most arguments in favour of doping control testing are related to issues of 'harm'. Other arguments are also put forward, such as, cheating and the perversion of sport.[2] For the purposes at hand, I will concentrate on the arguments from harm because the primary goal of this article is to pose a second question about the potential human rights violations and resulting harms that may be caused by a ban on doping in sport. I will argue that there is a serious invasion of privacy caused by effective anti-doping measures and that this violation cannot be justified solely by the good those measures seek to attain. From a human rights and ethics perspective, this leads to an impasse. For doping-free sport, which many want, including athletes, we need effective enforcement. But the steps required for effective enforcement can be very invasive of athletes' rights, particularly the personal right to privacy and confidentiality. Further, the culture of sport itself, in many cases, is not one that fosters protection of an athlete's human rights.

To understand the ethical aspects and implications of doping controls, it is important to understand a number of central terms or concepts. First, is the distinction between: (i) *competition testing* – drug testing that occurs at a sporting event (usually involving elite athletes) such as a regional, national or international sporting competition; and (ii) *out-of-competition testing* – drug testing that occurs at any time of the year and in any location, such as the athlete's home, training venue or even while overseas. Out-of-competition testing is usually conducted on a short-notice or no-notice (unannounced) basis.

If one bans drugs or practices from sport, one must necessarily take steps to enforce those bans. The only effective way to test for banned substances and practices is random, unannounced out-of-competition testing. This is because some substances, for instance anabolic steroids, can be discontinued before competition and still retain their effects, and also because of the prevalence of masking agents and the method of urine substitution with catheters.[3] It can be argued that the demand that athletes be prepared to submit to urine and/or blood testing at any time is a serious breach of their civil and human rights in most countries (this is particularly so in North American countries). This sort of intrusive intervention in athletes' lives could only be warranted, from most ethics perspectives (in particular John S. Mill), by the need to protect others from serious harm. Although few have done so, most likely because of its political incorrectness, it is possible to question whether the depth of harm required to warrant such extreme interference with personal liberty can be established with the case of doping in sport and, in particular, elite sport.

The terms that describe written procedures regarding anti-doping in sport have varying degrees of formality and detail. In doping, 'rules' generally (but not universally) describe the written procedures of sport organizations.

As part of the rules of sport, anti-doping rules are made by sport organizations for the internal governance of the sport and its participants. Governments and their public authorities make 'legislation'. It may take a variety of forms (e.g. laws, statutes, acts, decrees, policies) and can apply to the nation's population as a whole or just those engaged in a particular activity. The term 'regulations' is often used in a general way to describe either anti-doping rules of sport organizations or legislation of public authorities, or both. The term 'policies' is also used either generically, to describe an overall anti-doping programme (in general), or to describe the basic principles that underlie particular rules, regulations or legislation.

There are some finer points that should be distinguished for those who are not intimately familiar with the problem of doping in sport, in particular with regard to the types of drugs and practices for which testing is required. Broadly speaking, a banned substance or practice may be intended to enhance performance on the day of competition or to enhance training in preparation for a major competition. Although the vast majority of performance-enhancing substances, such as stimulants, depressants and narcotics, can, with a fair degree of reliability, be tested at the competition site, certainly not all banned substances and practices can be detected with accuracy at the time of the sport performance.[4] In addition, some performance enhancers work not by directly improving performance on the day of competition but, rather, by enhancing recovery from prior training.

In-competition testing used to be the primary form of testing, but it was deemed to be of limited value in detecting training enhancers and preventing doping.[5] In-competition testing was thus seen to be ineffective but still necessary. Thus, out-of-competition testing was deemed essential and to prevent athletes from using masking techniques to hide their doping, the testing had to be unannounced or short notice. These considerations formed some of the basis for introducing random, unannounced, out-of-competition testing. Randomness was necessary because the expense of testing everyone is too great.[6] Although not all of the out-of-competition tests are random, some are targeted to sports and athletes that have had a history of doping. The question of targeting specific athletes is still open because the selection criteria are often not transparent, thus leading to concerns about the role of hearsay.

This state of affairs can lead to the perception by some athletes that the testing is not random but on the basis of suspicion. Note the difficulties. If it is believed by some athletes that testing is targeted towards individuals on the basis of rumour, the scene is ripe for vindictive campaigns of harassment. Start a rumour about your primary rival for selection and you could make his or her life quite a bit more difficult. On the other hand, if the testing agency does not follow up on rumours, and test accordingly, it runs the risk of being accused of turning a blind eye to 'known' abuses and abusers, which is what has occurred in sports like cycling, weightlifting and athletics where there have been known abuses.

Thus we are faced with the enforcement of bans on doping, that potentially require athletes to be prepared to submit to a doping control test at any time of the day or night, without warning. This also means that an athlete is required to give information regarding their whereabouts at all times. Further, not only will the athlete be tested for a wide range of substances, which have included recreational drugs such as marijuana and cocaine, which have no proven training enhancing properties (although cocaine may well affect performance if used in competition and thus needs to be tested for in competition), but which do carry criminal penalties for ownership or possession in many countries because they are illegal. In broader society, the term 'illegal' usually relates to the laws of the country that are set by the Government. The law controls the availability, possession, manufacturing, supply, import and export of pharmaceutical substances in a country. The degree of control will vary depending on the substance. Some substances are only 'legal' if dispensed by prescription from a professionally qualified and government certified person. Some are 'illegal' under any circumstances (such as cocaine) and mere possession can lead to a criminal conviction and imprisonment. The consequences of a positive test can be enormous even if there is not a doping infraction.[7] Even a two-year ban for doping can spell the end of a competitive athletic career. Not only does this mean the loss of sporting opportunity but, for some athletes in high-profile sports, this can also mean the loss of enormous commercial possibilities.

In most up-to-date anti-doping rules, an individual may seek early reinstatement or a reduction of the sanction if they can demonstrate that the positive test was the result of inadvertence, reliance on another person (such as a team doctor) in a position of responsibility or even sabotage. What makes this process very difficult, however, is the rule of 'strict liability'. Strict liability means that the responsibility for a state of affairs or for an act regardless of intent, motive or will lies with the athlete. Anti-doping rules that define 'doping' as the presence of a banned substance in an athlete's system, make that individual responsible or 'strictly liable' for the presence of the banned substance – even if the individual had no knowledge of how the substance came to be in their system or did not intend it to be there. From the point of view of other athletes, how a banned substance came to be in an individual's system is irrelevant. It is the advantage the banned substance may have given that individual – whether known or intended – that matters. In other words, an individual's competitors will suffer (loss of opportunities to train or compete, loss of top placing in events, loss of associated endorsements or other opportunities) just as much from an unintended advantage as one that is planned.

Thus the 'burden of proof' and 'onus of proof,' terms used to describe both the level of proof one must meet and who has to make that proof, often lie with the athlete because of strict liability. The burden and onus of proof come into play when an individual is exercising their right to challenge a positive test result. Because challenges to doping decisions take place in different languages and different legal traditions, the terms used to describe the burden and onus of proof vary – but the basic principles are common to most procedures that govern challenges. The 'burden of proof' describes the quality of the evidence and arguments that an individual must submit to prove his/her case. The burden of proof is sometimes described as the 'civil' burden (something that is proven on a balance of probabilities) or a 'criminal' burden (something that is proven beyond a reasonable doubt). There is a level that is somewhere in between the two which is sometimes used in doping matters: proof of clear and convincing evidence. The 'onus of proof' relates to who must prove a case. Doping control authorities generally have the onus (responsibility) to show a positive test result is valid and accurate (by sample collection, chain of custody and laboratory analysis to an accepted standard) while the individual then has the onus (responsibility) of showing that there was some departure from the standard or some other error that calls the validity or integrity of the positive test result into question.

When reviewing doping rules and regulations, one prohibited substance in particular has generated a great deal of debate – marijuana. This case has raised some serious questions for the drafters of drug policy. Very few scientists seriously argue that marijuana improves training or performance. If anything, its use is likely to impair performance; so why does sport test for its use? Marijuana was not on the International Olympic Committee's (IOC's) list of banned substances, but rather on a list of restricted substances. These restricted substances are not banned outright, but their use was tested for at the request of the international federation of the sport concerned. But still the question arises: 'Why?' Why would anyone in sport care if an athlete has smoked a joint if it does not enhance performance? Why is marijuana on the banned list and not, say, tobacco or alcohol? Testing and punishment for marijuana use in sport has a controversial history. (The history of general prohibitions against marijuana use is equally interesting.) In Nagano, the vote of the IOC medical commission was only 13–12 to penalise Rebagliati,[8] and the vote of the IOC executive was only 3–2 to uphold that decision. The history of the inclusion of marijuana on the IOC restricted list was controversial from the beginning. One story has it that the IOC medical commission originally voted 32–1 against including marijuana on the restricted list but that decision was over-ruled by the IOC executive committee.[9]

From a purely sport perspective, it was felt quite simply that the IOC had no good grounds for including marijuana on a restricted list, or for testing for its use. The mandate of the IOC for drug testing was to ensure that athletes compete fairly. The rules against drug use were to ban performance-enhancing substances – marijuana is not a performance-enhancing substance, so the IOC had no business testing for it from a sport perspective.

However, at the recent World Conference in Copenhagen in March 2003, the IOC and the United States in particular, argued that the use of marijuana is illegal and also immoral and so the new World Anti-Doping list should include it. The counter arguments, which were not articulated very forcefully, perhaps because of political correctness or for expediency, asked what possible grounds there were for suggesting that WADA has a role in enforcing the law of any particular country. Further, the IOC is a sports organization not a law-enforcement agency. Similar arguments were suggested in regard to enforcing morals outside of fair play in sport. In all sorts of areas, community moral standards are contested and open to debate. There are many people throughout the world who believe that homosexuality is morally wrong – yet it would be both absurd and immoral to suggest that WADA or the IOC has a role in testing for, and prohibiting from competition, anyone who had engaged in same-sex sexual activity. As a vast and powerful social institution, the IOC has an obligation to uphold and respect our basic human rights. These rights involve the fundamental right of each of us to choose how we will live our lives (providing we do not harm others), and our respect for the worth and dignity of each human being. Athletes also have a basic right to privacy.

From a human rights perspective, the doping control system may well be intruding into something that is beyond its jurisdiction. Is it fair to athletes to test for more than is required to ensure fair competition in sport? Drug-testing in sport is an intrusion into an athlete's privacy. That intrusion requires an athlete's consent, something, which is, and should be, freely given when the test is conducted in order to ensure fair competition. However, the demand for consent to test for something that is irrelevant to sport is unfair and coercive. The demand for consent to test for marijuana is unfair because marijuana is irrelevant to sport and it is coercive because unless the athlete consents to testing he or she is prohibited from competition. 'Consent', also referred to as 'informed' consent, is the deliberate act of agreeing to something. It presumes that the individual giving consent has the mental capacity to appreciate the consequences of agreeing to something and does so freely and voluntarily.

Consent can be expressed or implied. For example, when an individual agrees to become a member of a sport governing body they agree to play the sport according to its rules. If the individual is not willing to follow the rules he or she does not have to participate in the sport. If the sport's rules include rules against doping, the individual is said to consent to those rules (even if he or she has not taken the time or trouble to read and understand them completely). However, there are important aspects of doping control protocols that require additional or express consent, such as written consent to permit blood sampling and analysis and/or research. It has been shown that both urine and blood analysis are effective methods of detecting the use of banned substances and methods. Some substances are better detected by urine testing as the drug and its metabolites are found in higher concentrations in the urine than in the blood, whereas other substances such as most peptide hormones are better detected through a blood sample. Recent advances in detection techniques mean that testing programmes can now involve a combination of the collection of urine and/or blood samples. Research over past years has culminated in the development of blood sampling to assist in the detection of the abuse of EPO. Further research was undertaken to develop detection methods for the abuse of other peptide hormones and agents used to enhance the oxygen carrying capacity of the blood. At recent Olympic Games, a combination of blood and urine sampling for the detection of EPO were used. When the blood sample failed the screen, the associated urine sample was analysed. Both the blood and urine samples were required to return positive results for the test to be considered a positive result.

Discussions have taken place to further refine this protocol, anticipating that a modified testing protocol would gain scientific approval, and that a new EPO testing programme be implemented. The programme involved two steps – the first step was the collection and screening of a blood sample. Where the screening of the blood sample indicated abnormal blood parameters, step two was initiated. Step two required a urine sample to be collected and analysed to detect the use of agents to enhance the oxygen carrying capacity of the blood, such as EPO. The result obtained from the urine test was considered to be valid to determine whether a doping infraction had been committed.

It could be argued that a prudent athlete, knowing that in-competition he or she may be tested, would scrupulously avoid marijuana, for example, for some time preceding the event. But the intrusion into personal liberty is even greater for out-of-competition tests. In most countries, the state is not permitted to subject its citizens to random tests for the use of illegal drugs unless there is some direct risk of harm to others (e.g. pilots). Thus it has been asked if there were compelling reasons why sports organizations have a power denied to the state?

A second example of a banned substance that seems to have gone further than is required from an athlete's rights perspective is over-the-counter cold medication.[10] The tragedies of athletes stripped of medals for doping infractions for these remedies, prescribed or approved by team physicians, raises a number of questions about cheating, morality and sport, about what constitutes fairness in sport, and just what it is doping rules are intended to achieve. Some of these questions need consideration in more detail. Did Silken Laumann or Andrea Raducan cheat? What exactly is cheating?

Cheating is the intentional violation of rules to gain an unfair advantage while trying not to get caught. Did either of these women (Raducan was actually a minor) intentionally violate the rules? No, by all accounts Laumann either tried to find out if the substance she was using was against the rules and she had a history of scrupulously avoiding drug use in her rehabilitation from a severe leg injury for the 1992 Olympic Games when she won a bronze medal. Similarly, Raducan was undeniably ill and the medication she took was prescribed by her team physician. These athletes did not try to hide the fact that they were taking medication. Did either of them gain an unfair advantage over their opponents? It seems clear that they did not intend to gain an unfair advantage. It is a separate question as to whether they, in fact, gained an unfair advantage, whether they intended to or not. From all accounts, it is highly likely that they did not gain an unfair advantage because the medications also contained substances that could as likely inhibit athletic performance. But, of course, no one tests for those substances.

So, it seems that these two athletes did not cheat and did not gain an unfair advantage. The doping test was positive but a doping infraction should not have been given because sport should rightly take into account intention, especially given the unlikelihood of an unfair advantage. These athletes should have been given a warning for inadvertent drug use. So, why were these athletes publicly humiliated and their teams stripped of their medals and who is to blame? Ultimately, an athlete has to be responsible for what goes into his or her body. Adult athletes should not be treated like children. Yet, we all count on medical advice in all sorts of areas. These two athletes both sought and relied on medical expertise and did not rely on themselves (e.g. just read the substances on the banned list available to all athletes). The physicians clearly made an error. So both sides made an error but, instead of spending our resources on finger pointing in these cases, we should have been asking ourselves why would the innocent use of an over-the-counter cold remedy result in stripped medals, press conferences, public recrimination and an assault on national heroines? The reason for this is that in some cases anti-doping programmes, and the resulting lists of banned substances, confuse the goals and glory of sport with an often well-meaning but misguided attempt to protect athletes from themselves and an unfounded notion of sporting purity.

So far, the focus of this article has been on the potential harm that can be done to athletes by the doping control protocols from a human rights perspective. Now the question that follows is, can that harm be justified? Athletes, like all people, have some right to privacy. Under what circumstances can the state, or other agencies, interfere with the autonomy of its members? It would seem that an intervention, such as a drug test, must be justified by its advocate. An intervention can be justified two ways. First, it can be justified by an overwhelming need to pursue other moral values.

Namely, the moral value of privacy is superseded by some other moral value, such as harm to others. Second, intervention can be justified by permission. Therefore, if consent is gained for an intervention, then that individual has waived his or her right to privacy. Many countries require national team athletes, or athletes who receive government financial support, to sign a contract agreeing to the testing (and many other things) in order to get their funding. Many national sport organizations, federations, and national Olympic committees – the organizations that would be in charge of selecting an athlete to compete internationally, require similar kinds of agreements.

The suggestion that there is an overwhelming public interest that could supersede the assumption of an individual's right to privacy is one possible argument. Such an interest in public safety has been postulated in some countries by proposed introduction of random drug testing for workers in, for example, the transport industry. These proposals are sometimes amended, since public interest, sufficient to justify the random testing of transport workers and pilots, has not always been perceived to exist. However, the principle of overwhelming public interest in safety is accepted in the case of random roadside breath testing for alcohol use (RIDE programmes) in many countries. If the public interest in safety is insufficient to justify random testing of transport workers, then the public interest in doping-free sport is likely to be insufficient to justify random testing of athletes. In the case of transport workers, the feared harm had to do with causing accidents, and the evidence was deemed to be insufficient for overriding rights to privacy. The arguments that are designed to show that doping should be banned because of the harm it causes should be reviewed to see if there is a sufficient justification to warrant the intrusions into privacy caused by enforcing bans through doping control protocols.

One of the most commonly cited category of arguments used to justify the bans on doping are those from harm. There are at least four types of arguments from harm: 1. harm to users; 2. harm to other athletes; 3. harm to society; and 4. harm to the sport community. The purpose of this section is to analyse these arguments to see if they will work to justify the forfeiture of an athlete's right to privacy. The first argument from harm – based on the harm that will befall the user – in its simplest form, runs along these lines. Substance or practice x harms its user. The user needs to be protected. Banning the substance can protect the user. Therefore, the substance should be banned.

It is important to note that this argument from the potential harm that befalls the user needs to be applied on a substance-by-substance basis. As seen in the above examples, we cannot simply assume that all substances and practices on the banned lists do indeed cause harm to their users. However, consider, for example, the general argument in respect of adult rational athletes and a particular substance – anabolic steroids. The argument can be examined in three quite different ways.

The assertion that steroid use harms the user is plausible. Some of the medical evidence is mixed and is derived from anecdotal testimony of athletes using very high doses in uncontrolled conditions. On the other hand, the hard medical evidence from controlled low-dose studies tends to show minimal harm. The overall abhorrence of the practice has prevented the gathering of hard, scientifically validated, evidence because such research has yet to pass ethics committees when volunteers, who are already using steroids, come forward just to be monitored where the scientist is not even administering the banned substance.[11] Therefore, for the first premise of this argument to work without question, better evidence would be required. There are two elements to the harm charge: bad effects and the causal linkage of these to doping. Currently the weaker link is science proving bad effects from controlled usage. This question about the first premise is, however, insufficient to dismiss the argument. So let us grant, for the sake of argument, that steroids do indeed harm their users, because it is not implausible.

The second premise runs into problems for different reasons, especially from a human rights perspective. The desire to protect some other 'competent' adult from the consequences of his or her own actions is paternalistic.[12] It can be argued that banning doping, in the elite sport context, would be a form of paternalism if it were done solely in order to protect competent adult athletes from the potential harm from usage. Paternalism has acceptable and unacceptable forms. For example, some have argued that banning doping for minors is acceptable and banning doping for adults is unacceptable. However, there are cases in societies where certain practices are illegal for adults (e.g. driving without seatbelts, riding motor bikes without helmets, use of cocaine, etc.). The relevant question to be addressed in the context of athlete's rights is: 'Is banning steroids and other substances and practices an example of acceptable paternalism?' For the purposes of this argument, the focus will be on the justification of bans imposed on competent adults.

The discussion of whether it may be acceptable to prohibit minors from doping is not as controversial because most writers assume that this is possible. However, this question raises an interesting difficulty. If, for example, steroid use is banned for minors but not for adults, and if adults and minors compete against each other in the Olympic games (which they do in some sports), then we would have the odd situation of different rules applying to different competitors. This would not be fair. One might, therefore, conclude that doping should be banned for adults so that the competition between them and children might be fair. An alternative would be to ban minors from competing in elite sport (there are currently minimum age requirements but most are below the standard age of majority in most countries). Given the enormous amount of time and commitment required to reach elite and Olympic levels, permitting children to compete may well be placing an intolerable burden upon them – a burden they may not be fully able to consent to or to choose anyway.

However, for the purpose of this section, because the focus is on adults, the kind of paternalism that will be reviewed is 'hard' paternalism – the view that paternalism is sometimes justified even if the action is fully voluntary.[13] W. M. Brown has most consistently argued the suggestion that paternalistic interventions in the lives of adult competent athletes are unwarranted.[14] In 'Paternalism, Drugs, and the Nature of Sports', Brown describes his position as follows:

> At this point, we may resort to something like a principle of 'hard' paternalism if we are to persist in our efforts to control the choices and options of [adult] athletes. We are in effect seeking to impose on those who resist it an alternative set of values. But what would justify such an imposition? There seems no reason to suppose that taking risk in sports, even great risk, is inevitably irrational, self-destructive, or immature, as we have seen. Nor is it plausible to suggest that we forbid all of the sports which involve such risk, such as mountain climbing, sky-diving, or even boxing. As Mill argued, such intervention in people's lives would itself be a greater wrong than the possible injury of activities voluntarily chosen...We can indeed forbid the use of drugs in athletics in general, just as we do in the case of children. But ironically, in adopting such a paternalistic stance of insisting that we know better than the athletes themselves how to achieve some more general good which they myopically ignore, we must deny in them the very attributes we claim to value: selfreliance, personal achievement, and autonomy.[15]

Generally speaking, many countries try to foster independence and the right of people to make the important choices that affect their lives: they seem to value autonomy.[16] Much of the thrust of modern medical ethics has been directed precisely against paternalism. To ban steroids solely to protect their adult competent users is to treat those athletes as children unable to make the choices that most affect them. As Brown points out in all of his writings on this topic, this position is generally inconsistent with the limit-pushing nature of high-performance sport. The question to be asked is, why this inviolable boundary? If Mill's 'harm principle' is accepted, paternalistic interference with the freedom of athletes is ruled out because we are only entitled to interfere with the behaviour of competent, consenting adults to prevent harm to others. If athletes choose the gains that some substances or practices provide along with possible harmful side effects over what they believe to be the alternative of less risk but worse performance, external interference with their freedom of choice seems unwarranted.

This second premise may be unsuccessful for other reasons too. It is inconsistent at the least, and maybe even hypocritical, for sports governing bodies to attempt to justify a ban by appealing to the athlete's health and well-being. There are many training practices and indeed many sports that carry a far greater likelihood of harm to the athlete than does the controlled use of a substance like steroids. In some cases the risk is so high that the national sport organizations demand that athletes sign a liability waiver in order to compete.[17] One need only note the deaths in cycling, boxing and alpine skiing.

There are some calls now for the reduction of the physiological severity of cycling's Tour de France, but they do not seem to be coming from the current riders, promoters, organizers or officials. Many team doctors see their athletes as patients requiring medical care but do not seem to be calling for change. Some authors have pointed to the striking passivity of high-performance sports physicians for whom the problem of 'inhuman' stress during training and competition never seems to be the issue:

> One of the remarkable aspects of the physicians' self-image is their constant boasting about their moderating influence, at the same time that they claim to be helpless when confronted with the prevailing [societal] conditions.[18]

Physicians' organizations worldwide have taken a stance against the sport of boxing because of its health risks, but there is no such stance taken for the Tour de France. Rather, there seems to be acceptance of a model of 'reduction of harm' to defend medical intervention rather that reduction of harm by reducing the physical stress requirements of the Tour. Many feel that some athletes have been traumatized by their ordeals at the hands of the French police since the 1998 scandal.

> In the beginning ... the officials in Lyons were friendly. But on Thursday evening the horror show began. I was put in an isolation cell and had to strip naked. I had to give up my belt, shoes, even my glasses. They inspected every body cavity, including my rear end. The night was bad, the bed was dirty and it stank. The next morning they confronted me with the compromising documents they had found. They said that they were used to seeing hardened criminals in the chair I was sitting on. But is that what we are? I wanted out of this hellhole, so I confessed.[19]

If the reason for banning doping in sport really was a concern for the health and well-being of athletes, there would be many sports and many more practices that should be banned. So at the very least, it seems inconsistent to argue in favour of the bans on doping and not the myriad other practices which are also harmful to athletes.

One might try to argue that risks incurred by the nature of the sport, such as brain damage in boxing, are different from risks incurred from practices that have nothing to do with competition in the sport per se, such as liver damage from steroid use. This suggestion works from the idea that we can distinguish between risks necessary in some sport and risks that are not. This is a promising suggestion, but one that is not yet complete. What is required is a method for distinguishing between a sport's necessary risks and those that are unnecessary. But this distinction is not going to be based on health.

Finally, the third premise is questionable because there is little evidence to date to suggest that banning substances like steroids really will protect athletes. All the time that a sub-culture exists which indicates that doping use brings benefits and that it is an occupational hazard of high-level competitive sport, athletes will continue to use it in clandestine, unsanitary and uncontrolled ways. This is not just a matter of better enforcement of the ban, but rather, it requires a change in values, and this will only happen after a logically consistent position for the ban has been put forward and the sub-culture in some sports changes.[20] Presumably the ban is intended as part of a larger process aimed at producing just such a change in values, but the evidence for this process is scant. Given the ban, for example, doping is cheating, and so the negative value placed on cheating would be extended to doping, which might change athletes' attitudes towards doping but for different reasons if they rejected it even if it was not on the banned list. Further, even if it were argued that we might protect some, if not most, athletes from harm and that this makes the ban worthy of enactment; there are other harms from the human rights perspective, caused by drug testing to enforce the bans – the violation of privacy – that must be weighed against this consideration.

Taken singly, the counter arguments, motivated by the antipathy to paternalism and the inconsistency of a ban predicated upon the desire to protect athletes, are sufficient to show that the first argument from harm does not provide sufficient grounds by itself. The rejection of the argument is strengthened by the lack of unequivocal scientific evidence with controlled use for harm and the contention that athletes may well not benefit by a ban anyway. The justification of banning doping based on protecting 'competent' and consenting adult users from potential harm, stands in need of considerable strengthening.

The second form of the argument from harm is based not on the harm that doping may cause to users, but on the harm its use causes to other athletes: the 'others' in this argument are usually deemed to be other 'clean' athletes. ('Clean' simply means non-doped.) Sometimes this argument is called the 'coercion' argument and it is more difficult to dismiss than the first argument based on the potential harm to the user. The same liberal tradition that prohibits paternalistic intervention permits interventions designed to prevent harm to others. The crucial questions will concern how great the harm is to other athletes and how severe the limitation on personal action. This second argument runs along the following lines. An athlete's use of doping causes harm to 'clean' athletes. The clean athletes need protection. Banning doping in sport will protect clean athletes from harm. Therefore, doping should be banned.

In order to assess this argument one needs to consider whether or not the potential coercion of clean athletes outweighs the infringement on the liberties of all athletes caused when a substance or practice is banned. Clean athletes are harmed, so the argument goes, because the dopers 'up the ante'. If some competitors are doping, then all competitors who wish to compete at that level will need to take steroids or other substances to keep up. Some have argued that the competitive sport environment is inherently coercive because when some athletes choose to dope to give them a competitive edge, others will be pressed to do likewise, or resign themselves to either accepting a competitive disadvantage or leaving the endeavour entirely.[21] This limited choice is considered a genuine threat to an athlete's life plan or their freedom, and further, it is a serious threat to human flourishing. Thus, doping is wrong because it is coercive (as well as for its potential for harm and because it advances no social value).[22]

The problem with positions like this is that elite-level competitive athletics is already a very high stakes game. In order to compete effectively one has to dedicate oneself totally and submit to a minutely controlled training regimen that will dictate almost all aspects of one's life. Why is the upping of the ante caused by the use of, for example, steroids, qualitatively different from the upping of the ante caused by the increasing professionalism of athletes and coaches and the mechanization of athletes that elite-level competition now requires? It might be argued that this criticism rests on the assumption that one must either ban all bad things, or none, and can be met with the reply: if we ban this one bad thing, that will at least be one bad thing the less. But what remains to be shown is why doping is the worst bad thing.

Any effective training practice 'ups the ante', and many training practices are extremely onerous. Further, libertarians have argued that the choice of whether the risk of drug use is worth the gain should be left to the individual athlete to make, just as in the case of other risky training techniques. The feeling that doping is worse than longer and ever more specialized training risks just raises the question of why it is worse. This is a qualitative question and the answer will inevitably appeal to a qualitative distinction.

A second potential group that could be harmed by doped athletes is the general public, in particular children. People look up to athletes and view them as role models. If they take drugs like steroids they are no longer suitable as role models and the general public has lost a significant benefit. There are several things to say in response here. The first will examine just why it is that doping disqualifies one from acting as a role model. The response might be that those who use steroids are cheats and, of course, cheats cannot be role models. And, of course, this is true, but this just begs the question as to their being banned in the first place. A further response to the suggestion that athletes should be role models, and in particular 'moral' role models, is to ask just why that should be so. We currently expect widely varying things of our public figures. No one seriously expects musicians or actors and actresses to be moral role models, why should athletes be singled out for special treatment? Why do we expect more from athletes than from other public figures? From a societal perspective, if the hero is morally despicable this will be a negative influence because young people will not separate the athletic abilities of their heroes from the quality of their personal lives, especially when fame and glamour surround the hero. Perhaps for these reasons we are more concerned about the moral image of athletes than other public figures.

For example, no one else is prevented from using cold remedies, even if they drive public transportation, or from using caffeine as a stimulant to work harder. So it is not even the case that we want athletes to meet the standards everyone else meets but, rather, that we want them to meet more rigorous standards in regard to substance use. What is missing is a clear and cogent reason to justify treating athletes differently from other public figures and clear causal linkage between their actions and harm to others in order to have a justification for the violations of privacy rights.

There is, thus, an insufficient justification in the harm caused by doping to warrant the intrusion caused by enforcing those bans. That leaves open the second option; that we might allow dope-testing because the athletes consent to it. However, elite athletes living below the poverty line may well feel that they are coerced into giving consent because they cannot continue to compete without financial aid, unlike wealthier athletes. To satisfy the stronger aspects of autonomy, a person must make decisions which affect his or her welfare. The athlete, therefore, is the person who has to decide if he or she will follow the procedure. To satisfy the demands of autonomy, the athlete cannot simply acquiesce to the procedure chosen by the coach or team physician, he or she must actively choose the procedure in the first place.

Another important issue is consent of minors because many elite athletes are minors. Any person consenting to an intervention must be competent to do so. It is generally assumed that adults are competent, unless shown to be otherwise, and that minors are not. In the latter case, usually a parent or a guardian may consent to an intervention on behalf of a minor. This has worked well enough in the case of consent to medical treatment designed to benefit a minor but not for non-therapeutic interventions.

Further, the inherently coercive power imbalance between an individual and a state agency that requests consent for a drug test is exacerbated by the possible consequences of the test result. In giving consent, an athlete is also consenting to being tested at any time for drugs that may have no relation to his or her training, but which do carry the risk of criminal prosecution. These potential consequences morally require that consent is genuinely informed and not coerced but, further, that there are accompanying educational programmes.

Privacy Acts exist, at least in part, to recognize the extreme imbalance in power between governments and individuals. This imbalance renders some requests by governments for permission from individuals inherently coercive. One objection to the requirement of consent is that sport is somehow different, in that the usual requirements of consent fail to apply. These arguments are not convincing. The suggestion is that participation in 'high performance' sport is a privilege, not a right. The argument runs like this; athletes are not deprived of their rights if they are deemed ineligible because they will not submit to a drug test, because they do not have a right to participate in the first place. The serious consequences of this argument are that it would allow the imposition of any rules no matter how absurd. However, the rules of sport are not arbitrary and they themselves are open to moral scrutiny. Just as a rule of eligibility that barred people on the basis of race would be objected to on moral grounds, other rules of eligibility for sport are open to similar moral assessment. If, therefore, doping control is unacceptable on the moral grounds that it invades privacy, it would be unacceptable for there to be a rule of eligibility that required it. Sport may well be different, but nothing is so special or different that it can escape all moral scrutiny from those outside of sport.

The harm arguments, on the surface, appear quite powerful. After all, the one, generally accepted, limitation on individual liberty is that one's actions might harm others. The harm argument comes in a variety of forms, some of which are more potent than others. There are also important limitations on the arguments from harm, limitations that stem from the requirements of consistency and balance. The argument that seeks to justify invasive doping control measures on the basis of the harm doping causes to the adult user may well be paternalistic and inconsistent. Harm to other athletes is probably the most cogent form of the harm argument. The best form of this argument is that doping harms other athletes in that it coerces them into accepting risks of harm that are not essential to the sport being practised. Banning, and the measures required to enforce it, are justified to protect other athletes.

However, the argument has its limitations. The first is that it needs to be applied practice-by-practice, drug-by-drug and sport-by-sport. Indeed it may even be necessary to evaluate not just substances but amounts ingested or methods of administration. The second is that not only would it work for some items on the banned list, but consistent application would require banning other non-essential, yet harmful, practices or sports. For instance, we might wish to limit certain kinds of training and certain kinds of sports. Third, the harm caused by the practices concerned has to be weighed against the harm caused by enforcing bans. While the harm caused by enforcing a ban on a performance enhancer, a test on the day of the competition, is relatively minor, the requirements of enforcing bans on training enhancers are quite onerous. The conclusion here is that while harm to other athletes may well feature in the justification for banning certain elements of doping it cannot stand alone as the whole story.

An alternative is to turn part of the formulation of rules, in particular rules of eligibility, over to the athletes, the ones to whom the rules apply. There is evidence that the majority of athletes would prefer doping-free sport if it could be guaranteed that the competition is fair. What is missing is the guarantee. If athletes agree that they want doping-free sport, and if they also agree that they are prepared to take the necessary steps to achieve the thing they want, then they could be in the position to request an agency to conduct testing on their behalf. Thus, instead of governments and the governing bodies of sport imposing rules, the athletes would set their own rules and request that an outside agency enforce them. So, athletes would be limiting their own liberty while their autonomy is clearly unfettered. They take steps to curtail their liberty in the short term in order to preserve or enhance their liberty in the long run. In this way, the agency conducting the testing is not acting on behalf of governments or sports bodies, but on behalf of athletes. The government or governing bodies of sport cannot then be seen as interfering in the lives of its citizen athletes. This means that the power of the justification relies essentially on genuine athlete agreement. There are immense practical difficulties in introducing an athlete-driven system that would provide the protection athletes want while truly honouring their autonomy and their privacy. If athletes view the rules as imposed from the outside, and fundamentally against their own personal self-interest, we will be doomed to the ultimately fruitless and self-defeating game of tester against cheat. The outcome of that game will be the eventual abandonment of doping control.

NOTES

1. Most recently, the President of the United States has announced that the White House wishes to organize a summit of representatives from the major sports leagues and US Olympic Committee to discuss steroid use by athletes. There seems to be some resistance from the baseball players union (*Associated Press*, 1 March 2004).
2. These other arguments are dealt with in detail in earlier publications: A. J. Schneider and R. B. Butcher, 'Why Olympic Athletes Should Avoid the Use and Seek the Elimination of Performance-Enhancing Substances and Practices in the Olympic Games', *Journal of*

the Philosophy of Sport, XX and XXI (1994) 64–81; A. J. Schneider, 'Doping in Sport and the Perversion Argument', in G. Gaebauer (ed.) *The Relevance of the Philosophy of Sport* (Berlin, 1993) pp.117–28.

3. This is still true despite more positive tests. The game of testing and masking is constantly evolving. If one knows when one is to be tested one has a far greater opportunity to seek to thwart the test.

4. For example, the entire group of peptide hormones, analogues, human growth hormone, and EPO could not be detected until recently and there has been much debate about adding substances to the list for which there is no sound test. But, more interestingly, there was also much debate about the criteria of 'performance enhancement' for any justification for the banned list because scientists have pointed out that the evidence is mixed in several cases with regard to the performance-enhancing abilities of the substances and practices on the banned list.

5. For example, athletes may use a training-enhancing substance like anabolic steroids and discontinue use prior to competition, rendering the detection of these compounds extremely difficult at the time of competition, particularly if masking agents are also used. This is so, despite the contemporary use of endocrine profiles that allow us to trace changes in the body. The logical problem is that endocrine profiles are only useful as a testing criterion for those with a long history of previous tests.

6. The costs of tests vary from country to country, but the average range is about US $500–$1,000.

7. Not all positive tests have lead to a charge of a doping infraction e.g. therapeutic exemption.

8. Ross Rebagliati, snowboarder.

9. A member of the commission who attended that meeting shared this information.

10. Previously, under the doping class of stimulants in the *IOC Anti-Doping Charter* products like these were listed on p. 24, 'Thus no product for use in colds, flu or hay fever purchased by a competitor or given to him/her should be used without first checking with a doctor or pharmacist that the product does not contain a drug of the banned stimulants class.'

11. Based on personal communication from scientists who have attempted to get ethics approval and from ethics committee members.

12. The basic notion is that individuals are deemed to be competent to make their own decisions unless they are minors or are demonstrated to be 'incompetent' from a medical/legal perspective.

13. See J. Feinberg, 'Legal Paternalism', *Canadian Journal of Philosophy*, 1 (1977) 106–24. This argument from paternalism operates only in the case of so-called 'competent' adults; different considerations apply to children or those deemed not competent to make their own decisions. The philosophical problems surrounding competence deserve a full study itself.

14. See W. M. Brown, 'Ethics, Drugs, and Sport', *Journal of the Philosophy of Sport*, VII (1980) 15–23; 'Paternalism, Drugs, and the Nature of Sports', *Journal of the Philosophy of Sport*, XI (1984) 14–22; 'Comments on Simon and Fraleigh', Ibid., XI (1984) 33–35; 'Practices and Prudence', Ibid., XVII (1990) 71–84.

15. Brown (note 14) pp.20–21.

16. As previously mentioned on competence, discussion of all philosophical problems with definitions of the concept of autonomy is too broad for the topic in this paper.

17. For example, the Canadian Alpine Ski Athlete Agreement (1995) reads: 'I release, indemnify and forever discharge the Releasees, their members, volunteer workers ... and I voluntarily accept the legal risk, thereby expressly giving up any right of action, and the physical risk arising from all liability... And, acknowledging that Alpine Skiing is extremely dangerous, I do hereby assume all Alpine Skiing's risks and dangers ... I understand that the Releasees will not permit me to participate in Alpine Skiing programs or activities unless I sign this *COMPLETE RELEASE, WAIVER OF CLAIM AND ASSUMPTION OF RISK AGREEMENT...*'.

18. See A. Singler and G. Treutlein, *Doping – von der Analyse zur Prävention* (Aachen 2001) pp.40–41.

19. See 'Hier sitzen nur Schwerverbrecher,' *Süddeutsche Zeitung* (27 July 1998).

20. The concept of positive deviance is proposed as an account of this type of behaviour by some sociologists of sport. In A. J. Schneider and R. B. Butcher, 'Fair Play as Respect for the Game', *Journal of the Philosophy of Sport,* XXV (1998) 1–22, it is argued that in sport there is an essential connection between playing and outcome. Doping does not enhance playing, and only enhances outcome when one competes against someone who does not dope. See also Schneider and Butcher (note 2).
21. See T. M. Murray, 'The Coercive Power of Drugs in Sports', *The Hasings Center Report,* 13 (1983) 24–30.
22. Murray (note 21) p.3.

Breaking Post-War Ice: Open Fun Football Schools in Bosnia and Herzegovina

PATRICK K. GASSER AND ANDERS LEVINSEN

> Football is merely a continuation of war by other means.
> (Franjo Tudjman, from Karl von Clausewitz)

In recent years, many scholars have examined how sports in general, and football in particular, influence identity and social relations in different parts of the world. A complicated picture emerges: in some situations sport contributes to social harmony, and in others it feeds conflict. In spite of this ambiguity, many still have strong faith in sport's potential for mending social cleavages.

This faith is not a new one. For centuries governments and leaders have used sport as a tool to overcome old divisions and mould new identities; the idea that sport can foster peace between nations has been enshrined in the Olympic concept. What is new is how the international community is recasting the strategy to fit current problems, identifying sport as an important element of civil society and adopting it as a tool within international peace-building strategies. A growing number of programmes are designed to use sport to strengthen links between polarized communities, and are funded by international organizations.[1]

Making ideals fit reality is often quite a challenge. Peace can be a complicated matter, and the tools of sport are not always user-friendly. A survey of initiatives to foster peace through sport produces a number of examples of good intentions gone awry.[2] For those responsible in planning, implementing, or funding programmes that are intended to help integrate divided communities, or to promote peace in other ways, these failures raise important questions: How do you know whether a 'peace-building through sport' programme is really building peace? Which strategies work, under what conditions? How do you prevent peace-building through sport initiatives from being derailed and actually contributing to inter-group tension? What are the warning signs, and how might these be effectively challenged? In short, exactly what are the best usages of the tools that sport can offer, if one wants to foster the peaceful co-existence of hostile groups? While much has been written on a theoretical level about different aspects of the intersection of sport and politics, it is still hard to find information at a practical level on the successes and failures of programmes designed to help reintegrate divided communities.

The Open Fun Football Schools (OFFS) is one such programme. A grassroots youth football programme that works to encourage the reintegration of divided communities, it was opened in 1998 to help re-weave the social fabric of communities that had been torn by conflict in Bosnia and Herzegovina. Since then it has expanded to the Former Yugoslav Republic (FYR) of Macedonia, Serbia and Montenegro, Croatia and Georgia, and has organized tens of thousands of children from antagonistic communities to play football together. This article will describe the OFFS schools in Bosnia and Herzegovina, highlighting elements of its success and identifying the challenges that will mark its future.

Background: Football in the Balkans

Football came to the Balkans at around the beginning of the twentieth century, when the region was still part of the Austro-Hungarian Empire. When the First World War ensured the collapse of that empire, Serbs, Croats and Slovenes were grouped into a kingdom that struggled to unify these peoples through the new national identity of Yugoslavs (southern Slavs). By the 1920s, football had become the region's most popular sport, and it was intimately entwined with national identity struggles that pitted Serbian monarchists against Croat nationalists.[3] During the Second World War, the struggle escalated into a bloody civil war between the *Ustasha* (Croat nationalists led by Ante Pavelic), the *Partisans* (communists led by Tito) and royalist groups including the *Chetniks*.

The *Partisans* emerged victorious. Under Tito's leadership, they established the Federal National Republic of Yugoslavia, joining the republics of Serbia, Croatia, Slovenia, Macedonia, Bosnia and Herzegovina and Montenegro under the rule of a strong state apparatus. Tito suppressed nationalist opposition,[4] and mobilized mechanisms of the State, including control of the media, education, and economy to bury ethnic animosity, encourage contact between groups and develop interdependence as a means of reinforcing the Yugoslav identity that was the basis for the country's unity. Becoming a leader of the international movement for non-alignment, he established a distance from the Soviet Union that set Yugoslavia apart from the Eastern bloc. Sport was recognized as an important tool for reinforcing the State and strengthening the multiethnic Yugoslav identity. Sports clubs were closely linked to the aims of state,[5] and sporting activities, in providing one of the most important faces the country presented to the outside world, were accorded priority for funding. The good facilities and good-quality training and organization within Yugoslav sport paid off. In the 1960s Yugoslavian footballers won the Olympic title in Rome, and over the years achieved impressive results at club and national team level in European competitions. Clubs sponsored youth teams that were also competitive internationally. School sports programmes, run by trained sports teachers, gave schoolchildren good access to sporting activities around the country.

Starting with the death of Tito and ending with the fall of the Berlin Wall, the developments of the 1980s shook the foundations of Yugoslavia's polity and economy. Yugoslavia tumbled with the rest of Eastern Europe into an economic downspin; nationalism re-emerged and gained ground, led in Croatia by Franjo Tudjman and in Serbia by Slobodan Milošević. The federal structure of Yugoslavia weakened as independence movements in Slovenia and Croatia gathered momentum. During this period, football fan violence was gaining visibility around Europe; in the Balkans it was, as elsewhere, often oriented around ethnic tensions.

The use of football to intensify nationalistic sentiment has been most thoroughly documented in Croatia, where fan violence was instrumental in setting off violence that spread to the streets.[6] The famous football riot that occurred in Zagreb Maksimir stadium in May 1990, during a game between Zagreb Dinamo and Belgrade Red Star, is still remembered by some as the start of the war; a photograph of the Dinamo captain kicking a policeman became a symbol of nationalist heroism for many young fans. Before Croatia was recognized as a state, the formation of a national team was a landmark in Croatia's symbolic assertion of its independence. On both sides, members of football fan clubs were among the first recruits of the new fighting groups and paramilitary forces that were at the fore of hostilities. On frontlines and in war ruins, the names of football clubs were mingled with symbols of nationalistic extremists: swastikas, the 'U' used by Ustashas, and the symbol of the cross employed by Serbian paramilitary groups.

At many different levels, then, football imagery and symbols were associated with the struggle between Serbs and Croats that sparked the war in Croatia and soon engulfed Bosnia and Herzegovina. There, Muslim Bosnians, led by Alija Izetbegovic, constituted the third group in what quickly became a brutal war. As violence escalated, these groups competed for control of areas; where domination was achieved, competing groups were driven out in what the press dubbed 'ethnic cleansing'. At first fighting together against Serbian groups, Croats and Bosnians eventually fought each other, and the Croats declared their own state of Herceg-Bosna.

When fighting ended, some 200,000 people had died and two million had been forced from their homes. The 1995 Dayton Accord established Bosnia and Herzegovina as a single country with two entities: Republika Srpska and a Federation of Bosnia and Herzegovina (comprising Croat and Bosnian cantons).

The entities had separate armies, administrations, criminal justice and educational systems. Even if Croats and Bosnians were united officially, most power lay at the cantonal level, leaving Croats in full control of areas formerly declared Herceg-Bosna; tension remained high between Croats and Bosnians. In many areas, those in control of law enforcement, courts, and security forces had personally supported or even conducted the inter-group hostilities during the war.

Aiming to establish Bosnia and Herzegovina's economic and political viability, and to solve problems of refugees and displaced persons by permitting them to return to their homes, international organizations, including the United Nations (UN) and the European Union (EU) supported the vision of a multiethnic state. Through their control of reconstruction funding, they worked to undo the effects of ethnic cleansing by re-integrating polarized communities. Their programmes, however, depended for implementation on the cooperation of local governments who often had a competing vision of maintaining the ethnic boundaries that they had fought to create. People showed little willingness to cross the 'ghosts' of frontlines that divided Serbian, Croat and Bosnian communities in order to renew severed social and economic ties. If they did dare, they were often met with hostility, both from the public and from local authorities and police. In situations where the destruction of housing left a severe shortage of shelter and a devastated economy offered little employment or tax base to provide funding for basic public services, communities scrambling for scarce resources had little desire to share anything with the groups who had recently been shooting at them, and whom they blamed for their predicament.

The football establishment, like the rest of society, had been weakened by the economic decline that preceded the war and by the devastation of the conflict itself. Halting all play within Bosnia and Herzegovina, the war already had created a strong 'push effect', driving out the area's considerable football talent; in 1996 the Bosman ruling added a 'pull effect' by enabling more players to join clubs in neighbouring European countries. The Football Federation of Bosnia and Herzegovina (FFBH) was formed, and became a member of the International Federation of Football Associations (FIFA) in February 1996, and of the Union of European Football Associations (UEFA) in 1998; both bodies provided considerable assistance to help rebuild structures needed to re-establish play. The Republika Srpska formed its own football federation and organized a separate football competition; its teams rarely played FFBH teams. The Serbian federation was not recognized by FIFA or UEFA. Croat and Bosnian cantons, though joined in the FFBH on paper, still maintained separations at ground level, with clubs only competing with those from their own ethnic groups until they met in playoffs. Tensions between them led to squabbles over the use of stadiums.[7]

Football clubs, like most other organizations, were in a shambles: they had no money and were weakened by not only the flight of talent but also the 'ghettoization' created by ethnic divisions that limited match attendance, media coverage and the standards of competition. The clubs could barely manage to maintain professional play that provided their funding; youth activities lagged far behind in priority. Schools, whose few resources were controlled by segregated municipalities, also had difficulty re-establishing sports activities. In spite of the talent drain, many well-trained coaches and sports teachers remained in Bosnia and Herzegovina, but clubs and schools lacked the funds to employ them. As was common throughout the Balkans, club leadership was often closely linked to the local political leadership, and without independent means of finance, clubs sometimes depended on funding from municipalities.

It was in this environment that the OFFS first began to operate. Fighting had stopped, but the struggle to 'win the peace' was still very much alive between those subscribing to two opposing visions. On one side were the nationalists, who strove to maintain the recent separation into different ethnic-based units that had been achieved in the war and who preferred to orient themselves (at least in the case of Serbs and Croats) toward neighbouring states with the same ethnic origins. On the other side were those who strove to preserve the integrity of the Republic, and to establish independence as a multiethnic nation. In the service of this second vision, the OFFS was designed to give children from Serb, Croat and Bosnian communities the chance to move over the old frontlines, breaking invisible barriers to play with children from nearby communities that were recently considered as enemies.

Open Fun Football Schools

The Open Fun Football Schools programme was initiated by Anders Levinsen, who also founded the non-governmental organization (NGO) Cross Cultures Project Association (CCPA) to organize them.[8] In a five-day grassroots football programme, which is organized during school vacations, OFFS brings together children from different ethnic groups, with different skill levels, to play football together on the same teams. Using a variety of games and exercises, not limited to football, OFFS works to develop confidence, skills and teamwork. In addition to the schools, the programme organizes three to five-hour street events. These may include children in OFFS, but are not limited to the schools, and can be organized independently.

Open Fun Football Schools were first organized in the communities of Bosnia and Herzegovina that were divided by the recent conflict. By the end of the 2003 season, there were 99 Open Fun Football Schools in the country, involving 20,000 children and almost 1,700 trainers.[9] Over 60 per cent of the municipalities in the country have participated in the programme. OFFS expanded in 2000 to FYR Macedonia, in 2001 to Serbia and Montenegro and in 2003 to Croatia and Georgia. By the end of 2003, over 3,900 local leaders and coaches had organized a total of 237 OFFS schools for 48,000 children. In 2003, activities included 78 football schools with leaders, trainers and children from 173 municipalities and 264 football clubs. The OFFS is now formulating plans to expand to Azerbaijan, and Armenia. In what follows, we focus on the experiences of the programme in Bosnia and Herzegovina.

OFFS is based on the concept of 'fun football', as developed by the Danish Football Association. Their philosophy is derived from the Danish public sport culture that is characterized by a strong local focus, democratic principles, volunteerism, parent support, and the basic principle of 'sports for all'. Levinsen got the idea of setting up OFFS when he returned from working for the UN in war-torn Bosnia and Herzegovina, and witnessed how Danish children benefited from attending the summer fun football camps.[10] Applying the concept to the Balkans and other areas of Eastern Europe, he has also taken inspiration from the work of Danish sport sociologists Henning Eichberg and Claus Bøje.

Fun is at the heart of a pedagogical method that has been developed in close detail. Competition is played down to preserve the joyful, playful aspects of the game. There is no physical or tactical training, but rather a focus on techniques children can refine after leaving the school: the unusual strike on the ball, the delicate pass, or the elegant dribble. Exercises are not limited to football skills, but also include other play sports such as rope games, balancing games, communication games, and floor hockey. The coaches are trained and the activities designed to make participants feel that they succeed many times during each game or practice; the schools are set up to nurture community spirit and social relations fuelled by the positive energy generated by this sense of success. Deliberately designed to create the feel of festivity and foster a sense of the magic of the game, the schools pack the activities of 12 teams into a single playing field, using upbeat piped-in music. De-emphasizing the competitive aspects enables schools to be more inclusive in a 'sports for all' philosophy. Developing the concept of 'attentive areas'[11] OFFS aims to sharpen trainers' abilities to develop children's social skills, confidence, and trust. The goal is to encourage children to dare to use their imagination and play freely, reassure them that mistakes are permissible, and teach them to take responsibility and to make a positive contribution.

Each school in Bosnia and Herzegovina involves around 200 children and 15 leaders, and is jointly organized by OFFS, local football clubs, school leaders and municipalities. Through a national office, staffed exclusively by national employees, OFFS provides equipment and educates the trainers. Local organizers (clubs, municipalities) choose trainers and participants, organize events, and cover costs such as stadium rent, transport of children, and meals. Cooperation is based on an agreement drawn up for each school: it specifies the geographical, social and ethnic balance of trainers and children, trainer requirements (being unpaid volunteers and attending training courses), and contributions of each party, including the quantity of equipment to be provided by OFFS. The supplies and equipment are left behind afterwards for clubs and trainers. An advisory board which determines the location of football schools includes donors, senior OFFS group leaders and senior football organization representatives from the different entities. Sports faculties from local universities are involved in training events, and local OFFS leaders/trainers are involved in designing training materials. The whole scheme of cooperation is outlined in a letter of mutual intent signed by ministries of sports and national football organizations.

At first each school was organized by a single municipality, but in 2000 OFFS adopted the 'twin city' approach. With this new approach, neighbouring municipalities with different ethnic orientations (i.e. Muslim, Serb or Croat) were obliged to work together to organize each school. Adopting the twin city approach in Bosnia and Herzegovina broadened the utility of the programme as a peace-building tool, applying it not only to promote contact between children, but also establishing sustainable contacts which foster relationships between the adult trainers, schools, clubs and municipalities that are involved in organizing the school, and potentially even spectators (presumably mostly parents) from antagonistic communities. Trainer seminars are multiethnic. Football schools are led by three leaders each, at least one from each community involved, and the hosting of the school rotates between stadiums in participating towns in a system which serves to divide responsibilities equally, assure that no single group is excluded by a hostile arena, and demystify 'enemy territory' by bringing both children and adults over the ghosts of the old frontlines. OFFS aims to engage all participants sufficiently to help them forget, at least for a while, the fear and discomfort of crossing the lines.

Participants

Children

OFFS camps are open to boys and girls from ages 8 to 14. The Balkans has not been one of the areas of the world where children were recruited to participate in armed conflict, but they were often victims: many have strong memories of the war and its effects on their families,[12] but with each passing year, fewer are old enough to remember living in a peaceful multiethnic Bosnia and Herzegovina, sharing activities and experiences and having fun with members of groups now cast as enemies. They generally go to segregated schools and have few opportunities for contact with children from other ethnic groups who live in nearby towns or neighbourhoods. Their motivation to join the programme is straightforward: fun speaks to children around the world, and in their post-war communities, group activities for children have been rare. OFFS aims to use fun to strengthen their confidence and encourage them to play football, and to enable the contacts and generate the warmth that are needed to demystify 'enemy territory' and to thaw the psychological freeze between groups. To accomplish this, it has to maintain balance across the ethnic groups of participating children, and to preserve an apolitical and informal forum where everyone is welcome.

Trainers

The creation of the apolitical and informal forum depends entirely on the schools' trainers and leaders, in terms of their skills and motivation. Creating and maintaining the proper atmosphere is the focus of their training, which goes to great lengths to emphasize the coaches' duty in creating an environment where everyone is comfortable and feels secure enough to participate. The training of coaches also provides detailed exercises and methodology for practical use as educational tools. Trainers and leaders are very often teachers, particularly sports teachers. Unlike the children, many of the trainers participated actively in the fighting; but while they may have shot at each other over the frontlines, before being divided by the war, they spent many years going to school, working, and often playing and watching sport together. Trainer training is obligatory, and workshops are always run jointly with trainers from all sides. A survey that examined the motives of trainers for participating in the programme showed that many were attracted by the chance to meet old friends and associates at training workshops.[13]

Another motivation is the love of football: because OFFS was started at a time when football activity was nearly dead in Bosnia and Herzegovina, many well-trained professionals (coaches, trainers, players, sports teachers) were jobless and desperate to become active in football in any way possible. As reconstruction progresses and the football establishment is rebuilt, the programme has to retain a high professional standard to maintain interest. OFFS has achieved this largely through the training and experience of instructors.[14]

OFFS does not choose school trainers and leaders nor does it demand a particular political orientation: it simply requires proper ethnic balance, and depends on that balance and everyone's mutual commitment to playing football to maintain the fairness and transparency needed to make the schools work.

Clubs and Municipalities

Clubs and municipalities host OFFS, providing the stadiums, buses and other 'hardware' that are essential for running the programmes. They also choose the participants and trainers. In return they get footballs and other equipment left behind after the schools are over. Often closely linked to local political forces and oriented more to the competitive approach of elite sports, clubs are not necessarily in line with the philosophy of OFFS. On the other hand, football is their *raison d'être*, hence there is a strong convergence of interest in a setting where football activity requires re-establishing. By 2003 OFFS had left more than 17,000 balls to clubs in Bosnia and Herzegovina (based on football association estimates) – that constitutes approximately 70 per cent of all balls in the possession of clubs. While most are the number four balls used for children's football, they always include some number five balls suitable for adult competition. In this way OFFS encourages and enables clubs to set up youth activities, but at the same time provides some perks to help them develop their priority area – professional football.

With municipalities, OFFS leverage comes not only from the support it offers to the local football team, but its provision of youth activities: municipal leaders might have diverging political visions, but they only stay where they are by providing valued services to their communities. Being able to choose trainers and participants also empowers clubs and municipalities. The participation of clubs and municipalities is voluntary; they only apply if it offers something that is valuable enough for them to comply with OFFS conditions by working with clubs and communities 'from the other side'.

Parents/Public

As the ones most invested in the welfare of the children, and as community members and constituents, parents are an important vector for the programme's impact on the community. They too are drawn across lines when they come to watch their children play and have fun; once there, they find themselves cheering with former enemies who have children playing for the same team. When successful, the football event has made parents' mutual concerns for their children outweigh the mutual hostility bred by the war; this can have a symbolic value in restoring confidence that public life can be normal again. If it works, it is because the community is war-weary enough to tip the balance toward peace. The success of the event, the imagery of children having fun again in normal activities, is an effective tool to build confidence that people can live and work together again. This symbolism is spread beyond the stadium by media coverage, both local and international.

Football Association

OFFS depends on the football establishment for its long-term survival. If they are to take over funding from international donors, national level football officials have to be involved in planning and decision-making from the beginning. Since 1998, the OFFS Advisory Board has included members from both football federations concerned. Although the Serbian federation did not officially participate before 2001, it was through individual connections within the federation that the OFFS held a trainer-training seminar – the city's first interethnic event after the war – in Pale in 1999. In May 2002, the two federations agreed to a unified competition structure, the *Nogometni Futbalski Savez-BiH* (using both languages' terms for football!).

Donors

The programme in Bosnia and Herzegovina has been funded by UEFA, the Nordic countries (Denmark, Norway and Sweden), the UN High Commission on Refugees (UNHCR), and European Commission's Humanitarian Aid Office (ECHO). The interest of these donors lies in the social impact of the programme, and they depend on expatriate staff to ensure that the programme reinforces integration of ethnic communities.

The Practical Elements of Success and Potential Pitfalls

OFFS builds upon a double agenda: a political one (integrating communities) and a sporting one (promoting grassroots youth football). Local football organizations, players, and communities, from the grassroots level up to the national level, also have double agendas, both political and football. By finding common ground in the sporting agenda, OFFS aims to bring them together to find compromises with the political agendas that oppose reintegration. Making it work depends on two things: preserving the ethnic balance, and maintaining the motivation that springs from the love of football and the commitment to children's welfare. Programme success lies in preserving both. In OFFS, this has depended on maintaining a delicate balance between local and international control.

Local control ensures that the programme provides something communities need, in a way that matters to them. OFFS has fostered local ownership by including local and national groups and individuals at all levels, in all stages of programme planning and implementation. This has depended on engaging the considerable talent, experience, passion and infrastructure that existed already and only needed a relatively small international input to be tapped. Because there is enough local know-how to organize events, and enough motivation to do it even under the conditions imposed, the programme works with minimal expatriate input in funding or expertise: until 2003, the OFFS had only one expatriate staff member. Because it depends on the trainers' voluntary contribution of time, and the infrastructure of clubs and municipalities, the OFFS preserves local leverage: clubs, municipalities and trainers only participate for as long as their own interests in football and children are served.

A heavier dependence on international resources or expertise would weaken local leverage and thus dilute motivation. It would also compromise the very popularity of the programme that provides the source of international leverage. A heavy international hand in shaping the programme would smother the popularity that powers the programme's success. Paying trainers, or providing infrastructure or in other ways relying on more external resources could have the effect of 'buying' cooperation that would evaporate as soon as the money stopped.

But maintaining some international control, through conditionality of funding, is important in early stages to ensure that quotas are respected and that ethnic balance is preserved so that all groups profit by working together. It is here that the expertise of expatriate staff counts: not football expertise, but an intimate knowledge of the country and its politics, to anticipate problems, to activate the right parts of the local and international power structure to navigate around them, and to insist that on the points of ethnic balance and the politically neutral forum of the stadium, there are no compromises. Reliable statistics are key to keeping an eye on what is going on without having to be present everywhere: the OFFS collects figures for each school on the number of trainers from each area, attendance at trainer training, and the ethnic group of children participating. It also monitors media coverage of its events.

The 'twin city' concept has been the essential mechanism in OFFS for maintaining local control without sacrificing ethnic balance. This permits the programme to give local leaders, regardless of their political orientation, a good deal of leeway in planning and implementing the programme; the counterweight of other groups' equal participation, rather than the interference of expatriate staff, ensures that the programme is run in a way that benefits all groups. OFFS, in clear terms set out in agreements ahead of time, will participate in areas where its conditions are accepted, while sharing the venue and responsibility for covering costs maintains each local group's power within the overall equation. Once power-sharing is established, clubs and trainers get on with working out between them how they will make schools happen. The expatriate staff's only role is to monitor results in the atmosphere of training and events, the respect of quotas, and the preservation of transparency.

OFFS conditions can only be imposed so long as the popularity of the schools maintains high demand, so that it can turn down clubs and communities that do not agree to its conditions. It has cancelled plans with communities that would not accept its conditions or did not abide by them. In a few cases, trainers from specific localities have resisted attending multiethnic training seminars; OFFS has also had to resist pressure to include the symbols or terminology of a single side, which would be interpreted as excluding other sides' ownership.

Evaluating Success

Staging a large number of football schools which have good participation from all ethnic groups is already an accomplishment. One only has to know a bit about the conflict in Bosnia and Herzegovina to be impressed to hear the names of places where OFFS schools have been held not only without incident, but with enjoyment. Only a few years after fierce fighting and brutal ethnic cleansing there, in periods when hostility still ran high and there was little interaction between communities, OFFS held multiethnic events in Gorazde, Mostar, Sarajevo, Bjeljina, Sanski Most and many other sites that had been the focus of the conflict. When OFFS brought Muslim children into Srebrenica, UN forces considered that the risks justified not just vehicle escorts, but helicopters; while emotions on all sides ran high, the event was a success. Participation rates have remained high, and ethnic balances, closely monitored through programme statistics, have been respected. It is enough to attend the events to be caught up in the fun that kids, spectators, and trainers are sharing: fun may not be quantifiable, but it is real, and at OFFS schools it is palpable.

Apart from this subjective evaluation (which is the most important real test of success, even if not quantifiable), OFFS systematically collects information on the number of events; the number of staff, monitors, school leaders and coaches deployed; the ethnic balance of children and coaches participating in the schools; the number of children participating in the schools; the number of street events organized; and an evaluation of press coverage. These, however, only chart performance: they tell us that the programme did what it planned and for how many people, not whether it had the impact it promised. While a prerequisite for long-term impact, good performance does not alone guarantee it.

Making a Long-Term Difference

The future of OFFS lies in the national football establishment. Its challenge in Bosnia and Herzegovina is to create a sustainable platform for the programme within the new unified football association, one that preserves its commitment to grassroots football and which will preserve its inter-ethnic, social, and pedagogical premises. Balance and transparency are keywords in the process of building a financial platform that allows international input to be gradually replaced by local funds. Setting itself a goal of financial and institutional sustainability within three or four years, the success of the OFFS 'football agenda' will be reflected in how much OFFS funding is assumed by actors from Bosnia and Herzegovina, how much its pedagogical concept is adopted by local educational institutions, and how youth football activities have developed in areas where OFFS has been active.

In terms of the 'social agenda', anchoring progress is trickier. Once international funding dries up, how do you preserve ethnic balance? OFFS faces the same question that hangs over every 'peace-building' activity based on an international initiative. While it has been designed from the beginning to ease this transition away from international control by basing as much as possible on local motivation and resources, it is clear that OFFS has also depended on its contribution of balls as a key motivator. Even if commitment to grassroots youth football survives the transition away from international funding, will youth football activities continue to be organized on a multiethnic basis and serve to reintegrate communities, or will they be used to freeze barriers between groups, leaving OFFS accomplishment of interethnic cooperation just a short parenthesis in an ongoing story of inter-group hostility?

This returns us to the issue of impact, as opposed to performance. Even if it is a roaring success at getting children to play football and have fun together, and spectators to cheer together, and organizers to work together, what is the impact of OFFS outside the stadium? The idea that it can have a lasting effect on interactions that are not sport related is based on several assumptions that are articles of faith for many of those designing or funding sport programmes with social goals. These assumptions include that playing football together, having fun together or cheering for a team together has a positive and lasting effect on interactions in other domains; that personal relations at grassroots level either have an impact on the decisions and developments leading up to violence, or at least are a factor that can modify them; and that symbolic gestures and acts in this one domain have an impact on peoples' behaviour and beliefs elsewhere. It is only to the extent that these assumptions are correct that a successful sporting programme will have an effect on the community at large.

Testing those assumptions with regard to OFFS, though, is difficult when the desired outcomes depend so much on factors beyond the programme's control. It would be interesting to evaluate community relations in the areas where OFFS has football schools, to see how these relations have changed since 1995, and to investigate how contacts made through the schools have contributed to the changes. But how would you control for the effect of other factors to isolate the impact of football schools? The contact that the schools facilitate is only a prerequisite: just breaking the ice does not guarantee that people will jump in the water, whose temperature depends far more on the economic situation, the criminal justice system, and the political climate. Having fun playing and watching sports together may help rekindle relationships and influence visions of group identity, but if it were enough to keep people from fighting each other, then this war would never have happened. The tragic irony of the 1984 Winter Olympics, which less than a decade before the start of the war had projected Sarajevo throughout the world as a symbol of interethnic harmony, was often highlighted during the war. Now it serves as a cautionary tale.

Conclusion

OFFS in Bosnia and Herzegovina has been strikingly successful, not only in getting children from across frontlines to play together, but also in getting their families and communities to cheer for them, and their local football clubs and town leaders to cooperate so that they can play. This makes it one of the most noteworthy in a growing range of projects that use sport to address social problems in post-conflict settings.

In the pursuit of both its 'football agenda' of supporting grassroots youth football, and its 'social agenda' of helping re-establish ties between communities recently opposed in war, OFFS has depended heavily on several factors peculiar to the Balkans. In football, these have included the widespread popularity of the sport, the availability of highly qualified human resources with much experience and training in the fields of football and youth sport, and a well-developed (if sometimes damaged) football infrastructure. In working to develop inter-group contact and cooperation, OFFS has taken advantage of the fact that communities' isolation from each other is not longstanding, or hostilities deeply ingrained; only a few years ago, people now cast as enemies were playing, watching sports events, working and going to school together. Compared to some conflicts, where hostilities have isolated populations for generations, the historical ice that has to be broken to re-establish contact and cooperation is relatively thin.

OFFS has been designed to profit from these resources and advantages, limiting international input to what was necessary to maintain the ethnic balances required to make the programme work, and offering maximum local control in all other aspects of running the programme. Demanding that trainers are volunteers and that communities and clubs cover a portion of expenses and provide infrastructure, has helped ensure that cooperation is not merely bought, and that schools are driven by local interests. The football establishment from all sides has been involved in planning and decision making since the beginning. At the same time, providing highly valued equipment that helps them re-establish their own football activities, and facilitating the establishment of professionally organized and fun youth activities that offer something to both communities and leaders and trainers, has given OFFS the leverage it needs to impose conditions of inter-ethnic cooperation. Points of no compromise have included the twin-city organization of schools, the ethnic quota of participants and the integration of trainer training.

While OFFS achievements have been impressive, its longer-term impact and sustainability have yet be seen; and it will be instructive to follow how the programme navigates the transition to local funding. The final outcome depends heavily on the interactions between local, national and international players as they struggle to advance their multiple agendas in both the little game (football) and the big one (winning the peace). OFFS long-term success hinges on the successes of the local officials, international organizations, international and national sporting bodies and others who work to develop Bosnia and Herzegovina as a multiethnic nation.

Though it has its moments of magic, football is not Quidditch:[15] it is played on the ground. As a terrain for re-integrating communities polarized by war, football is something like frontline farmland: fertile, but likely to be mined. Those who choose to support football in post-conflict settings need to navigate with care, keeping their eyes wide open and using all available knowledge regarding the successes and failures of strategies in other settings. They also need to have intimate knowledge of their own terrain and its particular risks and advantages. Without a heavy input from local actors at all stages of planning and implementation, programmes run the risk of being designed only to reinforce donors' image and ideals, backfiring at the expense of both; and worse, at the expense of the communities involved.

NOTES

1. See ⟨www.sportdevconf.org⟩ for examples.
2. See A. Rashid, *Taliban: Militant Islam, Oil, and Fundamentalism in Central Asia* (New Haven, CT: Yale University Press, 2000) p.3 on the Taliban use of UN-renovated stadiums for executions; see also D. Tuastad, 'The Political Role of Football for Palestinians in Jordan', in G. Armstrong and R. Giulianotti (eds.), *Entering the Field: New Perspectives in World Football* (Oxford: Berg, 1997) p.110 on how sports in UN-sponsored youth activities became a focus for expressing nationalism.
3. During this period the Yugoslavian football association was moved from Zagreb (Croatia), to Belgrade (Serbia), the capital of the Kingdom of Yugoslavia; its name changed from *Jugoslavni nogometni savez* (using the Croat word for football) to the *Jugoslavni fudbalski savez* (using the Serbian word).
4. Many of the survivors fled the country to Canada, Australia, and Western Europe, in communities where opposition to Tito's government remained strong. For explorations of the role of football clubs in maintaining community identity and nurturing nationalism in Australia, see P. Mosely, 'Balkan Politics in Australian Soccer', *ASSH Studies in Sports*

History 10 (1994); R. Hay, 'Croatia: Community Conflict and Culture: the Role of Soccer Clubs in Migrant Identity' in M. Cronin and D. Mayall (eds.), *Sporting Nationalisms: Identity, Ethnicity, Immigration and Assimilation* (London and Portland, OR: Frank Cass, 1998); and R. Hay, 'Those Bloody Croats: Croat Soccer Teams, Ethnicity and Violence in Australia, 1950–99' in G. Armstrong and R. Giulianotti (eds.) *Fear and Loathing in World Football* (New York: Berg, 2001).

5. Leading teams were those supported by the army, including the Belgrade football team, *Partisan*, and their leaders were often high-ranking officials.

6. For the role of football in Croatia see A. Sack and Z. Suster, 'Soccer and Croat Nationalism', *Journal of Sport and Social Issues* 24 (1999) pp.305–21; and also S. Vrcan and D. Lalic, 'From the Ends to the Trenches, and Back: Football in the Former Yugoslavia' in G. Armstrong and R. Giulianotti (eds.), *Football Cultures and Identity* (Basingstoke: Macmillan, 1998) and S. Kuper, *Football Against the Enemy* (reissue, London: Phoenix, 2001) pp.228–35. For more on links between Arkan and his Serbian paramilitary group the Tigers, one of the key groups in ethnic cleansing in both Croatia and Bosnia and Herzegovina, and the football fan club Deliye, see J. Borgber, 'Serbia's Dark Prince of War Dies as he Lived: by the Sword', *The Age* (23 January 2000); T. Judah, *The Serbs: History, Myth, and the Destruction of Yugoslavia* (New Haven, CT: Yale University Press, 2000) p.186; and C. Stephen, 'Arkan Raises 'Cleansing' Fears', *The Irish Times* (29 March 1999).

7. The playoffs for the UEFA club championships were cancelled in 1999 because of disagreements between Croats and Bosnians about stadium use in Mostar.

8. For more information on OFFS, see ⟨www.openfunfootballschools.org.mk⟩.

9. The actual number of individuals involved is smaller, since the statistics do not reflect repetition of the same person from one summer to the next.

10. Lars Barendt, Head of Communications for the Danish Association, points out a special connection between Fun Football and the Balkans: the Danish camps were developed largely with money that the Association received from the Euro 1992 Championships, which Denmark won. Denmark only entered the tournament because Yugoslavia had been disqualified due to the imposition of UN sanctions.

11. This is detailed in the 2003 *OFFS Manual for Trainers and Leaders*.

12. In an open street event organized in Srebrenica, 40 of the 60 Muslim child participants had been expelled from the city; 12 had lost parents.

13. Other motivations cited included obtaining footballs and enjoying the 'fun football' ethos.

14. In 2003, OFFS instructors included seven current or former national team coaches.

15. Quidditch is Harry Potter's favourite sport, played with other sorcerer students in the air on magic broomsticks.

The Lords of Misrule: Football and the Rights of the Child in Liberia, West Africa

GARY ARMSTRONG

In July 1998, as Liberia celebrated its 150 years of independence, an observer could gain some indication of the state of this West African nation by combining a reading of the local press with the reality of lived experience. Only a year after the cessation of hostilities, and an election that had produced a 75 per cent vote for Charles Taylor, the country was evidently not at ease with itself. While the rape of an 11-year-old girl by a man of 34 could have occurred in most countries on earth, the abduction of a woman in her 40s by members of the President's personal security force suggested a people living in fear. The discovery of her dead body days later, while reported, came with no explanation as to the progress into the hunt for her killers. On the same day as the body was discovered a man lost his eye following an altercation with police who were reported to have stolen money from his pockets as he lay in agony. Other monies were pocketed by the military personnel from drivers stopped at the ubiquitous road blocks in the capital city of Monrovia as they executed an unsophisticated form of taxation. In the hinterland ten people died in an outbreak of malaria. Returning a year later, things were not much improved. In the south of the country the discovery of a dismembered body saw some 18 people arrested for their part in a ritualistic killing. In the capital, journalists and police officers were arrested for their part in a scam that had seen contaminated meat rescued from destruction to be re-sold at the market-place. A dreadful traffic accident, some 200 metres from my abode close to the governmental offices of Charles Taylor in the capital, saw two small domestic use cars ripped apart following a collision with a military carrier belonging to the Anti-Terrorist Unit of the President. The hopelessly drunk driver of the carrier was found berating the three dead occupants of the two vehicles for the damage they had caused to his transport.

Some three years later, in late November 2001, Charles Taylor, caned his 13-year-old daughter in a Monrovian school. Accusing her of lacking discipline, he forced her to lie across a bench then beat her in front of a silent but seemingly approving audience of dozens of journalists. By way of explanation he stated that such an action was his duty to ensure 'the responsibility of nationhood will be passed onto reliable custodians'. The statesmanlike and paternalistic Charles Taylor was a busy man; part-owner of a US evangelical

TV station he, as a committed Baptist, liked to preach on the virtues of the Bible. Such words were seemingly incongruous while concomitantly a slave-owner and an alleged participant in the ritualized killings of human beings and subsequent cannibalistic practices. On a more leisurely level, he was a keen tennis player and had proclaimed himself the 'Chief Patron of Sport' a position that saw him direct public monies towards a variety of sports projects which he saw as useful to reconciliation and nation building.

A Sporting Chance?

Many people similarly believe that sport has an inherent property to integrate people at odds with each other or function as an antidote to social disorder. Certainly it can contribute to the quest for a shared identity but beyond this an observer may ask what is it exactly that sport is expected to promote? This begs the further question as to what state of existence or, to use a more fashionable term, what 'civil society' is it that a people, through sport, may wish to attain, share and sustain? In a post-war milieu we would do well to ask what it is that provides for a sense of national consciousness and where this can be most obviously witnessed. On first appearances, the game of football in Liberia could be said to be functional in this regard. As the national sport par excellence, football and the players that constitute the national team personify and sustain the idea of the nation. In times of victory for the national side the game is capable of evoking national pride and a sense of collective belonging.

The game has produced the most famous Liberian on earth in the person of George Weah. Known colloquially as 'The King' his footballing ability attracted the attentions of a Cameroonian club who took him from his homeland, at the age of 18, in 1987. Months later his mercurial abilities saw him transferred to Monaco and in later years he was to wear the shirts of Paris St Germain, AC Milan, Manchester City, Chelsea and Marseille. Twice afforded the accolade of European Footballer of the Year and once World Footballer of the Year, he was given the honorary titles of the International Federation of Football Associations (FIFA) Ambassador for Football and the United Nation, Economic, Social and Cultural Organization (UNESCO) Ambassador for Sport. He was thus, in the eyes of the world's footballing and cultural bodies, a man that represented all that was good in the game. He was a footballing force for good, originating from a society that brought only bad news to a Western media and was synonymous with the violation of human rights and dignity.

Assumed by many to be above politics and culturally neutral, sport is akin to a bubble separate from the baser instincts of humanity. Consequently, rhetoric about sport and human rights is available on both an institutional and common sense level. The Universal Declaration of Human Rights (Article 24) states that: 'everyone has the right to rest and leisure . . .'. Article 1 of the UNESCO International Charter states: 'the right to physical education and sport is fundamental for everybody'. Similarly, the Olympic Charter states: 'The practise of sport is a human right...' and '... sport in the service of the harmonious development of man, with a view to encouraging the establishment of a peaceful society concerned with the preservation of human dignity'.[1] Evaluation as to the validity of such rhetoric or the implementation of such an idea is very scarce.[2]

Sport need not correlate with human dignity. One could argue it is a pastime fraught with ideas of exclusion, elitism, militarism, ethno-political tension and used as a political vehicle the world over. More specifically one need ask; can the game of football stop conflict and induce dignity in its subjects? The unofficial peace that broke out for an hour or so around football in a few yards of the hundreds of miles of the no-man's lands of the First World War trenches may well be cited as evidence of the pacifying power of the game, but then one would have to forget that the Civil War in the former Yugoslavia began around the football match of 1991. For some the game dramatizes conflict and acts as a useful metaphor in place of the real conflict. But what can the game do in a place which is nihilistic?

Rights and Wrongs in the Land of the Free

Political upheaval in Liberia, beginning in the late 1970s, resulted in a civil conflict lasting between 1989 and 1997. The conflict was at times nihilistic in its practices and confused in both its origins and factions.[3] The conflict resulted in the death of 10 per cent of the population, i.e. circa 150,000 people, and the displacement of around a million people from a pre-conflict population of around 2.5 million both domestically and throughout West Africa.[4] The conflict touched upon the life of every Liberian, all knew someone or were close to someone murdered. To a military strategist the hostility was a guerrilla conflict fought by irregular armies using a range of weapons ranging from primitive machetes to state of the art machineguns. The combatants' demeanor and deportment was frequently one characterized by a dependence on a cocktail of drugs and alcohol, the bravado further enhanced by a pervasive belief in the mystic-induced powers of indigenous cults. These secular societies, prevalent among many ethnic groups in Liberia, are believed to invest spiritual powers in their followers and have been used for decades in conflict resolution.[5]

The enduring international image provided by TV footage was of boy soldiers carrying guns, at times almost the same size as them, while dressed in a bizarre variety of looted clothing which at times included women's dresses and wigs. The logic that informed the combatants will never be known, suffice to say that the conflict was to a Western audience atrocious in its brutality yet highly theatrical.[6] Around 10 per cent (15,000) of the combatants were aged 15 or under, the victors – the National Patriotic Front of Liberia (NPFL) led by Charles Taylor–even had a Small Boys Unit containing armed combatants as young as eight.[7] When hostilities ended, the former combatants and civilians had to come to terms with a plethora of personal traumas provided by, variously; bereavement, rape, torture, mutilation and witness to massacre. Then came the added problems of starvation and malnutrition not forgetting mass displacement and homelessness.

In the turbulent history of post-colonial Africa, Liberia, the oldest Republic on the continent, was regarded by the more naive of political analysts-ignorant of the dominant role of the Finestone Rubber Corporation – as a beacon of light, untainted as it was by white colonial rule. This political history, unique to the continent, explains both Liberia's decades of relative political stability and the ferocity of the conflict once the existing civil society broke down. The initial 100 years of relative stability was due in no small degree to its never having been the colony of a European power. Instead, Liberia was able to preserve its independent status and nomenclature as the 'Negro Republic of Liberia'. This status arose out of a form of colonialism which had its origins some 3,000 miles away in the United States where the 1790s abolition of slavery in the northern states saw immediate freedom offered to over 160,000 Africans, a figure that would rise to 250,000 by the 1820s. Freedom, however, did not come accompanied with economic assistance and the ensuing racial tensions and periodic revolts of those who remained in conditions of indenture, in the state of Virginia, inspired the local political elite to seek to repatriate the former slaves. Those that boarded ships to Africa and survived the journey were taken to the West Coast and the land that was to become Liberia.[8]

At the constitutional level, human rights were integral to the foundation of this nation. Adopting a model of the US Constitution in 1847 saw a nation governed by replica institutions but a disregard for the philosophy of the Founding Fathers. A Senate and House of Representatives headed by a President and Cabinet became the preserve of the newly arrived (or returned) people who were to become known then, and even 150 years later, as Americo-Liberians. However, the neo-colonialism of the Americo-Liberians subjected the indigenous 90 per cent of the population, consisting of 16 ethnic groups, to their political whims which were to see them emulate that which they were subject to in the USA, namely slavery. This time, however, the 'settlers' enslaved the indigenous people on their plantations. The latter in varying degrees of contempt referred to the new arrivals as 'Congo-people' a term that derives from the fact that such people originated from the Congo and were among the cargoes sent into slavery in the Americas. The term has become more pervasive in the late 1970s and 1980s in preference to the previously more used Americo-Liberians. The minority was to dominate the political, economic, judicial and social life of Liberia for the next 130 years in their Metropolitan society modelled on the southern states of the US.[9] Human Rights had little influence in this strange society.

Liberia has been one party state for all its history.[10] For the Liberian social scientist, Stephen Jubwe, the formation of Liberia has been characterized by a constant struggle along the lines of race and class.[11] The issue is a clash of two cultures – settler and indigenous – which has manifested itself periodically in ethnic uprisings against the neo-colonialists' central government mostly around issues of land ownership.[12] The settlers colonized via mercantile expansion imposing a monetary economy on the indigenous people. This paved the way for modernization and its consequences: rural-urban migration; a reserve army of labour; slum living; disruption of family structures and the alienation of the majority from the land.[13] The class struggle was between 1944 and 1971 a contest between indigenous versus settler, since then the struggle has been characterized between conflict internal to the indigenous peoples.[14] It took until 1944 when William Tubman assumed the role of President before the exclusivity of the ruling class was lessened. In a rule lasting until 1971 Tubman encouraged other ethnicities to become involved in politics. The same man permitted foreign capital to exploit resources in the hinterland using indigenous labour. Concomitantly, despite his sloganeering he restricted the educational opportunities of those ethnic groups he did not like.[15]

From 1870 to 1980 politics was controlled by the True Whig party who managed to pass on the Presidency without any threat to their political hegemony. This tranquility ended in 1971 when Tubman was succeeded by his former Vice-President, William Tolbert, who presided in a dictatorial manner[16] and met his demise in 1980 when disemboweled in his bed by 17 soldiers during Liberia's first military coup. Taking control of government was Master Sergeant Samuel Doe who assumed the role of the armed forces Commander-in-Chief. From the renowned warring ethnic group called the Krahn, Doe became the country's first indigenous President in 1986 following rigged elections. The ensuing years of Doe's rule saw widespread corruption, economic decline and violence merited on political opponents. His reign did not fundamentally alter the socio-economic system nor integrate people. Instead it produced a 'militarized ethnicity' and yet more stratification in a stratified society.[17] The fall of Doe was inevitable but his murder on the beach by Prince Johnson and the subsequent parading of the dead man's head around the city unleashed a variety of hitherto latent ethnic tensions.

The Theatre of the War Child

Without a doubt the dislike of the government had taken an ethnic angle but other factors were as significant.[18] It has been argued[19] that an over-centralized state following a failed coup attempt on Doe in 1985 resulted in pogroms against those he perceived as his ethnic opponents.[20] This produced an over-representation of Krahn people (a mere 5 per cent of the population) in positions of power.[21] In these paranoid times the over-concern with security was detrimental to the economy and the good years that characterized the country from the mid 1950s began to crumble 30 years later particularly when the labourers' jobs in the plantations ended. In the ensuing unemployment and hardships Stephen Ellis argues that war became thinkable.[22]

A civil war began in December 1986 originating in the district known as Nimba County adjacent to the border with the Ivory Coast. A multi-ethnic militia, numbering 209, trained in Libya and titled the National Patriotic Front of Liberia (NPFL) was led by Charles Taylor. Seeking to overthrow the dictatorship of Doe, the conflict took on dimensions of ethnicity: the Mano and Ghio people were fighting the Krahn of Doe. This ethnic division continued even after the murder (captured on video) of Doe in September 1990 after prolonged torture at the hands of his captors.[23] Following his death the conflict became confused as a variety of individuals claimed to be the new head of state. Seeking the precise cause of the subsequent conflict is impossible.

Religious belief had an understated role to play in what was to follow. The population is nominally two-thirds Christian, 14 per cent Muslim and 18 per cent traditional African. The traditional societies, found in abundance outside of the capital, meant that people looked to religious leaders to solve their problems and not politicians. Furthermore, the fighting took on the characteristics of a country that had little by way of industrial production and mercantile capitalism. Unable to move easily and distant geographically, politically, and morally, from the government, meant that people looked to strong leaders in times of distress or threat. As a consequence when armed conflict began a variety of 'Big Men' were to assume the role of faction leaders or, if one prefers, 'warlords'. Ideology seemed to play second string to economic opportunity. At one time no fewer than eight rival factions existed who were to make various alliances only to break them. Some have argued[24] that these individuals could be termed 'military entrepreneurs' because while in part they were motivated by a form of tribal-based ideology they primarily sought a share in the profits of the diamond, iron-ore and timber trades that found a market from the British and French who traded throughout the war.[25] This very rational economic motivation was combined with traditional forces of indigenous cults and the secret societies, which were the major form of rural political activity and law enforcement.

Democracy and Human Rights?

Once a useful Cold War listening post and aircraft base, the US was tolerant of decades of Liberian governments who treated the indigenous people appallingly. After the US military left, the politics of Liberia sank to new depths of depravity. In truth, the US had no desire to get involved in Liberian affairs. Its involvement in the immediate post-war decades was more about strategic and military considerations in the Cold War than the politics of 'development'. The US government supported the regime of Doe despite the rigged elections and brutal politics he perpetrated. When the conflict began in 1990, the US was stretched by the Gulf War and was thus not willing to deploy troops. The only troops that landed did so to evacuate US nationals. The arrival in the 1990s of some 11,000 neighbourhood 'peacekeepers' in the shape of ECOMOG (Community of West African States Armed Monitoring Group) troops saw them secure the country for the benefit of the 1997 election but at times shoot suspects at random, make full use of child prostitutes, assist in the looting of state utilities, and supply arms to rebel leaders in exchange for diamonds.

Following 12 peace accords and 25 ceasefires, the conflict formally ceased in July 1997 following an election contested by 13 candidates. Charles Taylor won with a landslide 75 per cent majority;[26] the 49-year-old Taylor assumed the role of President. The educated and the rich fled the country and Taylor governed via a personalized and completely de-institutionalized political network.[27] Shortly after, in October 1997, the Liberian government established the National Human Rights Commission, composed of representatives from five non-governmental organizations (NGOs). Groups that had spoken out about abuses by Taylor's forces in the conflict were excluded. Charged with promoting and protecting human rights, they began their task a month after UN observers had left the country. Established in 1993, by the UN Security Council to monitor the Peace Accord in conjunction with EGOMOG forces, the three individuals who constituted this mission were to report violations of human rights directly to the UN Secretary-General. Neither this body nor the newly established Commission could prevent detention without trial, torture in custody and politically inspired executions.[28]

In 1999 Taylor and his ministers accused human rights groups of promoting publicity that was detrimental to the economy. The publicizing of forced child labour and the abduction of political opponents saw the withholding of international financial aid.[29] Two NGO personnel were taken to court by Taylor – others faced intimidation by security forces. In the post-election society, people were murdered on the orders of Taylor, the wider hostilities which had never actually ended came to the fore in 2003 when six months of fighting saw around 10,000 Liberians lose their lives and another million become either displaced persons or refugees. Once again the forces of Charles Taylor included child soldiers as did the insurgent militia known as Liberians United for the Restoration of Democracy (LURD) a coalition of some 18 anti-Taylor groups. Combat in the streets of Monrovia destroyed much of what had been achieved over the previous four years.

The UN dithered for months before a Security Council vote authorized a multi-national force to enter Liberia in late July with a view to giving way to a UN peace-keeping force some two months later.[30] A small group of US military personnel entered the city to ensure the safe passage of US citizens. George Bush, somewhat ironically considering his war in Iraq in spite of a UN mandate, spoke of the need for a UN mandate in Liberia which would allow him to not deploy US troops on the ground but to have them provide logistical support to regional peacekeepers. Weeks later, military peacekeepers from West African countries entered Monrovia. Their presence and pressure from the UN, the European Union (EU) and the US produced a meeting between the rival forces in Accra, Ghana.

Facing military defeat, Charles Taylor resigned in August and now resides with his family and an entourage of around 100 in protective custody/house-arrest in Calabar, Southern Nigeria. The victorious factions agreed to replace him with a Liberian businessman who was to head a transitional government, which was expected to yield to an elected government in 2005. If this was a local version of the New World Order, we might at this moment step back and ask what happened to previous attempts to make the world a better place.[31]

Rights, Wrongs and Rhetorics

The 1948 Universal Declaration of Human Rights (UDHR) came in response to the barbarity of the Second World War and the decade that preceded it. It was also a product of the rise of the nation state. Drafted by Christians, Muslims, Confucianists, Liberals, Socialists, Social Democrats, Communists and signed by 48 countries, it became one of the most agreed upon documents on earth. Implicit in the ideology of Human Rights is a belief in the innate moral worth needed to fulfil human potential. Some 150 years previously, the American and European declarations of the Rights of Man (Thomas Paine) and Rights of the Citizen (Thomas Jefferson) accredited the *person* as the focus of rights in the face of the potentially arbitrary authority available to the Church and State. However, one could favour the notion of Rights as a *collective* entity applicable to groups even to the extent of national population, a thinking that informs the two United Nations Human Rights Covenants of 1986; the Economic Social and Cultural Rights and the Civil and Political Rights. Enshrined in both is the belief that all *people* have the right to self-determination. The 1981 African Charter on Human and *Peoples* Rights exemplifies this.

Various philosophical doctrines are enshrined in the idea of rights. The philosophers of the ancient Greeks and Romans spoke of 'right behaviour'. Not all seek origins in antiquity, for some rights are a Western philosophical idea bound up in the Magna Carta and the seventeenth-century moral philosophy of John Locke who spoke of rights and duties stating: 'No-one should harm another in his life, liberty and possessions.' Some philosophies reject outright the notion of rights. The Utilitarian, Jeremy Bentham, argued that man has been born into subjection and was not equal in rights due to a dependency on parents and the inevitability of hierarchies. Only from codified law did any sense of rights arise. Similarly, eighteenth century philosopher Edmund Burke saw Rights as a product of 'entailed inheritance' arising out of specific socio-political conventions and therefore not a universally agreed upon entity.

Some 50 years later, Karl Marx considered the Rights of Man arising out of the French Revolution as a bourgeois ideal enshrined in competitive individualism and exploitative capitalism. Justice and morality are thus not universally agreed upon principles. Inseparable from the notion of rights are ideas around the exercises of power, which means any analysis of human rights needs to locate the enquiry within the technologies of state violence, legal systems, social classifications and ideas of self in relation to others. One can, by virtue of being the subject of a nation state, 'have' rights but not necessarily enjoy the very rights that your leaders have signed up to. Indeed, Western governments are very flexible on human rights and conveniently overlook abuses when it suits them politically and economically. Notions of personhood and identity are crucial to any debate on human rights.

Saving the Children?

International conventions are written and agreed upon with the aim of protecting children from all forms of physical and mental violence, exploitation, harmful occupations and imprisonment (barring exceptional circumstances). But one problem immediately arises when one realizes that there is no universally agreed upon definition of what constitutes a child. Childhood is culturally specific and many cultures the world over – particularly those in poverty – have little time for the concept of extended youth and cannot conceive of young people as beyond political, economic and military obligations. Most legal standards agree that a child is defined as anyone under the age of 18 including the African Charter on the Rights and Welfare of the Child. Until 2002, the 1989 Convention on the Rights of the Child had set a minimum age of 15 for child combatants. An optional protocol to the UN's Convention on the Rights of the Child (Children's Conventions) was introduced in January 2000 which sets 18 as the minimum age for military conscription. Liberia did not sign up to the protocol.[32] However, in 1999 the Liberian government at the African Conference on the Use of Child Soldiers stated its commitment to an age of 18 for participation in armed conflict. During the post-conflict situation, in Liberia in 1997, attempts sponsored by the UN to demobilize the combatants were slow and the majority of the estimated 15,000–20,000 child combatants were believed, over the following six years, to have returned to the militias awaiting the next military scenario.

The Children's Convention (Article 19) obliges states to protect children from physical and mental violence, injury, abuse, neglect, maltreatment and exploitation regardless of whose care they are in. Furthermore, Article 37 requests that the state seek to eradicate violence in the home, school and workplace. But such fine words are not enforceable. Implementation of the Children's Convention is monitored by the Committee on the Rights of the Child to which governments are obliged to report within two years of ratifying the treaty. The Committee in principle hears evidence from concerned parties and can recommend policy, in effect it monitors the nations that sign the Convention but does not have a procedure to hear or investigate individual cases of abuse. They can, however, meet government officials and review the work of signatories, but can only suggest 'concluding observations' for improvements.

The Committee has stated that corporal punishment is 'incompatible' with the Children's Convention, which specifies that children should be protected from 'all forms of physical or mental violence'. The UN Commission on Human Rights (Resolution 43, April 2000) stated that corporal punishment '... can amount to cruel, inhuman or degrading punishment'. But who, when the President of the nation recruits boy soldiers, murders opponents and perpetrates an act of corporal punishment on his daughter, will enforce the protocols? Furthermore, in the fog of war who will ask soldiers for their birth certificates? Even at the cessation of hostilities if there is a case to answer for the death and maiming of child combatants does blame lie with the politicians who declared war? The militia recruitment system, Or the commanding officers of the units both regular and irregular the child soldiers belonged to?

The End of Innocence

It could be argued that the words expressed in the above rhetoric had little validity in the Liberian context. Liberia was always a militarized society and its children were subject to brutality from many sources. In the analysis of Swedish anthropologist, Mats Utas, these were major contributions to the civil conflict. Racism, unemployment, economic exploitation and a decaying infrastructure created a massive stratum of disaffected youth for whom the militias and the conflict gave them the opportunity for individual agency. They were thus able to challenge tradition, in the shape of both the politically powerful urban leadership, and the restraints of the traditional *Poro* and *Sande* secret societies gerontocracy that demarcated the male passage to adulthood.[33]

In militias, young men ceased to be marginal and consequently the majority of fighters took up arms voluntarily in pursuit of social and economic mobility. As a consequence, looting became an aim in itself manifest in individualized competition for the limited items of modernity that Liberia held. Immediate financial gain could be earned from protection money extorted from fearful adults. A gun barrel brought power over elders and the company of females as concubines.[34] In controlling their lives they controlled space, but the levels of violence required went beyond what might be termed 'legitimate' to that which can only be described as atrocious. One might equate the term 'youth' as denoting a suppressed citizen with a dependency on elders. At the same time, the term 'rebel' applied by the elders to the personnel that constituted the militias is not as pejorative as the accuser might imagine, signifying, to those so labelled, agency above dependency.

One could blame the parents. A massive use of violence in child-rearing was a characteristic of Liberia.[35] Childhood was controlled by the violence threatened and actual of the secret societies. Away from the *rites de passage* children were given labouring duties and beatings (often in public) to illustrate culturally sanctioned ownership. The educational system was characterized by physical beatings and the prevalence of children living with foster parents and other non-kin family structures did not come with any promises of decent treatment. Perhaps it is no coincidence that many children in such domestic arrangements ran to join the militias.[36]

Traditional rural authority was located within the war-chief, accompanied by his warriors, and celebrated in the distribution of the spoils of war. His entourage always consisted of children, the young were expected to fight and partake of human sacrifice and cannibalistic practices.[37] But tradition, in the shape of the *Poro*, sought accommodation and stability above conflict.[38] Ironically, the efforts of the Liberian settlers and the Christian missionaries to control the influence of such elders paved the way for the power of the war-chiefs (who were often at loggerheads with the *Poro*) and ultimately armed youth rebellion. The elders in high (urban) political office offered little by way of an alternative moral guidance. From their first landing, the settlers were involved in acts of war with the peoples of the hinterland. Via the badly trained and undisciplined personnel of the Liberian Frontier Force the indigenous peoples who survived their murderous forays suffered sporadic looting, rape and extortion. But the state's military personnel held an appeal to disaffected youth in that it offered mobility via a wage and a chance to start anew away from tradition. Furthermore, the chance to carry a gun signified a commitment to modernity. War signified inclusion in the wider society.[39]

Positive adult role models from beyond the nation's boundaries were equally hard to come by. The virtual heroes of Hollywood bad boys provided fascination and imitation in nomenclature and style.[40] Thus one could witness the personal militia of Charles Taylor wearing the tie-dye blue camouflage uniforms (inappropriate to the Liberian military context) accompanied by the simply essential wrap-around reflector sunshades as they carried their rocket-launchers, hanging on to the sides of their Mercedes vehicles. Their football team, named Watanga after the barracks they lived in and worked out of and which was synonymous with torture and death, was a name borrowed from a Hollywood film. Such aspects of modernity combined with the sub-cultural kudos offered by the urban 'rascal boy' persona working in the plantations and mines, and the 'homeboy cosmopolitan' manifest by an urban individualism complete with drug use and commodity possession.[41] Central to both the political and military narratives was the belief that good leaders were ruthless. Not for nothing was the President known as Charles *Gankey* (Strong Man) Taylor. The admiration for ruthlessness did not make concessions to concepts around human rights.

Suffer the Children: Salesians of Don Bosco

Challenging such notions of masculinity and child-rearing was not going to be an easy task, but there were willing adults who hoped to offer Liberian youth an alternative way of living. Inspired by Christianity, a variety of brave men sought to make a difference bolstered by the knowledge that elsewhere in time their founder had done precisely that. The Salesian Society (originally the Society of St Frances de Sales) was founded in 1859 by Don Bosco in Turin, Italy. Basing his principles and those of the society on the ethos developed by St Francis of Sales (1567–1622) as a model of apostolic dedication and loving kindness, Don Bosco (1815–88) sought to serve the needs of the poor and abandoned young people. Energetic and charismatic the priest Don Bosco was moved by the plight of the destitute children, visiting them in prison and organizing elementary schooling for child factory workers. Scholarly yet capable of brawling, he established orphanages and tried to inculcate marketable skills in the children he looked after via education and evangelization based on the Oratory wherein each was made welcome, valued and encouraged to give and receive. In response, a group of neighbours tried to have him committed to a mental institution. His belief was that work and skills prevented social evils and to this end avoided involvement in the political upheavals evident in Turin. He was to open the first printing school in Europe in 1861 as well as trade and agriculture schools, and in 1869 provided education for young girls under the control of the Confraternity of Daughters of Mary, Help of Christians. His pedagogic methods were revolutionary, at the time, for their liberal and fun-centred approach to learning and informed child education techniques throughout the twentieth century.The French author

Victor Hugo considered him a legend and his legacy today is a religious order active in over 150 countries.[42]

The style of the Mission, which first entered Liberia in 1979 with the aim of preaching and converting, bears little resemblance to the work carried out by the late 1990s. Since 1979 some 17 Salesians have worked in Liberia; by 2001 only four remained. The primary aim between 1979 and 1989 was to build educational institutes; thus the Arthur Barclay Technical Institute was opened in 1988, shortly after the Don Bosco Polytechnic with five colleges and a high school in Tappita, Nimba County. However the civil war, beginning in 1989, changed the *raison d'être* of the Salesian Mission. Over the following decade, the Salesian personnel were among a handful of white Westerners who did not evacuate Liberia. Sustaining their mission they faced both looters and the barrels of guns. They also collected and buried hundreds of war dead. When the conflict ended the Salesian personnel realized that the educational content of their mission had to take second place to rescuing children. The surviving children were not homogenous in their needs. Some were ex-combatants who knew nothing about co-existence and everything about killing. Some had not seen war but were orphaned as a consequence of it and some were also the victims of war indirectly, in being abandoned when adults fled. The problem of street children was magnified by parents who refused to have their children back at the end of hostilities believing that they, namely the children, had perpetuated the war and were thus bad people.

The Don Bosco project had in the early days of the civil conflict promoted attempts at reconciliation through sport. After 1997 the Bosco project continued this idea, but introduced a child protection unit that existed concomitantly with the promotion of football clubs. Such processes were the efforts of two remarkable men. Working and living with the Salesian Mission in Liberia in 1988 was a Salesian-educated teacher of physical education by the name of Sean Devereux. Leaving a teaching job in Surrey, he volunteered to work in a Salesian school in Liberia for two years. Dynamic, opinionated and courageous, he was able to entertain hundreds of children with his skills as a magician and, at times, as a bingo caller. The civil conflict, which began a year after his arrival, eventually saw the Salesian school evacuated; shortly he joined the UN as a food and logistics consultant.

Establishing athletics meetings, Devereux obtained UN funding for an athletics tournament held at the National Stadium in 1991, which saw ECOMOG forces officiate. Establishing two football teams, he promoted football tournaments, which saw the combatants lay down their arms for the duration of the games. His philosophy was that sport might provide an alternative career to the militia; however, he was to leave Liberia in 1992 having been expelled from neighbouring Guinea when voicing his disgust at the misappropriation of UN foods by police and soldiers. In September 1992 he joined the United Nations International Children's Emergency Fund (UNICEF) in Somalia. Four months later, at the age of 29, he was shot dead by an unknown assassin.[43] Thankfully there were others prepared to continue the pursuit of reconciliation.

By July 2001 a football club scheme, begun by accident by the Reverend Joe ('Father Joe') Glackin, had grown to accommodate 116 neighbourhood teams in Monrovia and its suburbs. This Scottish-born 40-year-old Salesian missionary had lived in Liberia for a decade. His professed ignorance of the world game was of little hindrance to his being nicknamed 'Pappy (Father/Patron) Sport' by his legion of local admirers. In an attempt to occupy the children of the Bosco projects during daytime hours, Fr Joe acquired a football and a set of football shirts. From such a small acorn grew a football club, the Bosco United Sports Association (BUSA) that entered the Liberian First Division within two years of its founding. Nursery teams followed and then a neighbourhood network of feeder teams. In its origins, the team stressed the value of self-help and demanded self-discipline from all players. Miscreants, be they drug users, violent thieves or rapists, were thrown out of the club. It was thus necessarily exclusive in its pursuit of inclusiveness. The rewards for inclusion were not financial – only travel expenses were paid. Instead, in a society of displaced people, the squad was both a surrogate family and a resource network.

The Bosco projects promoted multifarious tasks and football was only one strand of an extensive network of agencies and ambitions. One of the central aims of the Bosco Child Protection philosophy was reconciliation. The crux of this was in their attempts to re-unify and reconcile the children with the families that had abandoned them. As Father Joe explained to me:

> We have nowhere to place the child in what might be termed a place of safety. For better or worse they return to the home and the adult. It would be ideal to have sheltered accommodation and surrogate parents and counselling and intervention for victims and assailants, but that would require a total overhaul of the economic system of Liberia.

When this was not possible the next step was to help such children discover their own potential, to empower them from dependencies or handouts. To achieve these aims the Salesians established three organizations under the banner of 'Don Bosco Programmes'.

The first, founded in 1991, dealt with community rehabilitation and skills training and was a joint initiative with UNICEF. Aimed at those aged between late teens to mid-twenties, the workshop-based programme aimed to teach marketable skills vital in rebuilding the country (carpentry, masonry, agriculture, plumbing, electrics and car mechanics).[44]

The second scheme, Don Bosco Homes, was founded in 1992 for the protection of children between the age of four and 19. Located in three sites in Monrovia, the aim was to offer night shelters to the orphaned, the unaccompanied and the abandoned either because parents could not afford to feed them or, in the case of one disfigured eight-year-old because, his father had thrown him on a fire accusing him of being possessed by witches. Among these were some ex-combatants and others who existed by a life of crime. The shelters offered a place of safety with an adult acting as a house master; the daytime would see the children depart to their various activities only to return for food and shelter as night fell. The night shelters offered a safe place for recreation and elementary counselling. They were soon followed by the establishment of transit homes, wherein family tracing and unification was pursued.[45]

Out of this system came WAYS – War-Affected Youth Support – funded by UNICEF which paid for outreach workers. Such workers establish good relations with the police to the extent of buying them ledgers to track those detained. Individuals under the care of the Bosco projects were given an identity card to show when approached by adults whose intentions may not have been honourable. The Bosco 'ownership' of such children also meant that if arrested by police aid might be available. Outreach workers would visit daily the 20 police depots in Monrovia to intervene on behalf of any arrested child. By 1998 Don Bosco Homes had chaperonage of some 500 street children; however they were just a drop in the ocean.

The third strand to the programmes was the Don Bosco Youth Centre. Built in 1991, located in Matadi and funded by the Catholic charity, Caritas Sweden.[46] Five programmes operated weekly. The first concerned recreation and sport and was used daily by up to 200 who would play kickball (rounders played with a football with the pitcher bowling underarm to feet) – the Don Bosco Queens were established in 1998. A football team was established in 1992, and by 1996 the Don Bosco Knights were in Division Three of the Liberian Football Association League. Male and female volleyball and basketball teams and table tennis and board games were also established. Christianity and civic awareness were also promoted via Bible reading and hymn singing. That known as 'cultural troupe', promoted theatre, dance and music, while 'mini skills' aimed to promote marketable skills – for example sewing and typing for women. The women's development programme, aimed specifically at war widows, sought to instil self-reliance via the UNICEF-funded scheme which taught small business skills, AIDS awareness, basic literacy, hygiene and hairdressing.[47] Such long-term development projects showed some signs of success, but immediate direct action was at times required for children in danger. In addressing these issues football and child protection became partners.

Saving the Children

The Child Protection Unit (CPU), operating under the title of the Auxiliary Unit of the Don Bosco Projects, and that known colloquially as the Rapid Response Unit, were formed from a group of outreach workers who would visit any home or prison at the slightest behest to help, what was believed to be, a child in distress or danger. When not involved in such action-oriented activities, the personnel would disseminate child awareness programmes to educate people in the basic rights of a child and, at the same time, encourage reports to its office that were perceived to concern the well-being of children. As Father Joe explained:

> We come to learn about a case . . . it could be violence or sexual abuse. We call it counselling, but it's not, it's advice. Many a child will face adults who for the first time will talk to them. Asking them how they felt about a situation and what happened and ask them did you realise this was wrong? We then send workers to confront the offending adult and inform the community. The community will normally say we suspected something was going on but did not know who to tell. We tell them what we've discovered and the miscreant has to face them and apologise and promises not to do it again. Then there's two things we can do. One is send a worker to the home daily to speak to the child to see that they are not suffering repeated assaults. The other is to warn the neighbours that should such activities be repeated the police will be drawn in and the resultant court case could make their neighbourhood look very bad.

By 2002 the football programme had developed to the extent that some 120 people were employed by the project and 4,500 children were identified as part of the protection scheme. The philosophy behind the work of Fr Joe was to protect all children at risk and, once they were secure in the relative safety of the various Bosco projects,[48] engage them in the language of the rights of the child in many cases via football. This required good local people to implement, one of whom was Rob.

Muscular and tattooed, Rob was a longterm Monrovian resident in his late twenties. With a booming voice and lacking any form of social embarrassment, Rob was street-wise and comfortable in any social situation. He had his own observations on the scheme and its methodology, telling me: 'to get anywhere with young people in Liberia, you need to use sport. Football is the gateway; everybody wants to be like George Weah'. I spent three days in Monrovia with Rob who now had the title of Community Supervisor, having formerly been a street outreach worker. His line managers were two Liberians, Brother Paul, the executive director of Don Bosco Homes and Joe Hena in charge of Outreach. The two had held their positions from 1997 until 2003.

The former was also President of the BUSA football club. Rob had been a footballer at the highest level in Liberia before an injury ended his career. Having learned of the Child Protection Unit he applied to join. The only job available, however, was for an office assistant, which he took, eventually being promoted to police depots visitor after attending three day workshops, operated by the Young Men's Christian Association (YMCA), Don Bosco Youth Centre and Don Bosco Homes, which gave instruction on how to work with children in difficult situations. School-based study produced for Rob a diploma in social work.[49]

Aware and informed, Rob explained the multiplicity of problems the children of Monrovia faced:

> Some have homes and families but the parents don't want them. Many are ex-combatants, in the past they would rob and steal and were rich, now they have nothing. Some live as pickpockets, others indulge in black taboo – selling stolen and false gear . . .The war changed so much . . . for some love and tenderness towards kids is a luxury they cannot spare in their effort to survive. Adults don't value kids. Parents can't afford in many cases to look after them. Then in the war many kids handled huge amounts of money and can't cope with living at home with parents anymore. . . . some youths had women ten years older than them when behind the lines. But they didn't save, they took what they could and lavished it . . .

Walking me around Monrovia and its suburbs I was to witness the appalling living conditions that tens of thousands of adults and children had to live in; conditions in which some children succumb to drink and drugs as a relief from their wretched state. The supply of locally brewed gin is plentiful (and cheap) and youngsters will mix the drink with an intake of marijuana, opium and at times crack cocaine. The locally produced 'dutel' powder provided for hallucinogenic experiences and pills colloquially known as 'bubbles' produces a similar effect. Those seeking an honest approach to acquiring wealth faced various forms of abuse. The most obvious is sexual and, indeed, that termed 'money love' could see young girls selling their bodies for less than one US dollar a time. Boys were not public about payments for sexual congress such is the stigma of homosexuality, but were witnessed daily and publically involved in a variety of labour practices which to Western eyes were dreadfully exploitative. Thus, children would break rocks for unscrupulous builders at a rate of pay one sixth that an adult would demand. Others fetched water and staggered with large buckets to homes which they were then instructed to clean. Others carried building blocks – three children cost the same as one adult. In this milieu, leisure activities like football are a luxury many cannot afford. However, the work of the Salesians brought leisure (and football) to thousands of Monrovian children and, via this seductive and 'acceptable' medium, an introduction to the elementary ideas behind the Rights of the Child. Such an initiative required considerable local knowledge.

A New Ball Game

Some degree of order was required to make such a project manageable. Seeking logic and quasi-structure in what resembles chaotic neighbourhoods was, to this observer, beyond hope. Yet locals told me of how the populace demarcated itself and were in some instances very clear as to who did (or did not) live in their community. The defined communities were facilitated to an extent by 1997 post-conflict food shortage. This had resulted in a UN-sponsored post-war food distribution programme. Areas appointed a committee to receive food and answer census inquiries. As Rob explained '... people would divide into blocks. People knew where they lived.'

Outreach workers on finding groups of children kicking a ball on elementary surfaces would approach them and leave leaflets informing them of the Bosco programme promising to return days later. At other times local groups would inform the project of their existence, a community worker would then visit the location to verify that a football team existed. As Rob explained:

> You would go down there and explain yourself – to whoever – but you verify by asking the name of the team to a player. Then you would observe them practising and call the player over and privately ask 'who are you? Does your team exist and for how long?' From there you would find the coach, then liaise with the community leader or the chief.

A football is the key to the existence of the neighbourhood team found in Seytown a mile outside of Monrovia near the Salesian Mission, which had taken the name Savio Pro in honour of Dominic Savio the second saint of the Salesians. The football was kept in the home of the team manager and brought out for the thrice weekly training sessions. The Club President once played in the highest division of Liberian football, but left the game to study law only to leave law due to an absence of funding. His employment for the previous two years as a security guard for a Don Bosco premise had recently ended. He was thus out of work, similar to the team manager who occupied his day 'taking care of the youth here'. Central to this self-appointed pastoral duty was his team which attracted players mainly from the immediate area but also, in a few cases, from up to three miles away. 'Because we need to be open to all people' and furthermore 'maybe they'll learn from us and go back to their area and start a team.'

The Club itself – in existence for just a year – consisted of a squad of 20 boys aged 12 to 15 who would train on a flat sandy pitch located in the centre of the neighbourhood. Each of the players held an identity card with a photograph stapled on with personal details listed, which satisfied the requirements of the sub-committee of the Liberian Football Association that operated the league such neighbourhood football clubs are affiliated to. A set of 16 jerseys followed the arrival of the ball paid by what Rob termed 'a friend of the neighbourhood' who was a friend of the son of the Minister of Education. The Vice-President, an unemployed economics graduate, explained to me how the set-up worked:

> The President, myself and the first team's coach and assistant meet in the home of the President weekly. Players call there too to discuss disciplinary matters or to suggest tactics and how to develop the team.

By virtue of being older than the squad the four have a degree of culturally inbred authority which they are careful not to abuse:

> Those who quarrel at training don't need harsh words. You tell them, 'Don't fight a brother. The goal is to play football.' We tell them 'If you are strong in unity, success is assured.' And we remind them to be proud of their team, their community and other people.

But what of the recalcitrants and those who would steal or cheat?

> They'd be suspended and told that charity begins at home. If you're bad out there you must change once here. We ask them to behave like a footballer. We try to impart what we've learned from the Don Bosco project, we owe it to them. It's like football, you receive it and pass it on to the next man.

His words made sense, but his was a project that was up and running and seemingly successful. What could an inquisitor find about the processes of emerging teams? An answer came days later when I met with Rob. He had discovered a youth football team in its evolution on the outskirts of Monrovia. Knowing that they met daily in the late afternoon he took me to see the set up. Having requisitioned a corner of a communal piece of land that was basically water-logged sand and tall grass, the team consisted of both male and female youngsters held together by two coaches in their late teens, one male the other female. Yet to establish an identity via a name, the football practice was more a matter of structuring the day and giving both adults and children something to look forward to. The coaches were educated to high school level but both were without work. The children, by contrast, had various 'occupations' most of which involved 'selling' and 'hustling', terms that covered a host of activities ranging from walking the streets with a tray of boiled eggs to sell to hungry by-passers, to selling T-shirts from a street barrow, to selling water in polythene bags. Such pursuits could see children (male and female) walking the streets for hours. Not all could guarantee to make it in time for training. A further problem for those with little was obtaining the items that footballers needed, such as playing kit and football boots. The latter were prohibitively expensive and could cost more than many an adult made in weeks of work or selling.

Once discovered, such clubs were encouraged to remain and expand. To this end the Bosco project donated a football. The process, however, had a mantra which Rob explained: 'we don't sponsor, we donate'. Repeat contact between Rob and the coached eventually resulted in an invite to the club to attend a day programme at a youth centre owned by Don Bosco programmes in Monrovia. The players and officials were collected and returned in a Don Bosco minivan alongside up to ten other teams from other neighbourhoods. A day seminar presented by various workers combined lectures on child rights using drama and dance with the incentives of free food and a football competition to end the day, wherein more footballs were made available to the victors. The pedagogic content sought to inform all present on what rights they had as children and that which they must not tolerate. In turn they were instructed in what behaviours they ideally would manifest as responsible citizens. From such contact future football fixtures were arranged and the sprawling neighbourhoods of Monrovia became personalized and more manageable. The outreach work would continue in future weeks with workers visiting the teams to seek feedback on the day and to remind them to inform the Don Bosco programme about mistreatment of children. Mistreated children were, sadly, a regular feature of Monrovian life, and their safety and survival was often dependent on the existence of a local football club and the Bosco project's Child Protection Unit.

Tackled from Behind

Rob was often at the forefront of interventions to protect children in danger from adults. One case he dealt with concerned a child who received burn wounds as a product of his stepmother's anger and desperation. Tasked daily with selling cake made by her, the boy would walk the streets with the cake tray on his head selling the product by the slice. On a good day this enterprise could produce a daily income of US$2. One day, however, torrential rain soaked the cake as the child used the tray as a shelter. Such momentary negligence resulted in permanent disfigurement upon his returning home when his furious stepmother took his hand and, intending to teach him a lesson, forced it into the baking oven. Neighbours witnessed this act and were alerted by the screams of the distressed child. Unsure of who to turn to for redress some neighbours contacted the football coach of the community team. The coach informed the community leader who contacted Rob. The three paid the mother a visit. Met with her abuse they fell back on the argument that the child was not biologically hers and she had no right to conduct such punishment. The meeting was not considered a success so the next day Rob took the initiative and found the person closest to the stepmother. This was a female relative whom he informed of events and who accompanied him to the stepmother's home. Introducing himself a second time, his protestations met with a response from the stepmother that his organization was spoiling the children of Liberia. In response Rob asked if the loss of a few dollars of cake profit merited burning the hand of a small boy?

The ensuing logic explained to me by Rob was not the height of Western liberal thinking on the status of children. He agreed that the child deserved punishment – but not to the extent of burning. The stepmother was reluctant to discuss the issue further and demanded he leave. A more collective action was thus required which involved religion, shame and football. Rob explained the circumstances:

> As I'm leaving one of the neighbours tells me to see the pastor of a local church that she attends. I arrange for him to come to the house and meanwhile tell the community leader to get all local people to gather outside the house. When I return there are some 20 people waiting which included the football team and concerned neighbours. We all sat on the porch of the house and she is embarrassed . . . we talk again, this time she promises publicly she will not do such a thing again . . .

This was not the end of the matter. For two weeks Rob visited the woman daily to ensure she kept her promise. The child started to attend school and was no longer forced into selling cake and the burned hand was treated at a clinic paid for by the perpetrator of the wound. The football club's involvement was in being called upon in the beginning and being the final actor at the end when the coach took the boy to the clinic on a daily basis until the treatment ended.

Football officials were also dealing with sexual abuse of both teenage and infant girls. In the former instance a 16-year-old girl was receiving the unwanted sexual attentions of the stepfather when her mother left home to work at night. His first attempt of forced sex resulted in her screaming which alerted neighbours who came to the house only to be told by the teenager that the distress calls were a product of a bad dream. The stepfather however continued his objectives and succeeded in his aim, but was witnessed by another man living in the house. However the rapist warned him that should he reveal to anyone what he witnessed then things would happen to him. It was a vague threat but loaded with implications. The girl meanwhile told her mother what happened. Her response was to accuse the girl of lying. Days later, while the mother was asleep, the stepfather attempted again to force sexual intercourse on the girl. The other man in the house was alerted to the commotion, as was the mother. Their joint presence had no effect on events. Arising from this the mother told the girl to say nothing to anybody. Fortunately for the girl her younger brother was a player in the neighbourhood football team and, made aware of the rapes, informed the Don Bosco project. To add to the validity of the accusations the girl herself told the captain of the same football team what happened, who in turn informed the Child Protection Unit.

By way of response the CPU turned up at the house late afternoon but the man was not home. Speaking to the wife they informed her of their intention of taking the matter to a court of law. Fearful of the publicity and stigma that would arise from this she pleaded with them not to. Meanwhile the CPU, having found the girl, arranged for her to leave the house and live with her grandmother. As Rob explained to me:

> If we can sort matters out at community level – fine. If not we bring in the CPU and they talk; if they get no joy then the law moves in . . ..

A much simpler but more appalling incidence of rape resulted in this sequence being used. The difference to the above was the age of the victim.The case is shocking in its facts: a 32-year-old male raped a three-year-old girl, the daughter of a neighbour left with him by her mother when visiting the market. Rob explained the circumstances:

> . . . the mother left the child and food for her with him. But the man put Vaseline on his penis and sat her on it when feeding her. When the mother came home she saw blood on the man's lap, realised what had happened and began yelling. This attracted people so the man ran away. The baby needed hospital treatment.

The neighbourhood football team drawn to the commotion, knowing of the procedures in such, cases contacted the Don Bosco project, which sent the CPU. The baby received medical care paid for by Don Bosco and the legal costs of prosecuting the man were similarly paid from the same source. In the short term the rapist was found and given a severe beating at the hands of members of the football club. When in court he received an 18-month custodial sentence and was informally advised that for his own good he should never return to the neighbourhood. Muscularity and Christianity could complement one another, in this context lives and souls were saved. But football could not save everybody in Liberia.

Return of the Killing Fields

The game of football in Liberia has been burdened since the 1960s with the task of engendering that which the politicians were unable and unwilling to do. Many Liberians claimed to speak via the game and we hear the opinions of various 'Big Men' whose voices were significant in the realm of local football but have had limited influence at national level and in the wider shifting and uncertain power hierarchies of Liberian society.[50] Football has, thus, not altered the problematic political structures, which seem endemic to the country.[51] Liberia's perennial problem remains that of building a sustainable civil society central to which is the need to make people think of themselves as homogenous or at least not too different. Central to this are: access to land, gainful employment, a more egalitarian distribution of income, elementary health provision, the construction of decent and affordable housing, elementary educational opportunities, the availability of clean water and a campaign that might somehow address the growing incidence of AIDS. The political and national units are not congruent. Football alone cannot solve this.

The game can undoubtedly provide national heroes and recognition for a nation, but football heroes are fragile objects and no one criterion ever defines a nation. The best that football can claim to be able to offer is an avenue to better health, lessons on morality, the sacrifices teamwork requires, the need for charity and selflessness, and generally offer itself as a workable metaphor.[52] The game offers a neutral arena in which ex-combatants and the wider society might begin to seek accommodation in the hard task of re-forming Liberian social identities and social understandings.[53] Football has provided an avenue for linking local populations and groups of displaced 'outsiders'. The burgeoning community football clubs provided a justified source of pride for thousands of young people, be it in playing, spectating or organizing.

Innovative and well run, the Bosco projects should not be seen as a model imported into Liberia via any neo-colonial philosophy. It sought co-operation and when football goods were available would channel them as it saw fit. It was a scheme recognized by local UNICEF representatives as the only one in Liberia that was effectively working with youths via football. It thus attracted admiration and possibly envy from other NGOs. One internationally well-known enterprise declared in 2001 that it too was going to locate community football teams and work with them to save children. This brought exasperation from Father Joe who predicted:

> They'll swamp the area. Give out footballs willy-nilly and have photos taken of kids with balls for their brochures. After six months it'll all end, the balls will burst, or get lost and there won't be any replacements.

The kids meanwhile get the idea that what they want some Western agencies will get for them – free. Some NGOs are without shame, they start an idea, spend a fortune in the short term and don't follow it through. But then their duty is to their policy makers . . . .

The good work of the Bosco project went up in flames in the three major battles that occurred in the capital, dubbed 'World War Three' by combatants, in the summer of 2003. The Salesian school named in honour of Sean Devereux was looted of sports equipment and destroyed, the Don Bosco Polytechnic was ransacked and the care homes for orphans looted and all materials in the workshops stolen by both rebels and governmental soldiers. The youth centre did, however, provide for refuge for some 1,500 displaced persons. According to UN sources around 40 per cent of the fighters were children.

Liberia is, in the exasperated words of Fergal Keane, the BBC's long time Africa correspondent, 'a basket case'.[54] There is no simple ethnic or religious divide, there is no single evil figure to remove, there is no single political doctrine that requires defeating, there are not elderly figures in some organization or singular sinister foreign power behind the atrocities. No one knows what can cure Liberia. Financial aid from the West has not improved the life of the majority over the past 20 years. A democratic election in 1997 only led to a repeat of the violence that characterized the society under one-party rule and military dictatorship. The growth of literacy and the commodities of modernity, in the shape of Hollywood videos, and new weapon technology made impressionable young men into celluloid warriors with weapons that were fired from distances without consequences as to where and upon whom they landed. Loyalty is still manifest more to factors of ethnicity and militia camaraderie than the concept of national government. Football cannot prevent this.

Liberty and Order?

So who do Liberians turn to for hope or guidance? Who fills the gap created by failed governments and a failed state structure? What can the world offer a citizenry that lives a life among the most wretched on earth? The willingness of the NGOs to intervene has to be done in the face of the promotion of free-market economics that the world economic system wants the African nation to join. This calls into question who decides what 'development' is and what is it Africa needs. Organizations that produce mountains of rhetoric have been ineffective in their interventions in Liberia. Created in 1945, the United Nations proclaimed that one of its aims was to 'save successive generations from the scourge of war' but the UN has no soldiers of its own – it borrows them from members. Thus UN declarations are merely agreements as to what an ideal world would contain. The UN Security Council has, in rhetoric, power to maintain peace where it thinks it is needed but it can only really issue resolutions. An irony seemingly lost on many observers is that the UN's five permanent members are the main suppliers of weaponry at the global level. Of these five the US has refused to ratify proposals to prosecute war criminals, the sale of weaponry and the production of chemical weapons. For all its declarations and conventions the fact remains that tens of millions of people have died in wars since the inception of the UN.

For the time being, Liberia is in limbo and the key personnel of this research are no longer in Liberia. Sean Devereux's beliefs got him murdered; Father Joe was forced to leave Liberia in 2002 due to cumulative illnesses and is currently convalescing in the UK. A return to Liberia is unlikely. The King of Liberia, George Weah, retired from football in the same year and now resides in the US. The peacekeeping force currently in Liberia numbers over 10,000 and is actively attempting to disarm an estimated 50,000 combatants offering UN funds of £180 and three months counselling in return for weaponry. But the peace remains fragile with the two rebel groups – LURD and the smaller Movement for Democracy in Liberia (MODEL) – demanding in January 2004, a mere three months after the agreement, the resignation of the head of the transitional government (and presumed 'consensus figure') Gyude Bryant, accusing him of bias and incompetence in the allocation of government jobs.

The man who left Liberia in dignity and to a life of luxury and fabulous wealth was Charles Taylor.[55] Residing in a complex of three hill-top villas overlooking a river in a Nigerian city renowned in times past for the export of slaves, his departure illustrates the inability of the UN to deal with mass murderers.[56] The UN Security Council in March 2004 unanimously indicted Taylor as a war criminal and instructed all member countries to freeze all economic assets belonging to him and his family and associates on a UN sanctions list.[57] The Nigerian government, however, refused to extradite him to the war crimes tribunal thereby defying the UN. On the day he departed there were cholera epidemics in Monrovia and tens of thousands suffering the effects of malnutrition. Days later, fighting resumed in the hinterland between the rebel factions of MODEL and the remnants of Taylor's forces.

Sport is a project of modernity, one of the central aims of its promotion was and remains the pursuit of a longer life via the mechanisms of the body over and above the belief in longevity offered via the soul by religion. Modernity and theology were combined in the ideas of Sean Devereux and Father Joe in their attempts to get young people playing football and in sustaining neighbourhood clubs the Don Bosco projects were tapping into something that mattered. Without formal funding for their projects they used what was available locally and, in Father Joe's case, relied on donations from foreign well-wishers. Keeping the theological input to a minimum the schemes did not preach the language of Christian salvation in the after-life preferring instead the rhetoric of rights in seeking to save lives in the here and now.

It was moving to see the *joie de vivre* of the youth involved in such games of football. But the micro-level projects of the Salesian work could not address the macro-level realities of tens of thousands of disaffected youths who were prepared to take up arms some six years after the ostensible ending of conflict. The football clubs gave thousands of Liberian children a pride in association and might have had far-reaching consequences if time had permitted. Standing up for what they believed in cost Sean Devereux his life and Father Joe his health. They had a vocation and a mission, and Liberia is a better place for their involvement. The pair engendered associations of thoughtful and committed citizens and with the groups they gathered via sport sought to change the world for the better. They achieved via their activism more than any declaration could or will ever do.

But rehabilitation and re-integration projects are doomed to fail if there is no better life offered to the disaffected de-militarized. Until that time young militias might still pass around to the curious the photographs they carried of themselves posing in the formation of a football team with the severed head of a victim in place of the ball. The pose symbolizes the egalitarian nature of their collective effort; the head illustrates the brutality of their lives and the appeal of the militia system. The evident pride in such teamwork, violence and imagery is what the game of football in Liberia has to overcome.

ACKNOWLEDGEMENTS

The author wishes to thank the editors for the invitation to publish and their helpful editorial input. Special thanks are due to the Salesians of Don Bosco, especially the Reverend Joe Glacken, the Reverend Joe Brown. Gratitude is also extended to the Salesian personnel who live and work at the Liberian Mission. The author is indebted to both Karen Kinnaird and Irmani Darlington for their invaluable assistance at the latter stages of production.

NOTES

1. See R. Giulianotti, G. Armstrong and H. Hognestad, 'Sport and Peace: Playing the Game', Paper presented at the Sport and Development International Conference. Swiss Academy for Development, Magglingen, Switzerland (2003).
2. The 1975 European Sport for All Charter states that 'Every individual shall have the right to participate in sport.' The International Charter of Physical Education and Sport (1978) spoke of how 'The practise of physical education and sport is a fundamental right for all.' Olympic Aid an NGO established prior to the Winter Olympics in Norway to support athletes in worn-torn countries evolved into Right To Play in 2003 and now advocates the right of every child to play sport. (See www.righttoplay.com/overview.wp) For an academic debate on sport and human rights see B. Kidd and P. Donnelly, Human Rights in Sport, *International Review for The Sociology of Sport* 35 (2000) 131–48.

3. S. Ellis, 'Liberia 1989–94: A Study of Ethnic and Spiritual Violence', *African Affairs*, 94/375 (1995) 165–97.

4. Q. Outram, 'It's Terminal Either Way: An Analysis of Armed Conflict in Liberia: 1989–96', *Review of African Political Economy*, 24/73 (1997) 355–71.

5. W. D'Azevedo, 'A Tribal Reaction to Politics (Part 1)', *Liberian Studies Journal* 1/2 (1969, 1970–71) pp.1–21 (Part 4) *Liberian Studies Journal* 3, 1–19 and Ellis, 'Liberia 1989–94' (note 3).

6. S. Ellis, *The Mask of Anarchy: The Destruction of Liberia* (Oxford: C. Hunt & Co., 1999). For analyses of the significance of cross dressing and mask wearing in conflict see M. Utas, *Sweet Battlefields: Youth and the Liberian Civil War* (Uppsala, Sweden: Department of Cultural Anthropology, University of Uppsala, 2003).

7. Human Rights Watch/Africa, *Easy Prey: Child Soldiers in Liberia* (New York: HWR/A, 1994).

8. C. Clapham, 'Liberia' in Cruise D. O'Brien *et al.* (eds.) *Contemporary West African States* (Cambridge: Cambridge University Press, 1989).

9. The Trans-Atlantic influences are evident to any outsider. The national flag, known as the 'Lone Star' was invented in the nineteenth century and consists of a single star in the top left-hand corner and eleven horizontal stripes to signify the eleven signatories of the Declaration of Independence – from the American Colonization Society, not the USA. Socially one can witness a plethora of female beauty pageants, school and kindergarten graduation ceremonies, the popularity of the game of basketball, and instructors of various sports being referred to as 'coach'. A multitude of Pentecostal and Baptist churches originating from the Southern states and the mid-West are evident throughout Monrovia competing with the recent arrival of the Evangelicals. Adverts for such denominations are regularly broadcast on state TV.

10. Both skin pigmentation and ideas of 'race' have been issues of political contention since the late nineteenth century. The first four Presidents were considered to be mulatto and hence partly white and the twentieth century saw periodic uprisings against the mulattos by the 'pure blacks' (S. Jubwe, 'Sources of Problems and Prospects in Post War Liberia: a Sociological Perspective', unpublished paper, Department of Sociology and Anthropology, University of Liberia, Monrovia, 1998. Being a flexible concept, ethnicity was manipulated both prior to the war and during it (Ellis, *The Mask of Anarchy*, note 6).

11. E. Osaghe, *Ethnicity, Class and the Struggle for State Power in Liberia* (Dakar: Codisera, 1996).

12. S. Jubwe, 'A Social Analysis of the Liberian Crisis' (unpublished paper Department of Sociology and Anthropology, University of Liberia, Monrovia, 1994) and S. Jubwe, 'Hegemony and Class Consciousness in Liberia 1944–1989: a Sociological Perspective' (unpublished paper, Department of Sociology and Anthropology, University of Liberia, Monrovia, 1997).

13. Jubwe (note 12). S. Jubwe, 'The Politics and Ethnicity of Gender: The Liberian Implications', Paper presented at the Edward Wilmot Blyden Forum of the Press Union of Liberia (January 1994). S. Jubwe, 'Sources of Problems and Prospects in Post War Liberia: A Sociological Perspective' (unpublished paper, Department of Sociology and Anthropology, University of Liberia, Monrovia, 1998).

14. Jubwe, 'Hegemony and Class Consciousness' (note 12).

15. J. Liebenow, *Liberia: The Quest for Democracy* (Bloomington, IN: University of Indiana Press, 1987). Jubwe, 'The Politics and Ethnicity of Gender' (note 12). S. Jubwe, 'Sources of Problems', (note 13).

16. E. Tonkin, 'Model and Ideology: Dimensions of Being Civilised' in Liberia, in L. Holy and M. Stuchlik (eds.) *The Structure of Folk Models*, ASA Monograph 20 (1981) pp.307–30. (London: Academic Press, 1981).

17. Jubwe, 'Sources of Problems' (note 13).

18. Africa Watch, 'Liberia: Flight from Terror: Testimony of Abuses in Nimba County', reprinted in *Liberian Studies Journal*, 15/1 (1990) 142–61. M. Huband, *The Liberian Civil War* (London and Portland, OR: Frank Cass, 1998).

19. Ellis (note 6).

20. The coup attempt saw the perpetrators shot dead and decapitated. Some of their internal organs were eaten by their killers. Their heads were then attached to government buildings as a warning to the wider public as to the consequences of treachery.

21. A. Konneh, *Religion, Commerce and the Integration of the Mandingo in Liberia* (Maryland, MD: University Press of America, 1996).

22. The dominant position of Monrovia with a population of about 800,000 and home to all foreign banks, business interests, centre of politics and cultural life was in sharp contrast to a neglected and under-developed hinterland.

23. R. Kapuscinski, *Shadow of the Sun* (London: Penguin, 2001). D. Johnson, *Reports from the Edge of America and Beyond* (Methuen: London, 2001).

24. Ellis (note 19).

25. W. Reno, 'Foreign Firms and the Financing of Charles Taylor's NPFL', *Liberian Studies Journal*, 18/2 (1993) 175–88. W. Reno, 'Humanitarian Emergencies and Warlord Politics in Liberia and Sierra Leone', Helsinki: paper presented to United Nations University/WIDER Conference (1996). P. Beaumont, 'How a Tyrant's Logs of War are Bringing Terror to West Africa', the *Observer* (27 May 2001). B. Berkeley, *The Graves Are Not Yet Full: Race, Tribe and Power in the Heart of Africa* (New York: Basic Books, 2001).

26. D. Harris, 'From 'Warlord to 'Democratic' President: How Charles Taylor Won the 1997 Liberian Elections', *The Journal of Modern African Studies*, 37/3 (1999) 431–55.

27. Reno (note 25).

28. See *Amnesty International Annual Report* (London: Amnesty Productions, 1998).

29. In 1998 the US State Department withheld $1.2m in aid intended for projects to strengthen civil society and human rights. See *Human Rights Watch* (London: World Report, 2000).

30. The UN urged West African forces to commit to a date but Nigeria, while pledging troops, sought US funding for what was expected to be a lengthy engagement. The US promised $10 million in August and deployed troops to support the UN peacekeeping mission.

31. Around 10,000, troops from Nigeria, Ghana, Togo, Senegal and Ethiopia are currently involved in a humanitarian duty in which their primary focus is the prevention of armed conflict among child combatants.

32. Liberia's constitution makes no mention of conscription.

33. Bush schools and the institutions known as *Poro* and *Sande* in the hinterland were the arenas that traditionally demarcated the passage from childhood to adulthood. But the latter notion could be regionally specific and the passage was dependent on adults submitting the child to the procedure.

34. Utas describes how military prowess attracted female company. While thousands were gang raped, others who formed attachments with militia members attained prosperity from the spoils of war. Female combatants numbered around 2 per cent of the militia (see M. Utas, *Sweet Battlefields: Youth and the Liberian Civil War* (Uppsala, Sweden: Department of Cultural Anthropology, University of Uppsala, 2003)) pp. 170–221.

35. See Utas (note 34) pp.85–108). Particularly harrowing was the application of chilli pepper onto the skin and orifices of a child, which was sometimes combined with being forced into the outdoors to suffer the effects of a scorching sun. Food deprivation was a common technique of child punishment.

36. See Utas (note 34) p.136.

37. Ibid. pp.86–90.

38. Ibid. (note 34) p.95.

39. Ibid. (note 34) p.40.

40. Ibid. p.142.

41. Ibid. pp.137–43.

42. From its origins the Order made room for cooperators and past-pupil associations to share in the Salesian Mission. Unusually for a Catholic religion, order women were always included in the Salesian entity. The first ever oratory in Turin contained Mamma Margaret, the mother of Don Bosco who jointly ran the home. Other women also collaborated. The presence of such women was considered vital in creating the desired family atmosphere and led to the recognition that girls needed the Salesians' help as much as boys. The Salesian Convention

numbers 19 and 20 recognized lay people as full sharers in the Salesian Mission. Since 1917, Salesian mothers were recognized in various forms and nomenclatures: the Zealots of Mary Help of Christians, Co-operative Oblates of Don Bosco, Don Bosco Volunteers, the Association of Damas Salesianos. While recognizing this feminine presence, the Salesian hierarchy have reaffirmed that Don Bosco was decisively oriented to boys and young men. At times critics have recognized the preponderance of women and spoken of the problem of possible 'feminization' of Salesian work. For further details on the Salesians read: A. Auffrey, *St John Bosco* (Longhope, Glos., UK: Salesian Publications, 1970); P. Brocardo, *Don Bosco We Remember You* (Madras, India: Salesian Institute of Graphic Art, 1981); G. Williams, *The Project of Life of the Salesians of Don Bosco: A Guide to the Salesians' Constitution* (Madras, India: Salesian Institute of Graphic Art, 1986); A. Pedrini, *St Francis de Sales: Don Bosco's Patron* (New Rochelle, NY: Don Bosco Publications, 1988).

43. The life of Sean Devereux was commemorated in a variety of ways. A postage stamp was made in his honour in Liberia. A bridge in Somalia is named after him and his life story can be read in D. Devereux, *While My Heart Beats* (London: Penn Press, 2001). A BBC *Everyman* documentary drama, *Mr Sean*, was broadcast in the mid-1990s around the same time as his life was dramatized by Yorkshire TV in *The Dying of the Light*. A sports ground in Surrey bears his name. The Sean Devereux Liberian Children Fund, managed by his family, aims to re-establish the school he first worked in Liberia. It also seeks to build a teacher training college. Integral to such projects is a curriculum that promotes sport as a way of rehabilitating the child victims of war.

44. Expanded from 1993 to actually producing low-cost building materials, such as concrete fibre roof tiles, terrazzo tiles and laterite bricks, those who had been through the programme could also give technical support to construction workers.

45. The transit homes became entrepreneurial; one housed 20 pigs that were bred and sold. A beat band was established and hired out to weddings and birthdays, and a bicycle courier service delivered letters and parcels in Monrovia. Small business enterprises in the shape of toolkits for variously pastry making, sewing, soap making, masonry and carpentry were available. Other kits included kitchen pans and basic cooking ingredients were distributed at a group, not individual, level. A grant of US$50 was also available, and another $50 could be received from UNICEF if, 12 months later, such entrepreneurship was showing signs of success.

46. In 2000 there were 154 Caritas organizations worldwide whose remit was to fund development and human rights projects wherever they were considered necessary.

47. The Don Bosco Polytechnic was begun in 1988 under the motto '*laborare et liberare*' (works sets free) as a tertiary institution offering technical and professional programmes with a view to nurturing local talent so as to lessen dependency on donor organizations. The polytechnic was divided into five subsections. The first, business, offered diplomas and degrees in accountancy and administration. The second, technical, offered the same except in electrical engineering and surveying. Teaching degrees and diplomas constituted the third section and the fourth and fifth, health science and agriculture, offered diplomas and certificates in the first instance in nursing and social work. The various stated rhetorics were available to those available to those interested in the pedagogic philosophy. A brochure, produced by the polytechnic in 1988, claimed it was 'developing the man power base for the active participation in the economic advancement of Liberia thereby increasing the number of trained workers needed to decrease the nation's dependence on expatriates'. The stress on practical application rather than abstract disciplines was no doubt to the approval of UNESCO, which in 1996 sponsored a study of the educational system of Liberia only to criticize the over production of social science and humanities teachers and students and the resultant under employment of graduates, stating that there was not enough study of technology and the physical and life sciences. A further document, 'The National Educational Plan of the Liberian Government 1978–1990', aimed to stimulate the economic advantage of the country to reduce the nation's 'excessive reliance on ex-patriots in middle-level and skilled occupations'. Furthermore, it aimed 'to instil in Liberian youth appreciation for the dignity of labour and the need to achieve self-reliance'. Hence, it was proud to declare,

the educational plan was geared to commerce and industry and to providing problem-solving skills rather than mere academic debate.

48. The Don Bosco Project had divided Monrovia into five sections in 1999. A year later the zones increased to nine because of the number of people applying to join. By 2002 Monrovia was divided by the Bosco project into 12 sections, with two districts outside the city, making it 14.

49. Instruction came from a Spanish lecturer who visited Liberia for nine months. Hands-on experience came from a local NGO titled the Children Assisting Programme. Further experience came via the French NGO Médicin Sans Frontières when a Belgian-born official from the organization, who had married a Liberian woman, gave instruction on caring for children.

50. For further analysis of this issue see G. Armstrong, 'Life, Death and the Biscuit: Football and the Reconstuction, West Africa' in G. Armsrong and R. Giulianotti (eds.) *Football in Africa: Conflict, Conciliation and Communit* (Basingstoke: Palgrave/Macmillan, 2004).

51. Tonkin (note 16). D. Brown, 'Bureaucracy as an Issue in Third World Management: An African Case Study', *Public Administration and Development* 9 (1989) 369–80.

52. G. Armstrong, 'Talking Up The Game: Football and The Reconstruction of Liberia, West Africa' in *Identities: Global Studies in Culture and Power* 9 (2002) 471–94.

53. P. Richards, 'Soccer and Violence in War Torn Africa. Soccer and Rehabilitation in Sierra Leone' in G. Armstrong and R. Giulianotti (eds.). *Entering the Field. New Perspectives in World Football* (Oxford: Berg, 1997).

54. *The Independent* (26 July 2003).

55. Dignity and even legitimacy were leant to Taylor's departure from Monrovia by the presence of three African Heads of State: Thabo Mbeki of South Africa, Olusegun Obasanjo of Nigeria and Joaquim Chissano of Mozambique (the latter was also Chair of the African Union). An American evangelist delivered a sermon which involved him laying hands on the President's urging them to cry for peace. In his departing speech Taylor spoke of himself as a 'black cow' ravaged by the lion of the USA stating further that 'Africans need to take care of their own problems'. Citing economic sanctions imposed on him and his nation by the USA and the World Bank, Taylor spoke of himself as the 'sacrificial lamb'. Addressing the US he ended his speech stating: 'They can call off their dogs now. I realised I could no longer see the blood of our people wasted. I must stop fighting now. I do not step down out of fear of fright. I step down out of love for you. God willing, I will be back ...' He was then escorted to Calabar by the visiting Heads of State. Taylor's departure could have been very different had a plot by an Anglo-American private security firm to kidnap him and turn him over to the War Crimes Court succeeded. Offering a 3,000 strong force of former military personnel from Britain, France, USA and South Africa, this private militia had established links with LURD.

56. In a deal brokered by US diplomats and Nigerian peacekeeping commanders, Taylor agreed to leave Liberia if the international court dropped the war charges against him.

57. A UN-backed court in Sierra Leone indicted Taylor on charges of crimes against humanity. Specifically, Taylor was accused of arming the Revolutionary United Front movement of Sierra Leone in the decade 1991–2001. This conflict saw Taylor supply the rebel movement with arms in return for diamonds. The rebels were responsible for the deaths of some 50,000 people. The court was established primarily to deal with Foday Sankor, the leader of the rebels, his death of natural causes in 2003 while under arrest meant that only nine defendants are now awaiting trial. Tens of thousands of young men remain in Liberia without hope of meaningful employment. In the absence of hope they await the next calls of the militias. The country faces the problem in the meantime of enforcing total disarmament and holding elections that are free of fear.

Notes on Contributors

Gary Armstrong is a lecturer in the Department of Sport Sciences, Brunel University, London. He is the author of *Football Hooligans: Knowing the Score* and *BladeRunners: Lives in Football*. He has also co-edited, alongside Richard Giulianotti, *Entering the Field: New Perspectives in World Football*, *Football Cultures and Identities* and *Fear and Loathing in World Football*. He is currently researching the role of football in the reconstruction of Liberia and the role that football has played in the politics of Malta.

Celia Brackenridge, formerly Professor of Sport and Leisure at the University of Gloucestershire, runs her own research company specializing in child protection and gender equity. She chairs the Research Task Force of the NSPCC/Sport England Child Protection in Sport Unit and is author of *Spoilsports: Understanding and Preventing Sexual Exploitation in Sport* (Routledge, 2001).

Peter Donnelly is Director of the Centre for Sport Policy Studies, and a Professor in the Faculty of Physical Education and Health, at the University of Toronto. Recent books include *Taking Sport Seriously: Social Issues in Canadian Sport* (1997; 2nd edition 2000), *Inside Sports*, and the first Canadian edition of *Sports in Society: Issues and Controversies* (both with Jay Coakley, 1999 and 2004). He is a former editor of the *Sociology of Sport Journal* (1990–94), current editor of the *International Review for the Sociology of Sport* (2004–06), and a past President of the North American Society for the Sociology of Sport (2001).

Patrick K. Gasser works in the Legal Services and Assistance Programmes Division of UEFA, where he manages development programmes for member associations and coordinates contributions drawn from fines imposed in tournaments. Before joining UEFA he worked for over a decade with the International Committee of the Red Cross (ICRC) in areas of conflict including Afghanistan, Iraq, the Balkans and Rwanda, and studied Business and Human Resources in Switzerland.

Richard Giulianotti is a Senior Lecturer in Sociology at the University of Aberdeen. He is the author of *Football: A Sociology of the Global Game* (Polity, 1999) and *Sport: A Critical Sociology* (Polity, 2004). He has written numerous journal articles on various aspects of sport, and has edited or co-edited eight other books including, most recently, *Sport and Modern Social*

Theorists (Palgrave, 2004) and (with Gary Armstrong) *Football in Africa* (Palgrave, 2004).

Dr Fan Hong is Reader in the School of PE and Sport Sciences and Acting Head of Research of the Faculty of Education and Contemporary Studies, De Montfort University in England. She is an editor of the international journal, *Sport in Society* and a member of the editorial board of *The International Journal of the History of Sport,* the *International Encyclopaedia of Women and Sport* and *Tiyu Xuekan* [*The Journal of Sport Studies*]. Her main research interests are in the areas of gender and sport and politics and sport with particular reference to China and Asia.

Barrie Houlihan is Professor of Sport Policy in the Institute of Sport and Leisure Policy at Loughborough University, UK. His research interests include the domestic and international policy processes for sport. He has a particular interest in sports development, the diplomatic use of sport, and drug abuse by athletes. His most recent books include, *Elite Sport Development: Policy Learning and Political Priorities* (with Mick Green, Routledge 2005); *The Politics of Sports Development: development of sport or development through sport?* (with Anita White, Routledge 2002); and *Dying to Win: the development of anti-doping policy* (Strasbourg: Council of Europe Press, 2002).

Helen Jefferson Lenskyj is a community activist and a full professor at the University of Toronto. She has written six books and over 70 articles on women and sport, and, more recently, on Olympic industry politics. A recent book, titled *Out on the Field: Gender, Sport and Sexualities,* was published by Women's Press in 2003.

Anders Levinsen is the founder and current managing director of the Cross-Cultures Project Association. He has held several senior posts in humanitarian NGOs including the UNHCR and the Danish Refugee Council. He was a professional football player in the Danish Premier League and lower divisions from 1979–86, and subsequently held various coaching positions until 1990. He has gained several honours for his work in humanitarian projects, notably the Michael Laudrup Award, the Danish Peace Award on behalf of Open Fun Football Schools, the Pioneering Prize, UEFA's Gold Medal for a special contribution to football, and the Gerlev Sports Award.

Dr David McArdle is with the Department of Law at the Aberdeen Business School, Scotland. He previously held research posts at De Monfort, Middlesex and Manchester Metropolitan Universities and is the author of *Football,*

Society and the Law (Cavendish Publishing) and has written more than 20 book chapters and refereed journal articles on sports law and employment law. He co-edits the journal *Entertainment Law* and teaches employment law, trade union law and health & safety law.

Dr Richard Parrish is Senior Lecturer in Law at Edge Hill. He specializes in the regulation of the professional sports sector in the EU. He has published widely in this area including, *Sports Law and Policy in the European Union* (Manchester University Press, 2003) and *Sports Law* (Pearson, 2005) a forthcoming co-authored textbook. He has delivered academic papers on sports law throughout Europe and North America and has taught sports law on many of the major national and international sports law programmes.

LeAnne Petherick is a doctoral candidate in the Faculty of Physical Education and Health at the University of Toronto. Her research interests include youth and physical activity and health issues, physical education curriculum policy and children's rights in education and sport. Her dissertation is an ethnographic look at the social construction of health and physical activity knowledge within the Canadian health and physical education curriculum.

David Rowe is Director of the Cultural Industries and Practices Research Centre and teaches Media and Cultural Studies at the University of Newcastle, Australia. His books include the co-authored *Globalization and Sport: Playing the World* (Sage, 2001) and *Sport, Culture and the Media: The Unruly Trinity* (Open University Press, 1999).

Angela J. Schneider has a PhD in Philosophy in applied ethics. She is an Associate Professor in the School of Kinesiology in Faculty of Health Sciences at the University of Western Ontario. Dr Schneider is the former Director of Ethics and Education for the World Anti-Doping Agency and currently conducting her research and supervising graduate students at the International Centre for Olympic Studies. She also won a silver medal for Canada in the 1984 Olympic Games in Los Angeles in the Women's Coxed Fours in Rowing.

INDEX